SILENT HILL

DEAD/ALIVE

Written by **Scott Ciencin**

Art by **Nick Stakal**

Colors by **Nick Stakal & Tom B. Long**

Letters by **Tom B. Long**

Cover by **Scott Keating**

Book Design by **Robbie Robbins**

Original Series Edited by **Dan Taylor**

Trade Paperback Edited by **Aaron Myers**

ISBN: 1-933239-94-8

09 08 07 06 1 2 3 4 5

KONAMI

www.idwpublishing.com

IDW Publishing is:
Ted Adams, Co-President
Robbie Robbins, Co-President
Chris Ryall, Publisher/Editor-in-Chief
Kris Oprisko, Vice President
Neil Uyetake, Art Director
Dan Taylor, Editor
Aaron Myers, Editorial Assistant
Chance Boren, Editorial Assistant
Matthew Ruzicka, CPA, Controller
Alex Garner, Creative Director
Yumiko Miyano, Business Development
Rick Privman, Business Development

SILENT HILL

DEAD/ALIVE

CHAPTER 1

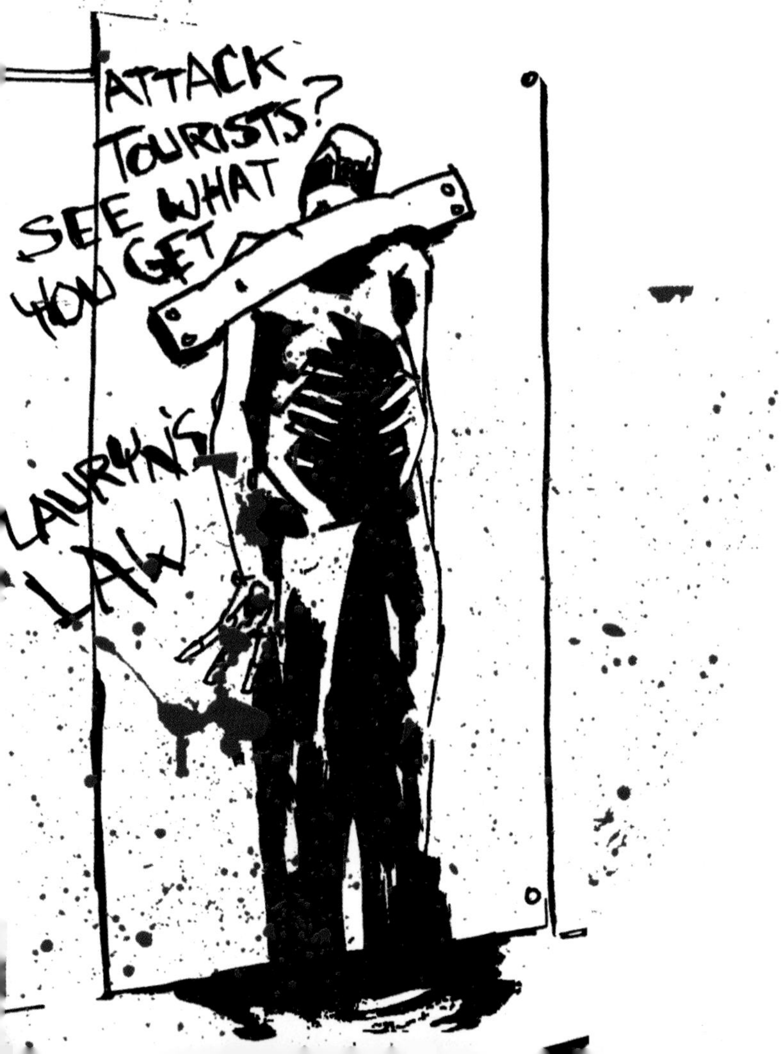
ATTACK TOURISTS?
SEE WHAT YOU GET
LAURYN'S LAW

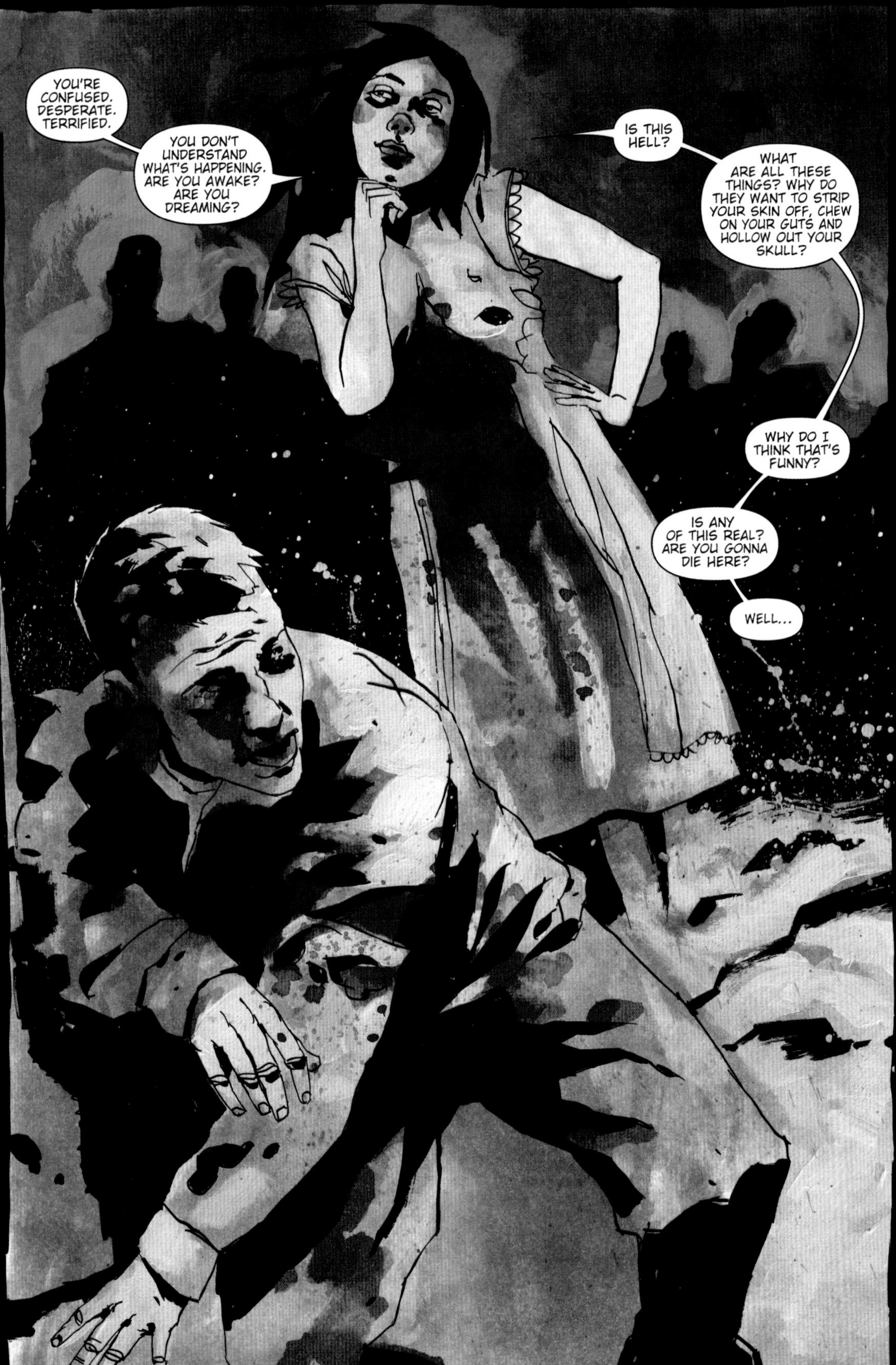
YOU'RE CONFUSED. DESPERATE. TERRIFIED.
YOU DON'T UNDERSTAND WHAT'S HAPPENING. ARE YOU AWAKE? ARE YOU DREAMING?
IS THIS HELL?
WHAT ARE ALL THESE THINGS? WHY DO THEY WANT TO STRIP YOUR SKIN OFF, CHEW ON YOUR GUTS AND HOLLOW OUT YOUR SKULL?
WHY DO I THINK THAT'S FUNNY?
IS ANY OF THIS REAL? ARE YOU GONNA DIE HERE?
WELL...

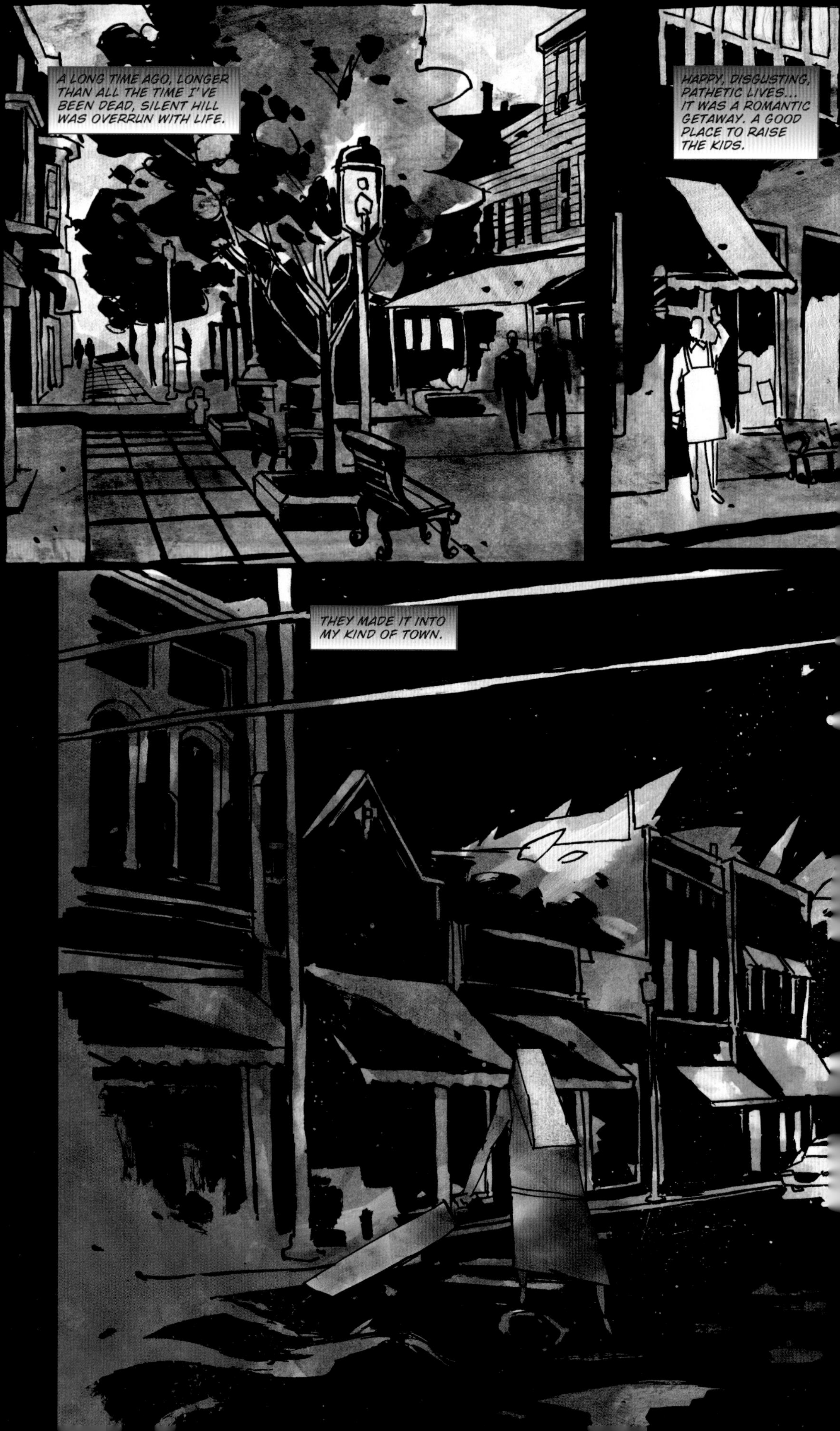
A LONG TIME AGO, LONGER THAN ALL THE TIME I'VE BEEN DEAD, SILENT HILL WAS OVERRUN WITH LIFE.
HAPPY, DISGUSTING, PATHETIC LIVES... IT WAS A ROMANTIC GETAWAY. A GOOD PLACE TO RAISE THE KIDS.
THEY MADE IT INTO MY KIND OF TOWN.

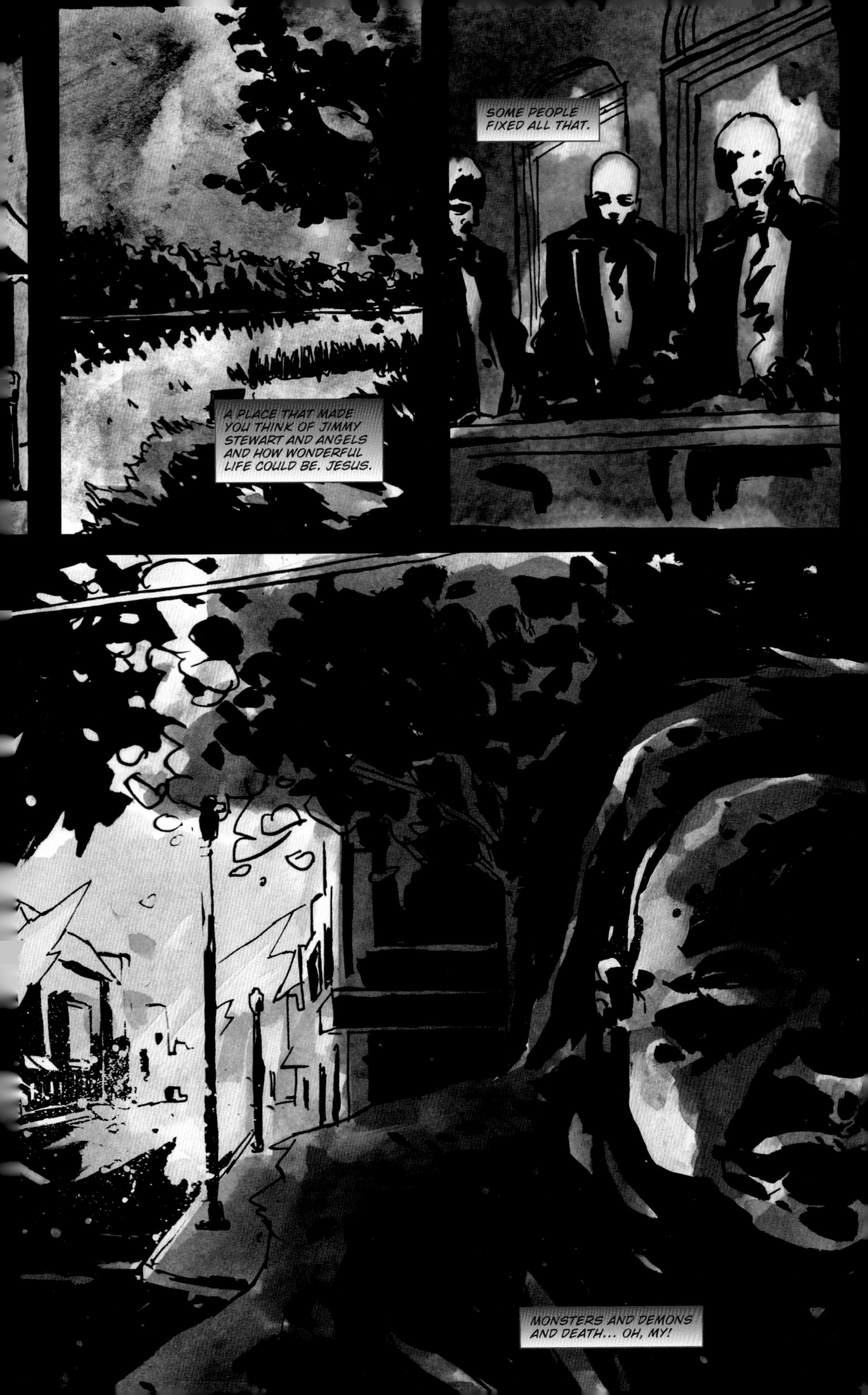
A PLACE THAT MADE YOU THINK OF JIMMY STEWART AND ANGELS AND HOW WONDERFUL LIFE COULD BE. JESUS.
SOME PEOPLE FIXED ALL THAT.
MONSTERS AND DEMONS AND DEATH... OH, MY!

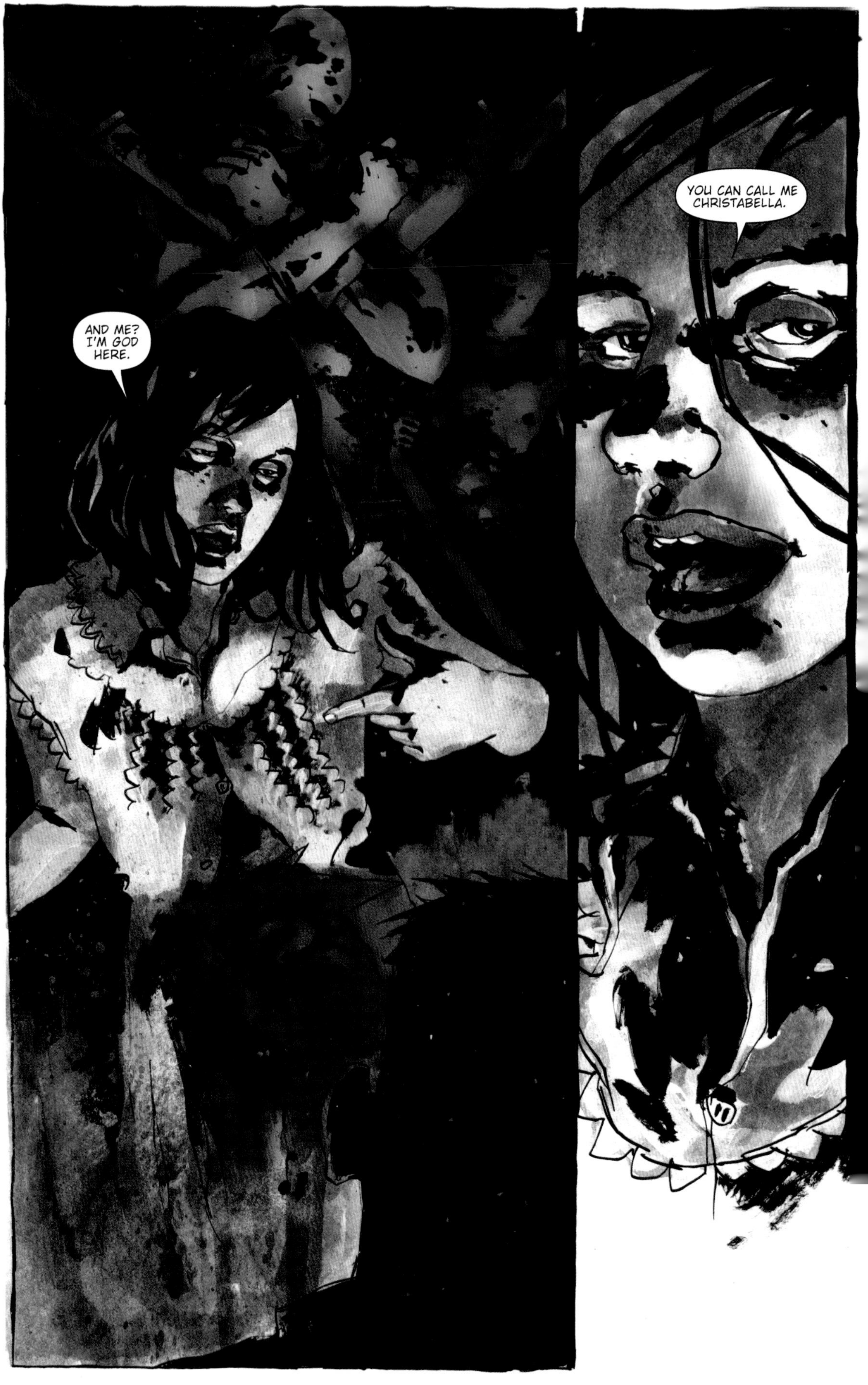
AND ME? I'M GOD HERE.
YOU CAN CALL ME CHRISTABELLA.

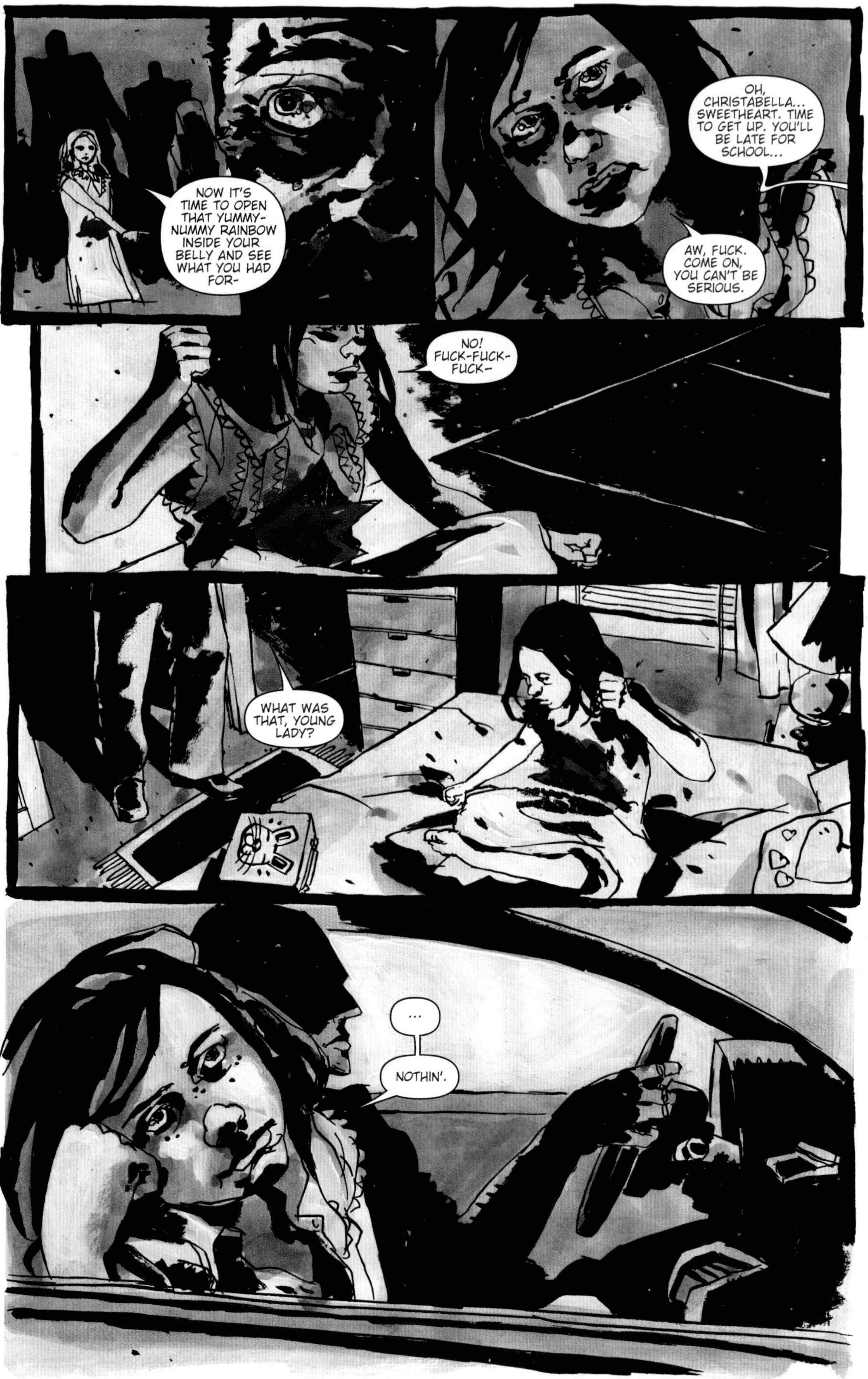
NOW IT'S TIME TO OPEN THAT YUMMY-NUMMY RAINBOW INSIDE YOUR BELLY AND SEE WHAT YOU HAD FOR-
OH, CHRISTABELLA... SWEETHEART. TIME TO GET UP. YOU'LL BE LATE FOR SCHOOL...
AW, FUCK. COME ON, YOU CAN'T BE SERIOUS.
NO! FUCK-FUCK-FUCK-
WHAT WAS THAT, YOUNG LADY?
...
NOTHIN'.

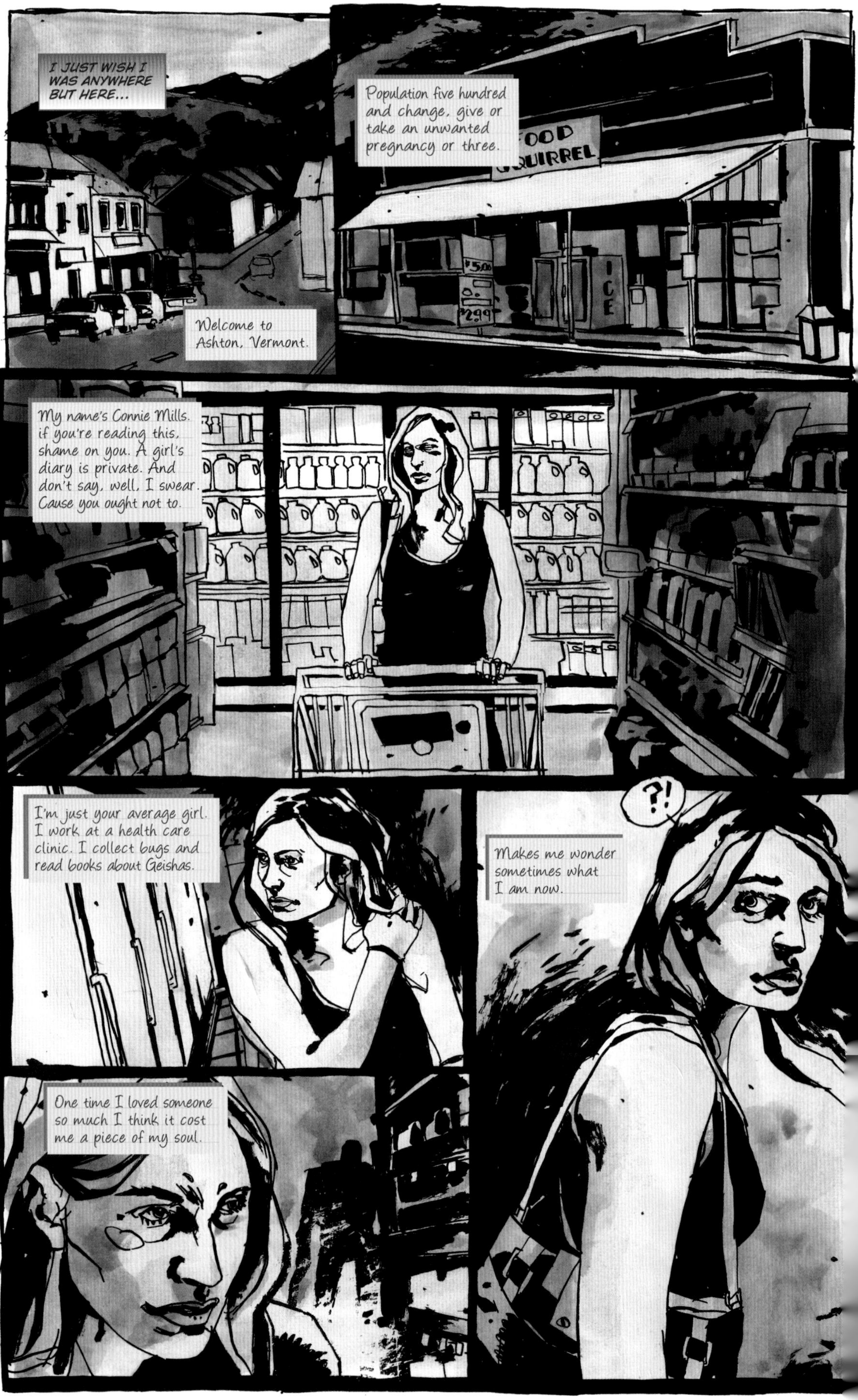
I JUST WISH I WAS ANYWHERE BUT HERE...
Welcome to Ashton, Vermont.
Population five hundred and change, give or take an unwanted pregnancy or three.
FOOD
SQUIRREL
ICE
My name's Connie Mills. if you're reading this, shame on you. A girl's diary is private. And don't say, well, I swear. Cause you ought not to.
I'm just your average girl. I work at a health care clinic. I collect bugs and read books about Geishas.
?!
Makes me wonder sometimes what I am now.
One time I loved someone so much I think it cost me a piece of my soul.

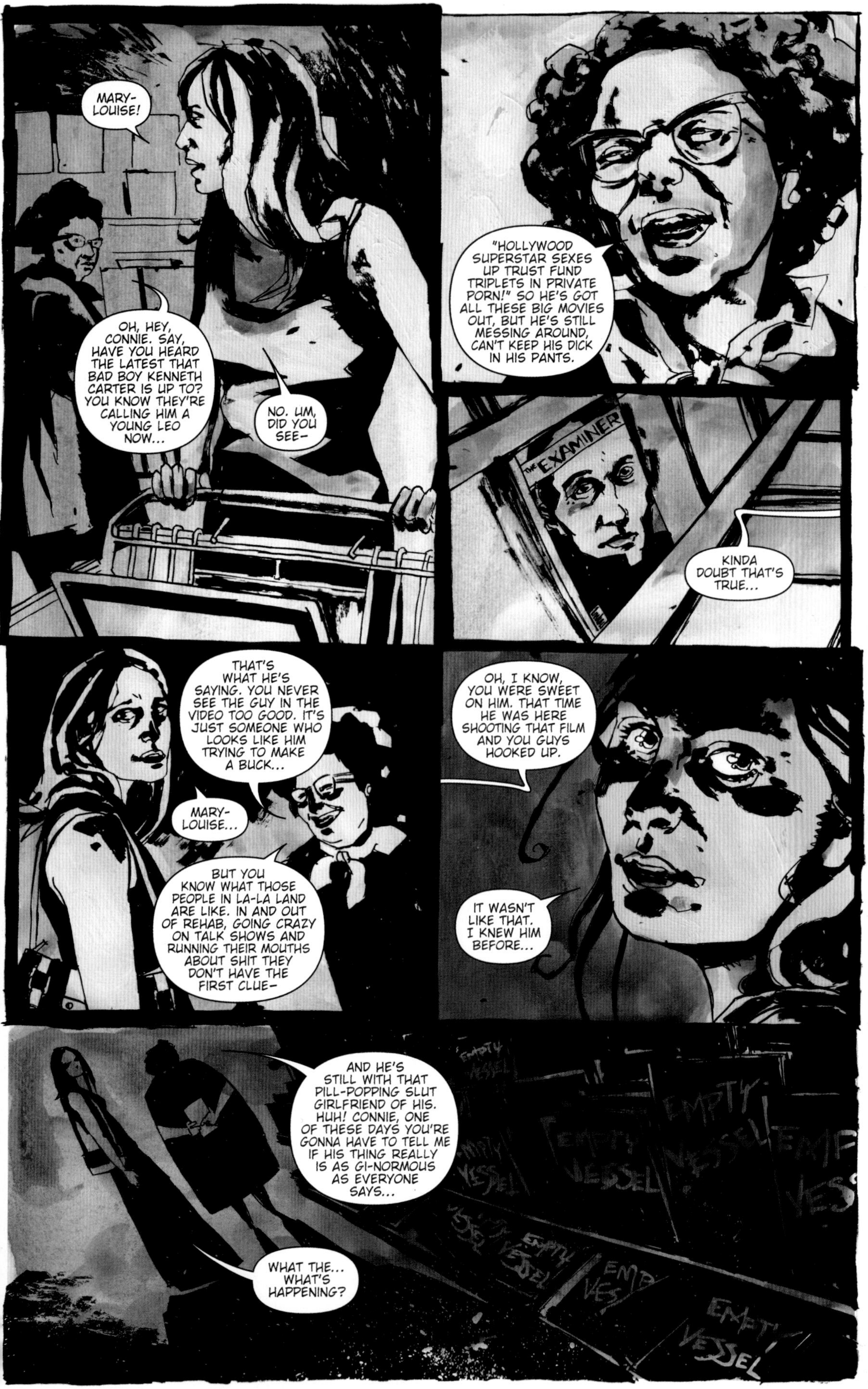
MARY-LOUISE!
OH, HEY, CONNIE. SAY, HAVE YOU HEARD THE LATEST THAT BAD BOY KENNETH CARTER IS UP TO? YOU KNOW THEY'RE CALLING HIM A YOUNG LEO NOW...
NO. UM, DID YOU SEE-
"HOLLYWOOD SUPERSTAR SEXES UP TRUST FUND TRIPLETS IN PRIVATE PORN!" SO HE'S GOT ALL THESE BIG MOVIES OUT, BUT HE'S STILL MESSING AROUND, CAN'T KEEP HIS DICK IN HIS PANTS.
THE EXAMINER
KINDA DOUBT THAT'S TRUE...
THAT'S WHAT HE'S SAYING. YOU NEVER SEE THE GUY IN THE VIDEO TOO GOOD. IT'S JUST SOMEONE WHO LOOKS LIKE HIM TRYING TO MAKE A BUCK...
MARY-LOUISE...
BUT YOU KNOW WHAT THOSE PEOPLE IN LA-LA LAND ARE LIKE. IN AND OUT OF REHAB, GOING CRAZY ON TALK SHOWS AND RUNNING THEIR MOUTHS ABOUT SHIT THEY DON'T HAVE THE FIRST CLUE-
OH, I KNOW, YOU WERE SWEET ON HIM. THAT TIME HE WAS HERE SHOOTING THAT FILM AND YOU GUYS HOOKED UP.
IT WASN'T LIKE THAT. I KNEW HIM BEFORE...
AND HE'S STILL WITH THAT PILL-POPPING SLUT GIRLFRIEND OF HIS. HUH! CONNIE, ONE OF THESE DAYS YOU'RE GONNA HAVE TO TELL ME IF HIS THING REALLY IS AS GI-NORMOUS AS EVERYONE SAYS...
EMPTY VESSEL
WHAT THE... WHAT'S HAPPENING?

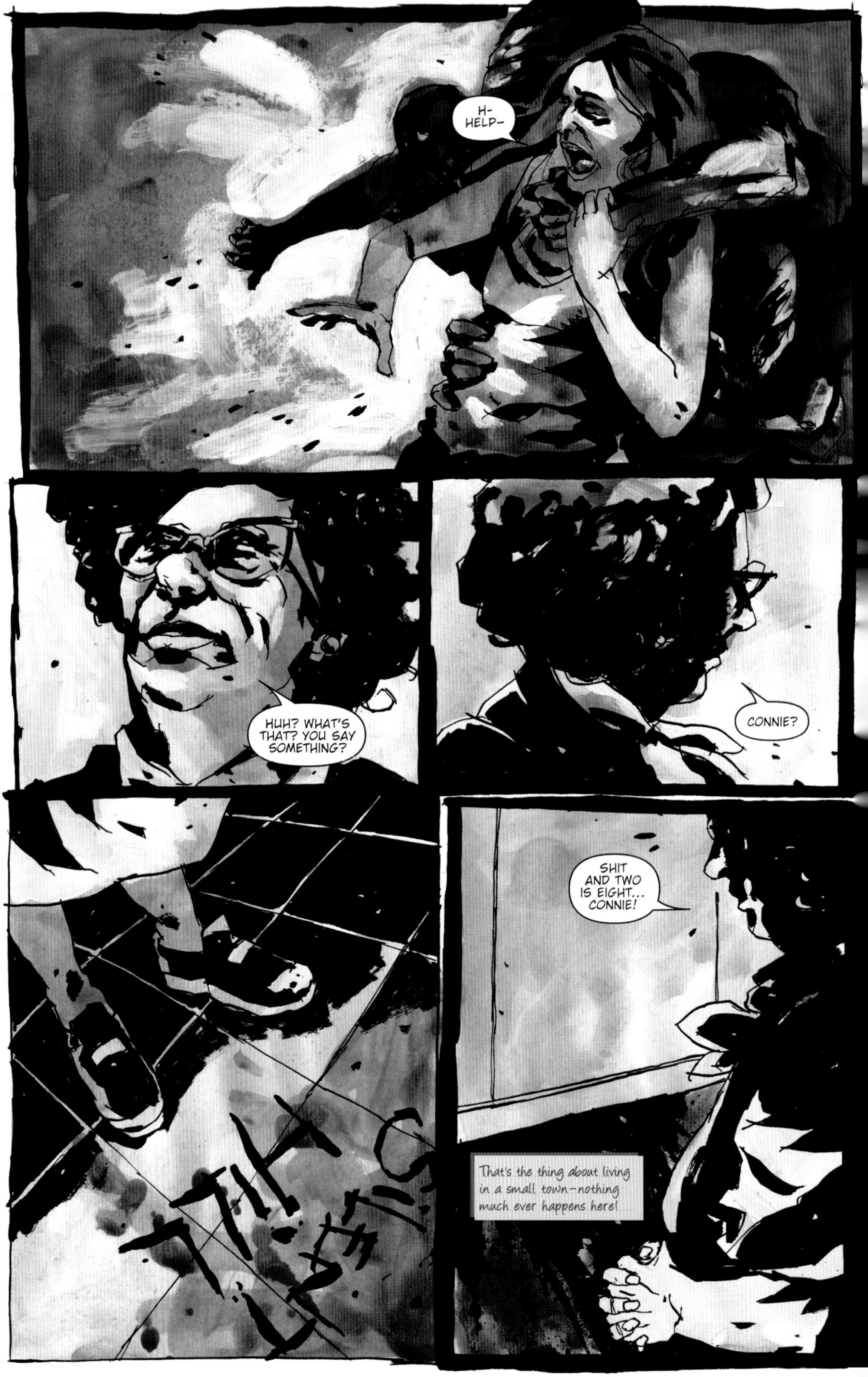
H-
HELP—
HUH? WHAT'S THAT? YOU SAY SOMETHING?
CONNIE?
SHIT AND TWO IS EIGHT... CONNIE!
That's the thing about living in a small town—nothing much ever happens here!

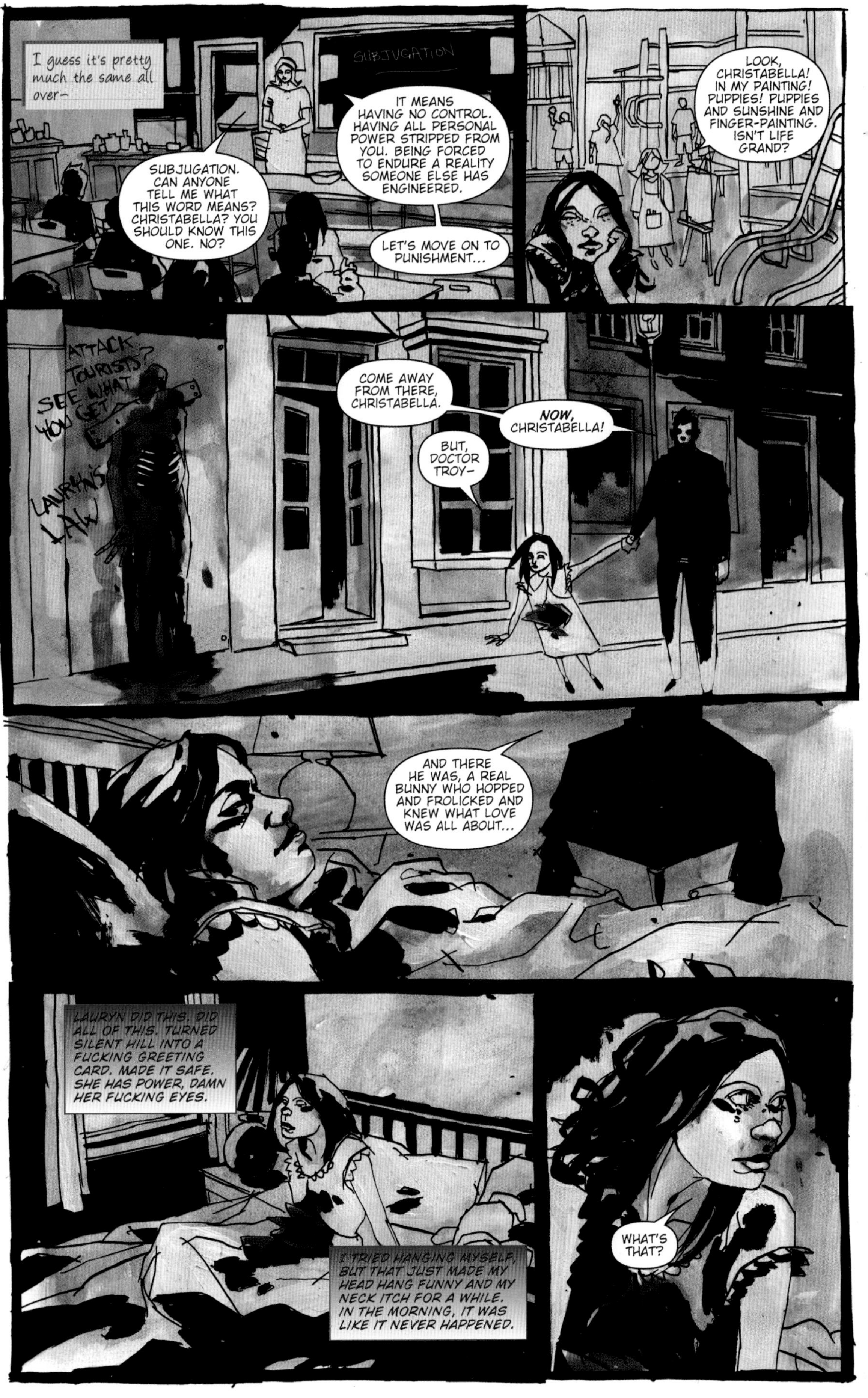
I guess it's pretty much the same all over–
SUBJUGATION
SUBJUGATION. CAN ANYONE TELL ME WHAT THIS WORD MEANS? CHRISTABELLA? YOU SHOULD KNOW THIS ONE. NO?
IT MEANS HAVING NO CONTROL. HAVING ALL PERSONAL POWER STRIPPED FROM YOU. BEING FORCED TO ENDURE A REALITY SOMEONE ELSE HAS ENGINEERED.
LET'S MOVE ON TO PUNISHMENT...
LOOK, CHRISTABELLA! IN MY PAINTING! PUPPIES! PUPPIES AND SUNSHINE AND FINGER-PAINTING. ISN'T LIFE GRAND?
ATTACK TOURISTS? SEE WHAT YOU GET
LAURYN'S LAW
COME AWAY FROM THERE, CHRISTABELLA.
BUT, DOCTOR TROY–
NOW, CHRISTABELLA!
AND THERE HE WAS, A REAL BUNNY WHO HOPPED AND FROLICKED AND KNEW WHAT LOVE WAS ALL ABOUT...
LAURYN DID THIS. DID ALL OF THIS. TURNED SILENT HILL INTO A FUCKING GREETING CARD. MADE IT SAFE. SHE HAS POWER, DAMN HER FUCKING EYES.
I TRIED HANGING MYSELF, BUT THAT JUST MADE MY HEAD HANG FUNNY AND MY NECK ITCH FOR A WHILE. IN THE MORNING, IT WAS LIKE IT NEVER HAPPENED.
WHAT'S THAT?

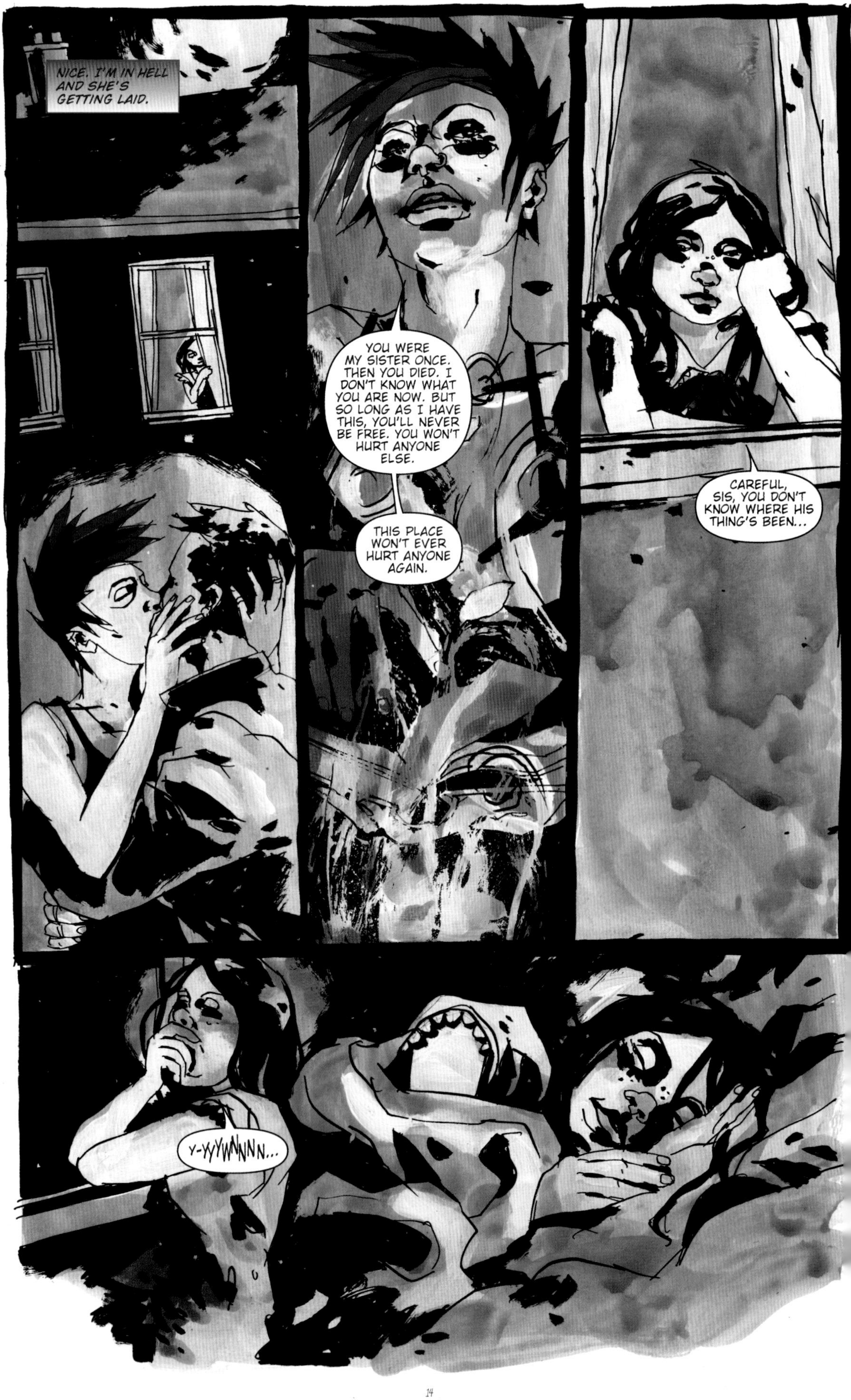
NICE. I'M IN HELL AND SHE'S GETTING LAID.
YOU WERE MY SISTER ONCE. THEN YOU DIED. I DON'T KNOW WHAT YOU ARE NOW. BUT SO LONG AS I HAVE THIS, YOU'LL NEVER BE FREE. YOU WON'T HURT ANYONE ELSE.
THIS PLACE WON'T EVER HURT ANYONE AGAIN.
CAREFUL, SIS, YOU DON'T KNOW WHERE HIS THING'S BEEN...
Y-YYYWNNNN...

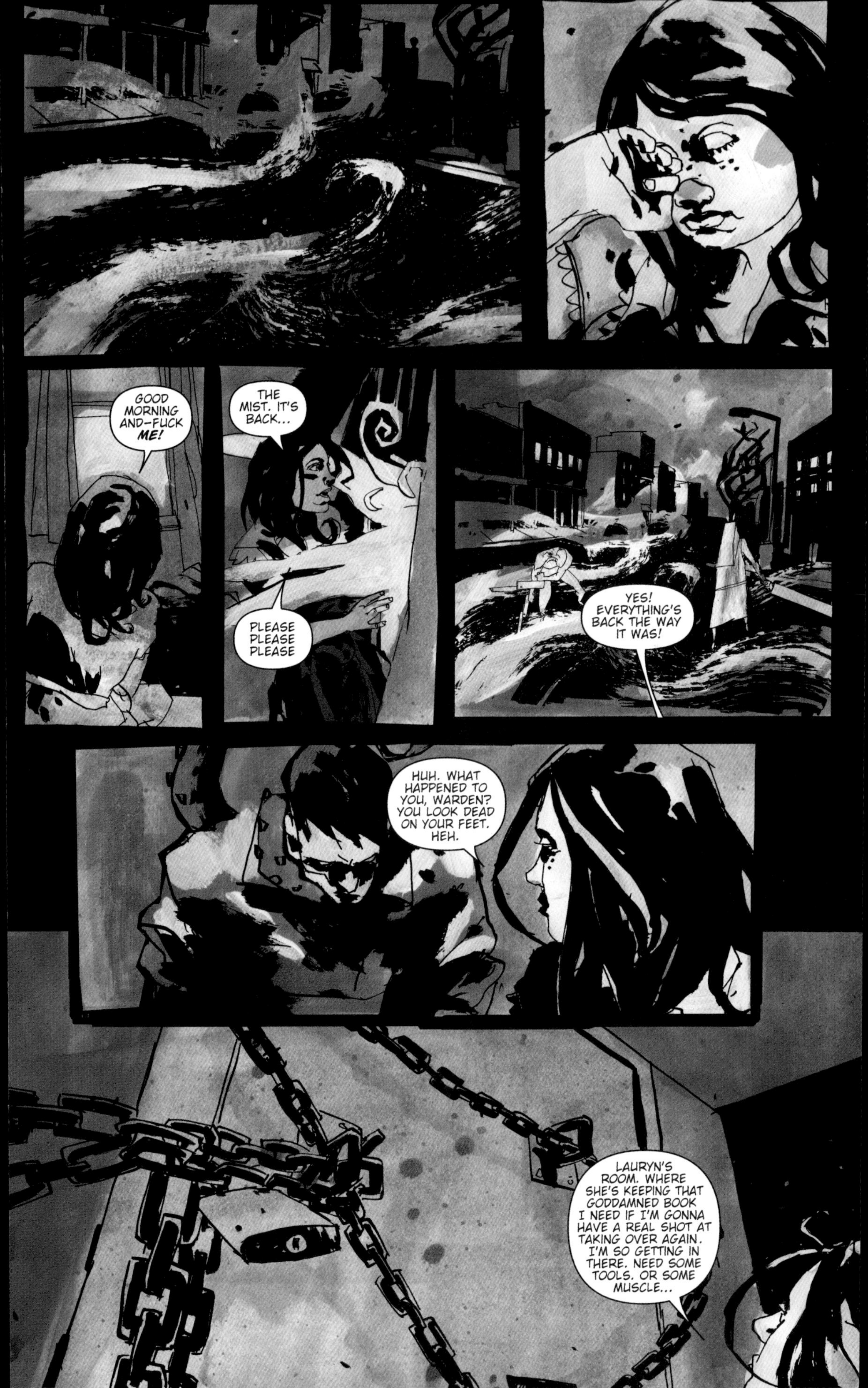
GOOD MORNING AND—FUCK ME!
THE MIST. IT'S BACK...
PLEASE PLEASE PLEASE
YES! EVERYTHING'S BACK THE WAY IT WAS!
HUH. WHAT HAPPENED TO YOU, WARDEN? YOU LOOK DEAD ON YOUR FEET. HEH.
LAURYN'S ROOM. WHERE SHE'S KEEPING THAT GODDAMNED BOOK I NEED IF I'M GONNA HAVE A REAL SHOT AT TAKING OVER AGAIN. I'M SO GETTING IN THERE. NEED SOME TOOLS. OR SOME MUSCLE...

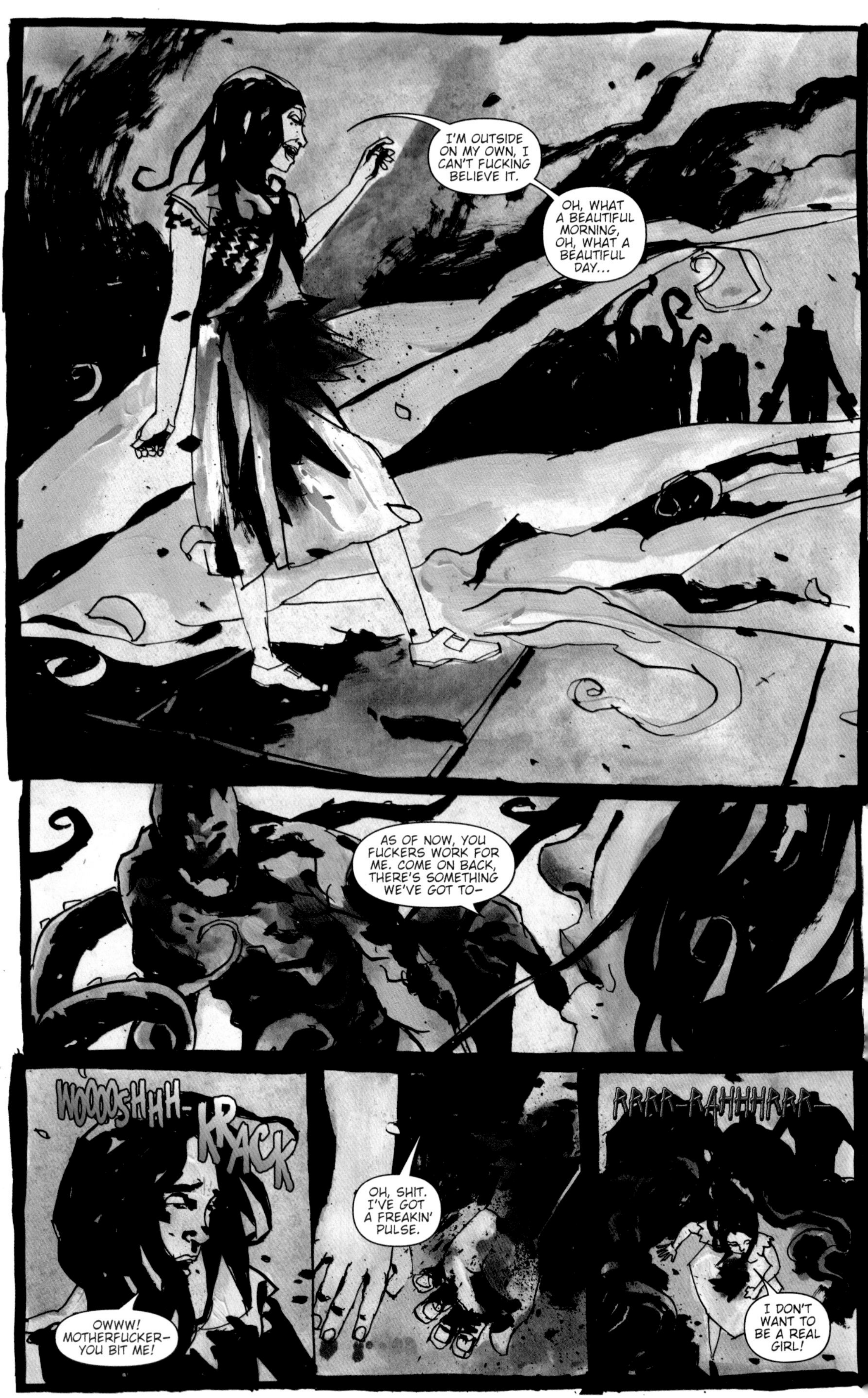
I'M OUTSIDE ON MY OWN, I CAN'T FUCKING BELIEVE IT.
OH, WHAT A BEAUTIFUL MORNING, OH, WHAT A BEAUTIFUL DAY...
AS OF NOW, YOU FUCKERS WORK FOR ME. COME ON BACK, THERE'S SOMETHING WE'VE GOT TO-
WOOOOSHHH-KRACK
OWWW! MOTHERFUCKER- YOU BIT ME!
OH, SHIT. I'VE GOT A FREAKIN' PULSE.
RRRR-RAHHHRRR-
I DON'T WANT TO BE A REAL GIRL!

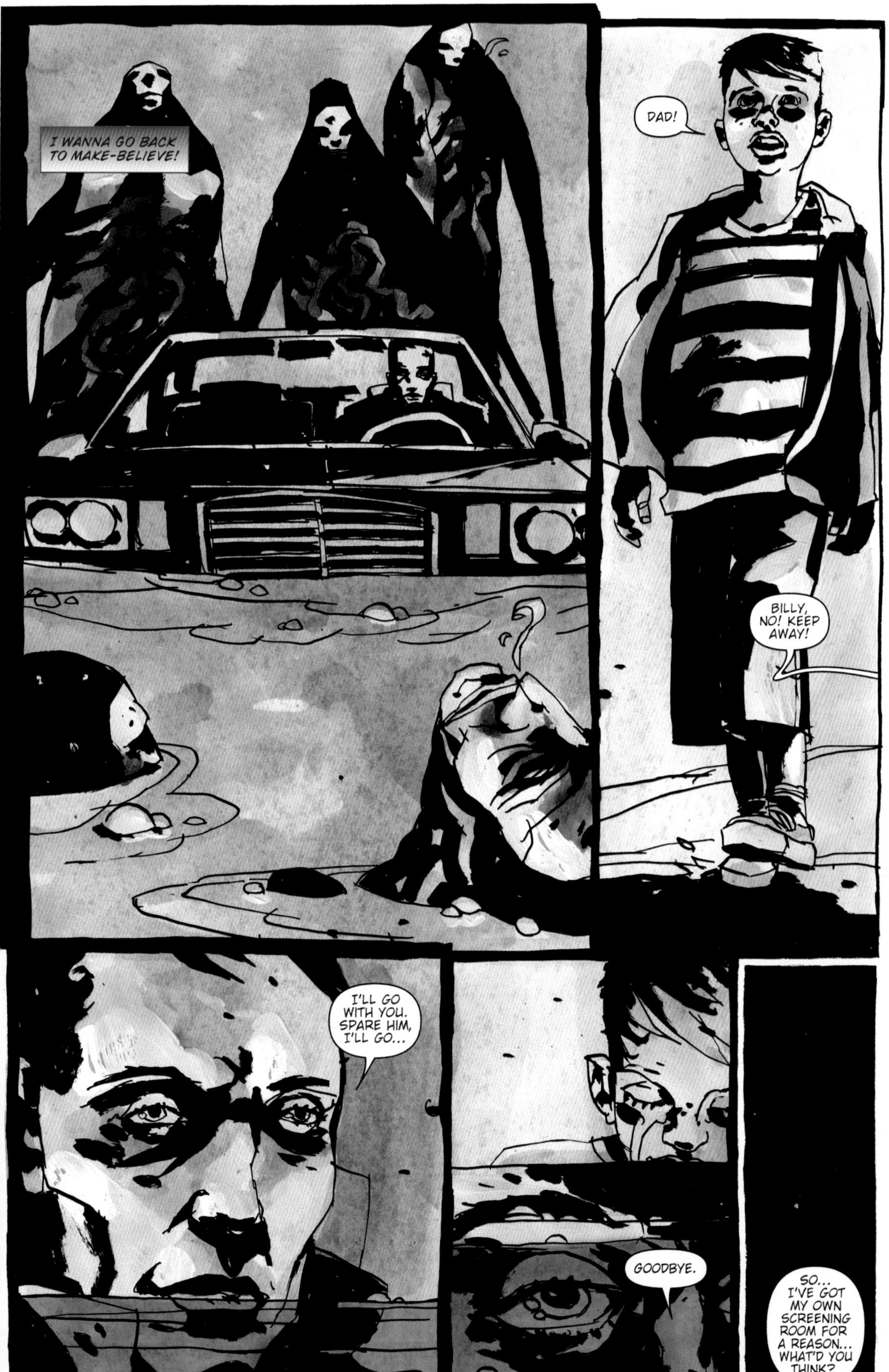
I WANNA GO BACK TO MAKE-BELIEVE!
DAD!
BILLY, NO! KEEP AWAY!
I'LL GO WITH YOU. SPARE HIM, I'LL GO...
GOODBYE.
SO... I'VE GOT MY OWN SCREENING ROOM FOR A REASON... WHAT'D YOU THINK?

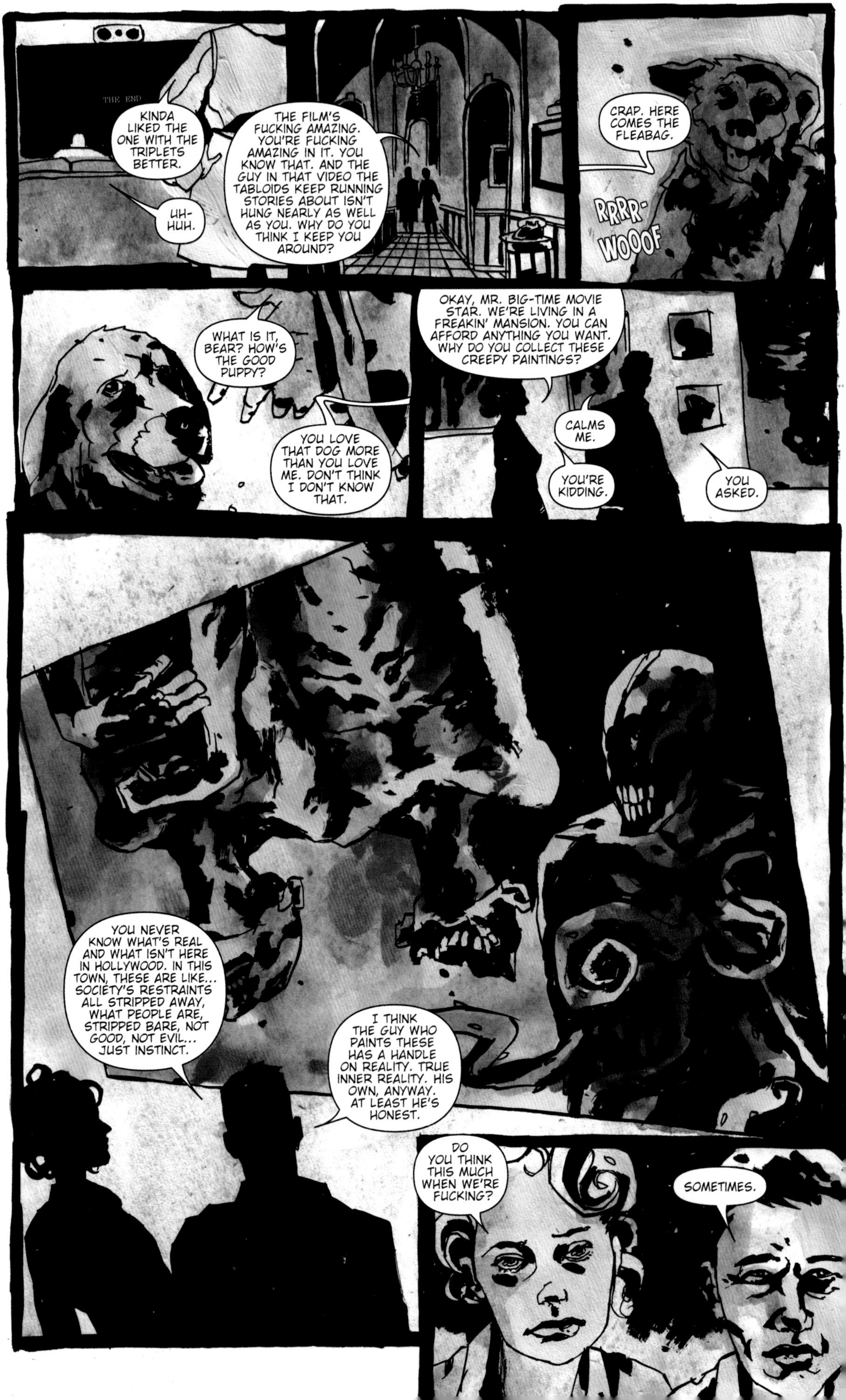
THE END
KINDA LIKED THE ONE WITH THE TRIPLETS BETTER.
UH-HUH.
THE FILM'S FUCKING AMAZING. YOU'RE FUCKING AMAZING IN IT. YOU KNOW THAT. AND THE GUY IN THAT VIDEO THE TABLOIDS KEEP RUNNING STORIES ABOUT ISN'T HUNG NEARLY AS WELL AS YOU. WHY DO YOU THINK I KEEP YOU AROUND?
CRAP. HERE COMES THE FLEABAG.
RRRR-WOOOF
WHAT IS IT, BEAR? HOW'S THE GOOD PUPPY?
YOU LOVE THAT DOG MORE THAN YOU LOVE ME. DON'T THINK I DON'T KNOW THAT.
OKAY, MR. BIG-TIME MOVIE STAR. WE'RE LIVING IN A FREAKIN' MANSION. YOU CAN AFFORD ANYTHING YOU WANT. WHY DO YOU COLLECT THESE CREEPY PAINTINGS?
CALMS ME.
YOU'RE KIDDING.
YOU ASKED.
YOU NEVER KNOW WHAT'S REAL AND WHAT ISN'T HERE IN HOLLYWOOD. IN THIS TOWN, THESE ARE LIKE... SOCIETY'S RESTRAINTS ALL STRIPPED AWAY, WHAT PEOPLE ARE, STRIPPED BARE, NOT GOOD, NOT EVIL... JUST INSTINCT.
I THINK THE GUY WHO PAINTS THESE HAS A HANDLE ON REALITY. TRUE INNER REALITY. HIS OWN, ANYWAY. AT LEAST HE'S HONEST.
DO YOU THINK THIS MUCH WHEN WE'RE FUCKING?
SOMETIMES.

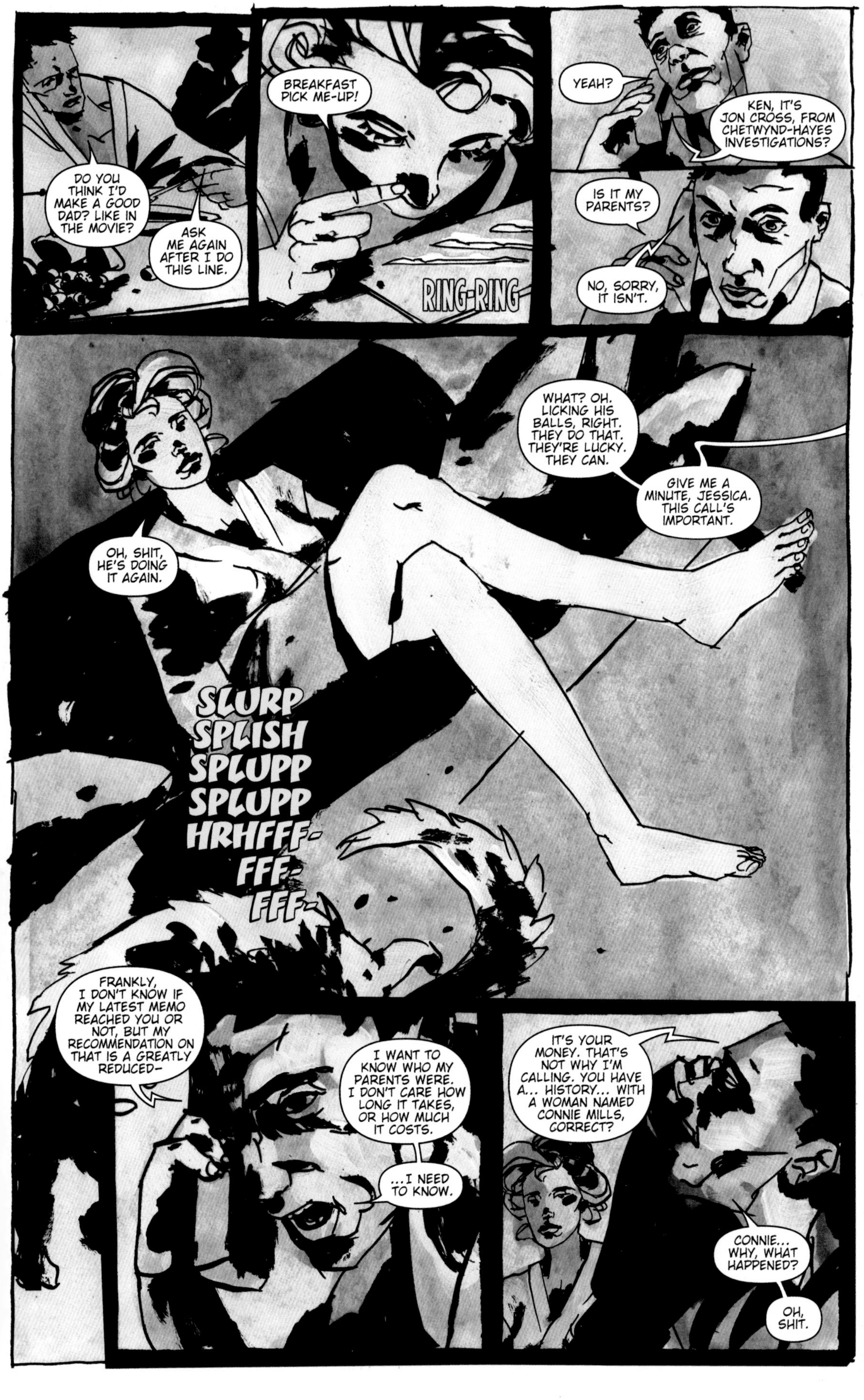
DO YOU THINK I'D MAKE A GOOD DAD? LIKE IN THE MOVIE?
ASK ME AGAIN AFTER I DO THIS LINE.
BREAKFAST PICK ME-UP!
RING-RING
YEAH?
KEN, IT'S JON CROSS, FROM CHETWYND-HAYES INVESTIGATIONS?
IS IT MY PARENTS?
NO, SORRY, IT ISN'T.
OH, SHIT, HE'S DOING IT AGAIN.
WHAT? OH. LICKING HIS BALLS, RIGHT. THEY DO THAT. THEY'RE LUCKY. THEY CAN.
GIVE ME A MINUTE, JESSICA. THIS CALL'S IMPORTANT.
SLURP SPLISH SPLUPP SPLUPP HRHFFF-FFF-FFF-
FRANKLY, I DON'T KNOW IF MY LATEST MEMO REACHED YOU OR NOT, BUT MY RECOMMENDATION ON THAT IS A GREATLY REDUCED–
I WANT TO KNOW WHO MY PARENTS WERE. I DON'T CARE HOW LONG IT TAKES, OR HOW MUCH IT COSTS.
...I NEED TO KNOW.
IT'S YOUR MONEY. THAT'S NOT WHY I'M CALLING. YOU HAVE A... HISTORY... WITH A WOMAN NAMED CONNIE MILLS, CORRECT?
CONNIE... WHY, WHAT HAPPENED?
OH, SHIT.

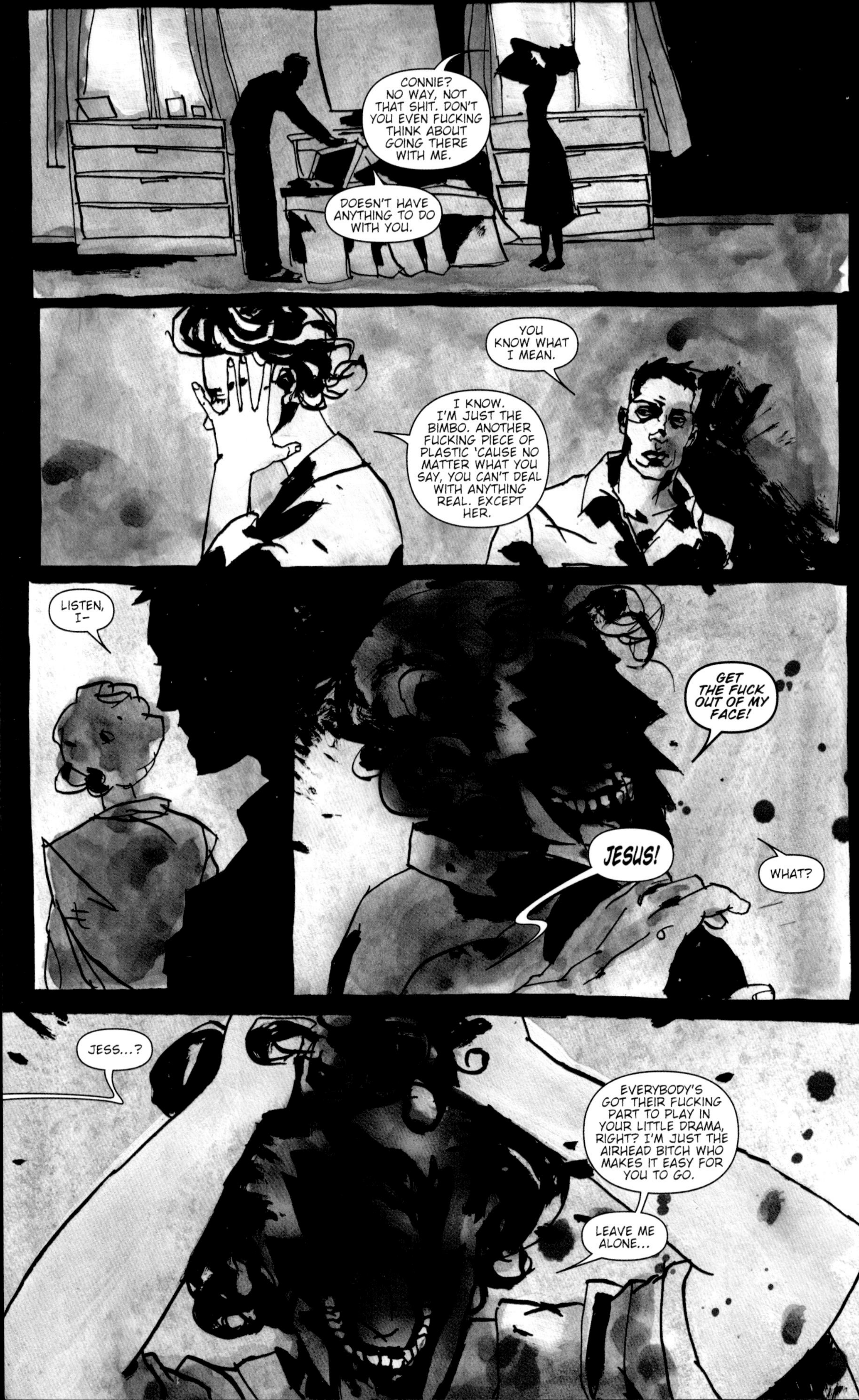
CONNIE? NO WAY, NOT THAT SHIT. DON'T YOU EVEN FUCKING THINK ABOUT GOING THERE WITH ME.
DOESN'T HAVE ANYTHING TO DO WITH YOU.
YOU KNOW WHAT I MEAN.
I KNOW. I'M JUST THE BIMBO. ANOTHER FUCKING PIECE OF PLASTIC 'CAUSE NO MATTER WHAT YOU SAY, YOU CAN'T DEAL WITH ANYTHING REAL. EXCEPT HER.
LISTEN, I-
GET THE FUCK OUT OF MY FACE!
JESUS!
WHAT?
JESS...?
EVERYBODY'S GOT THEIR FUCKING PART TO PLAY IN YOUR LITTLE DRAMA, RIGHT? I'M JUST THE AIRHEAD BITCH WHO MAKES IT EASY FOR YOU TO GO.
LEAVE ME ALONE...

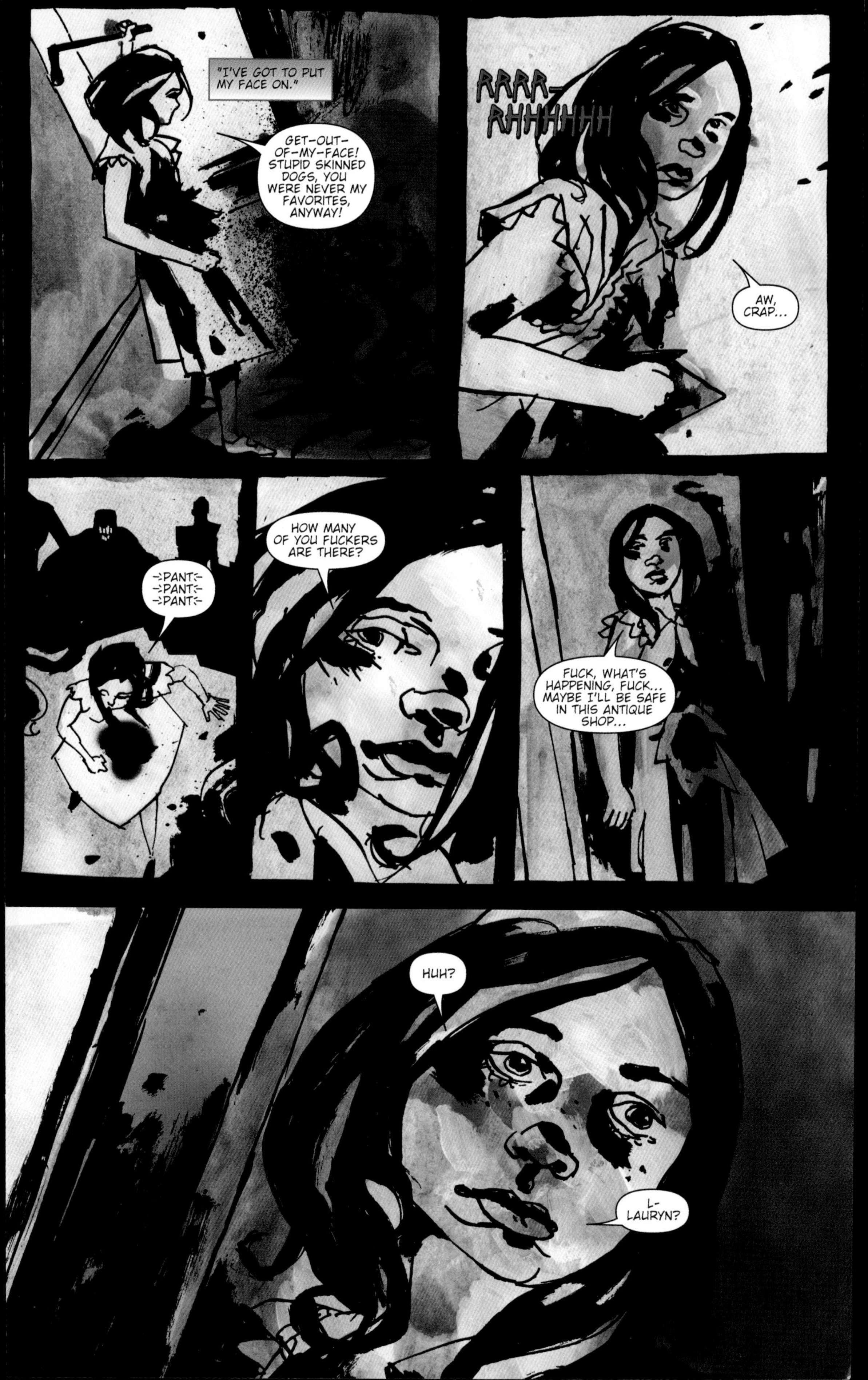
"I'VE GOT TO PUT MY FACE ON."
GET-OUT-OF-MY-FACE! STUPID SKINNED DOGS, YOU WERE NEVER MY FAVORITES, ANYWAY!
RRRR-RHHHHHH
AW, CRAP...
-PANT- -PANT- -PANT-
HOW MANY OF YOU FUCKERS ARE THERE?
FUCK, WHAT'S HAPPENING, FUCK... MAYBE I'LL BE SAFE IN THIS ANTIQUE SHOP...
HUH?
L-LAURYN?

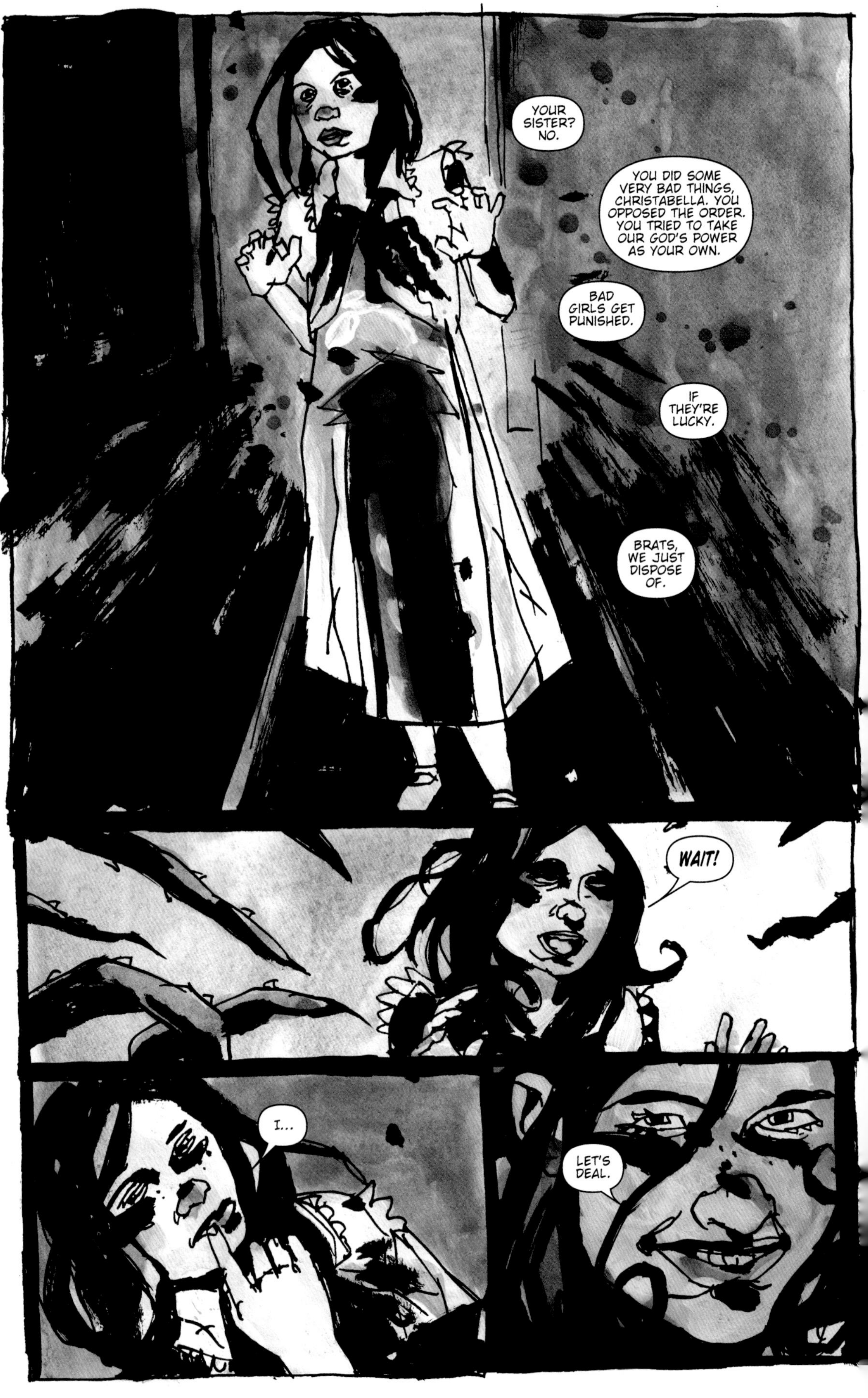
YOUR SISTER? NO.
YOU DID SOME VERY BAD THINGS, CHRISTABELLA. YOU OPPOSED THE ORDER. YOU TRIED TO TAKE OUR GOD'S POWER AS YOUR OWN.
BAD GIRLS GET PUNISHED.
IF THEY'RE LUCKY.
BRATS, WE JUST DISPOSE OF.
WAIT!
I...
LET'S DEAL.

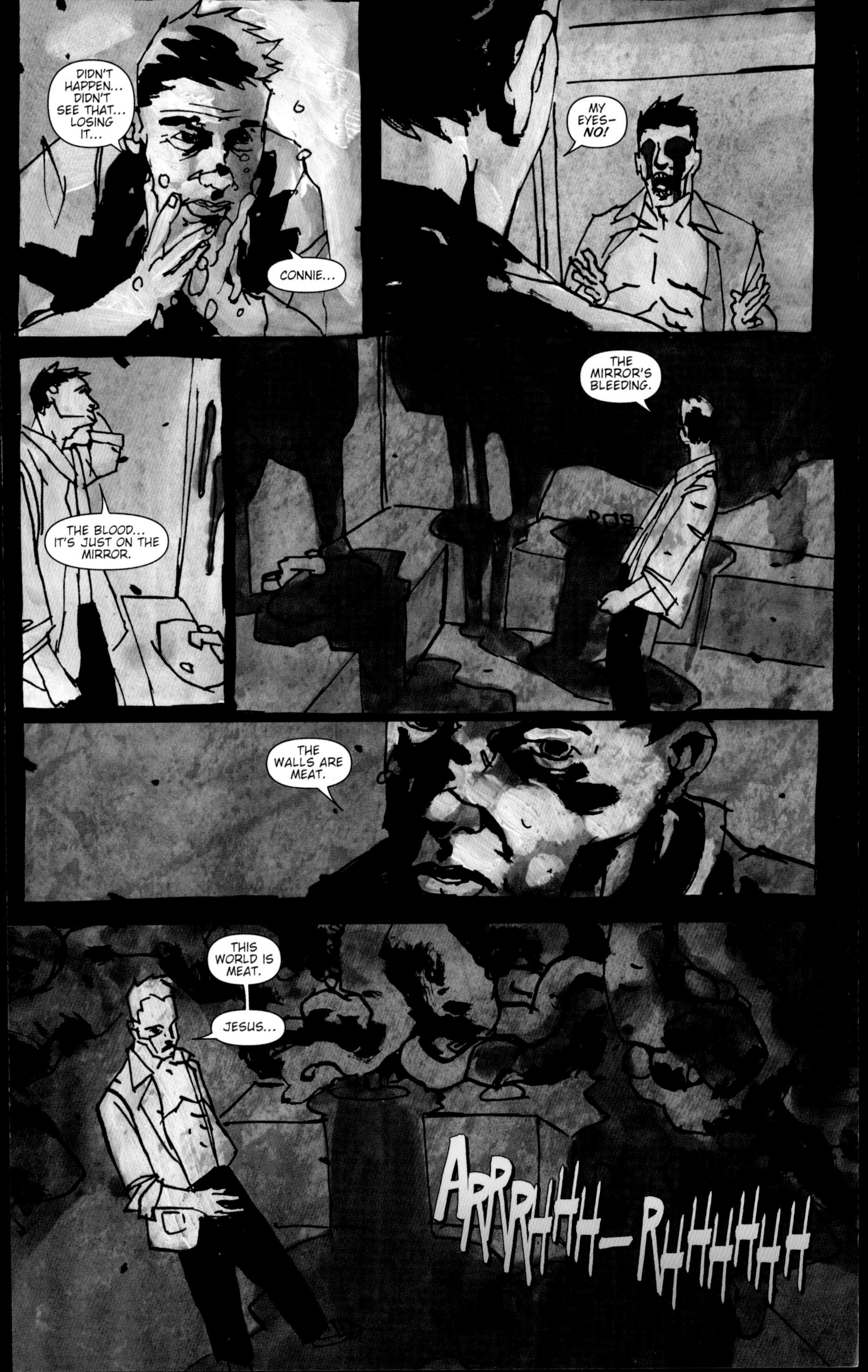
DIDN'T HAPPEN... DIDN'T SEE THAT... LOSING IT...
CONNIE...
MY EYES- NO!
THE BLOOD... IT'S JUST ON THE MIRROR.
THE MIRROR'S BLEEDING.
THE WALLS ARE MEAT.
THIS WORLD IS MEAT.
JESUS...
ARRRHHH-RHHHHHH

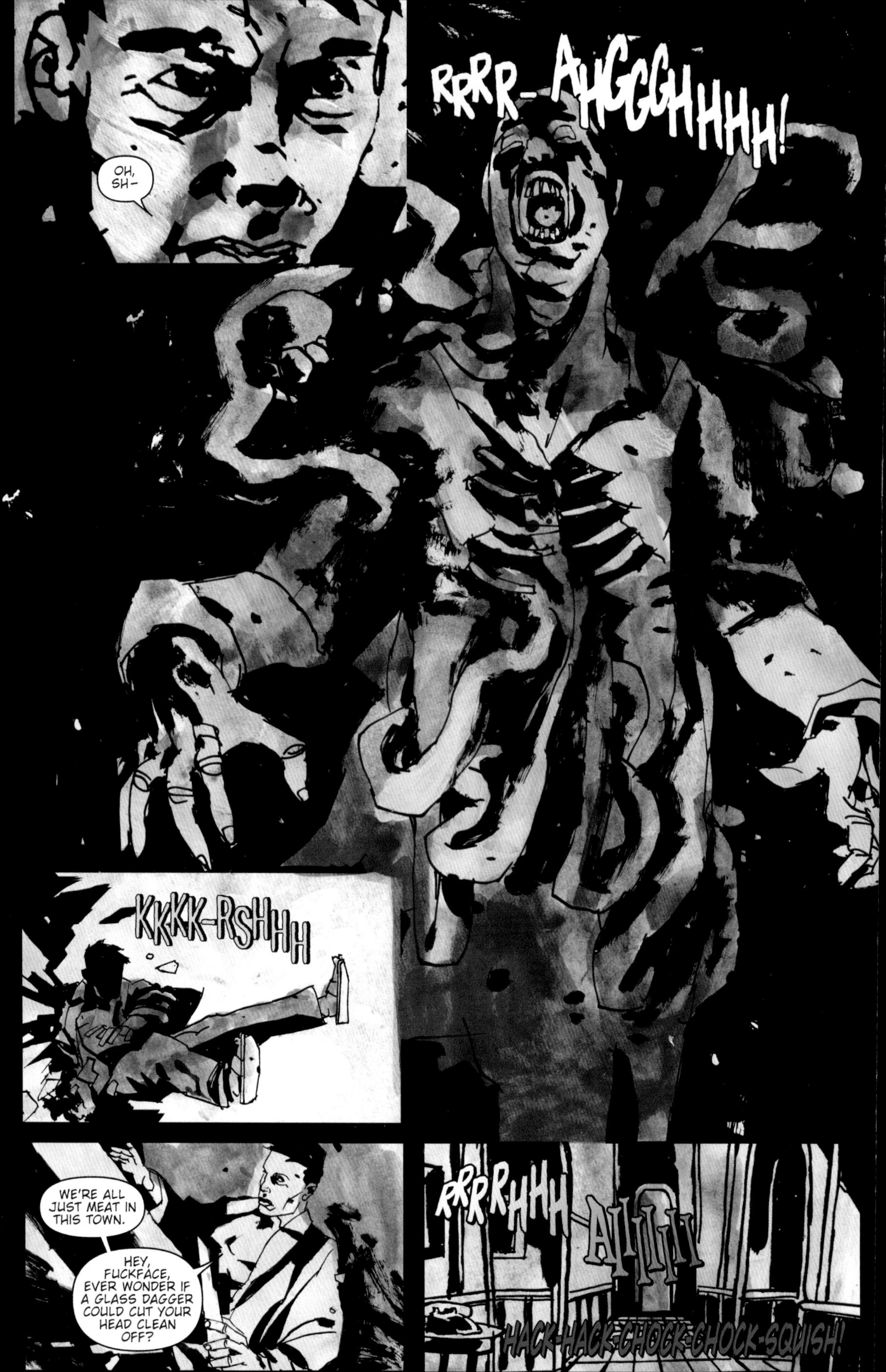
OH, SH-
RRRR-AHGGGHHHH!
KKKK-RSHHHH
WE'RE ALL JUST MEAT IN THIS TOWN.
HEY, FUCKFACE, EVER WONDER IF A GLASS DAGGER COULD CUT YOUR HEAD CLEAN OFF?
RRRRHHH AIIIII
HACK-HACK-CHOCK-CHOCK-SQUISH!

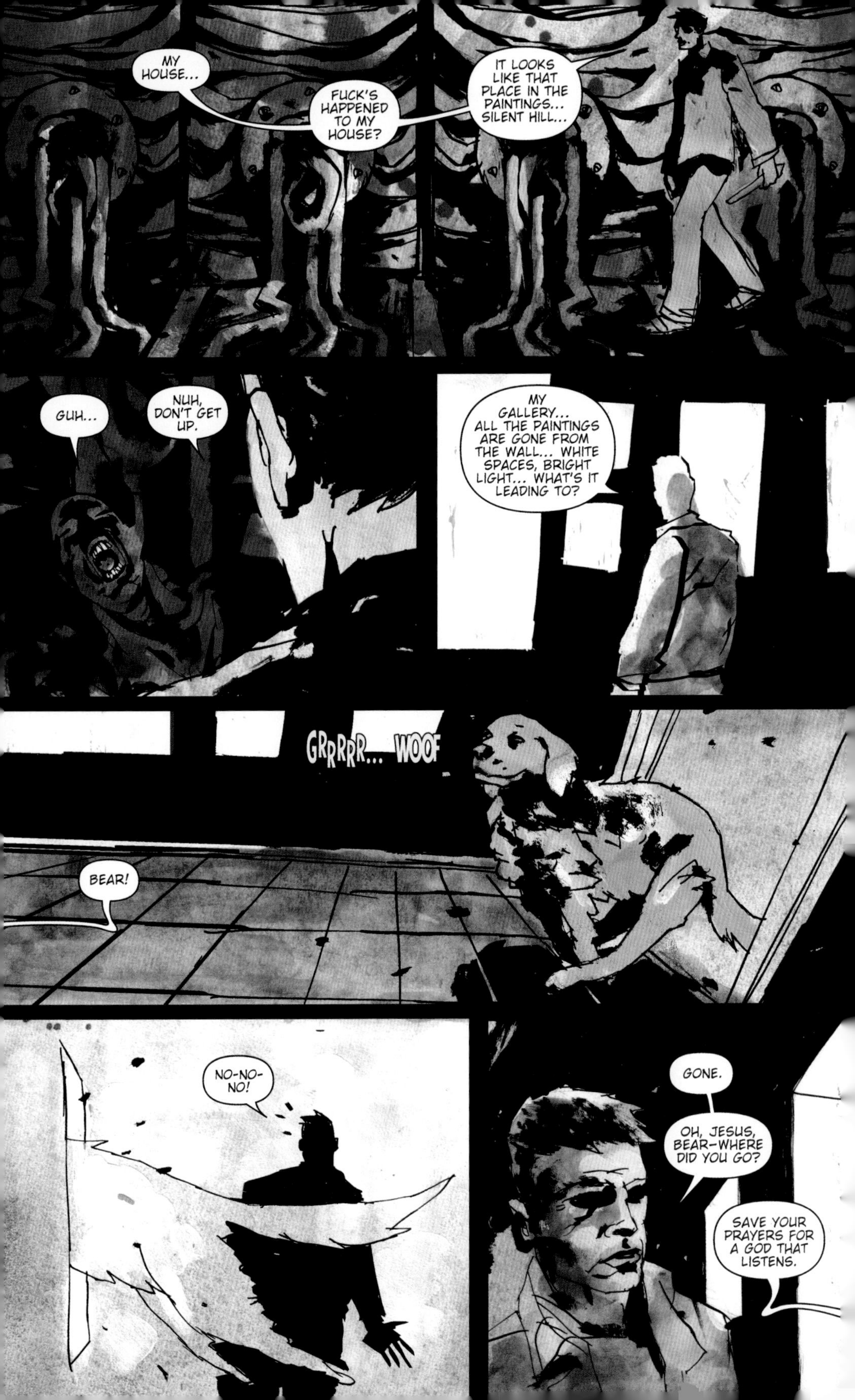
MY HOUSE...
FUCK'S HAPPENED TO MY HOUSE?
IT LOOKS LIKE THAT PLACE IN THE PAINTINGS... SILENT HILL...
GUH...
NUH, DON'T GET UP.
MY GALLERY... ALL THE PAINTINGS ARE GONE FROM THE WALL... WHITE SPACES, BRIGHT LIGHT... WHAT'S IT LEADING TO?
GRRRRR... WOOF
BEAR!
NO-NO-NO!
GONE.
OH, JESUS, BEAR—WHERE DID YOU GO?
SAVE YOUR PRAYERS FOR A GOD THAT LISTENS.

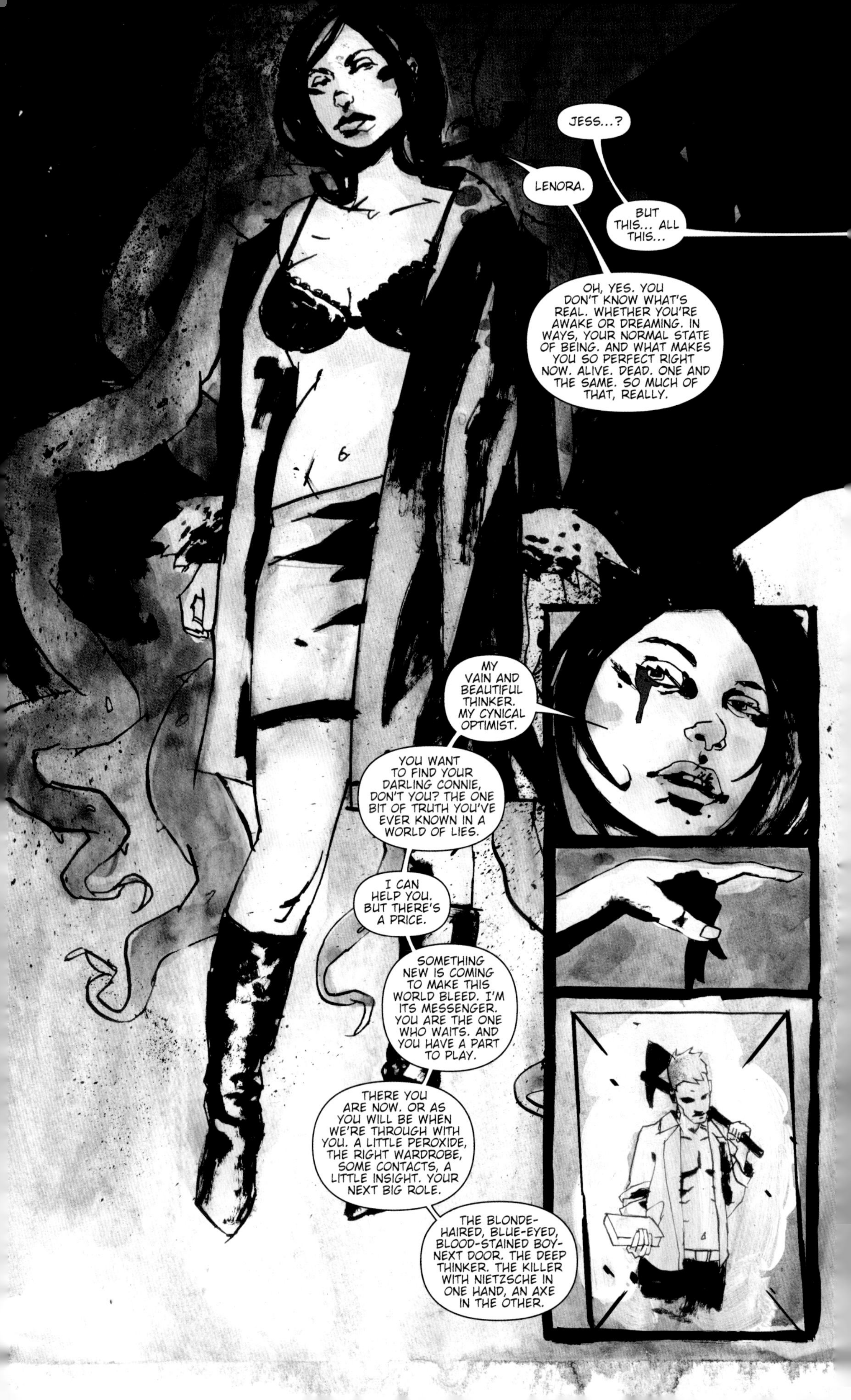
JESS...?
LENORA.
BUT THIS... ALL THIS...
OH, YES. YOU DON'T KNOW WHAT'S REAL. WHETHER YOU'RE AWAKE OR DREAMING. IN WAYS, YOUR NORMAL STATE OF BEING. AND WHAT MAKES YOU SO PERFECT RIGHT NOW. ALIVE. DEAD. ONE AND THE SAME. SO MUCH OF THAT, REALLY.
MY VAIN AND BEAUTIFUL THINKER. MY CYNICAL OPTIMIST.
YOU WANT TO FIND YOUR DARLING CONNIE, DON'T YOU? THE ONE BIT OF TRUTH YOU'VE EVER KNOWN IN A WORLD OF LIES.
I CAN HELP YOU. BUT THERE'S A PRICE.
SOMETHING NEW IS COMING TO MAKE THIS WORLD BLEED. I'M ITS MESSENGER. YOU ARE THE ONE WHO WAITS. AND YOU HAVE A PART TO PLAY.
THERE YOU ARE NOW. OR AS YOU WILL BE WHEN WE'RE THROUGH WITH YOU. A LITTLE PEROXIDE, THE RIGHT WARDROBE, SOME CONTACTS, A LITTLE INSIGHT. YOUR NEXT BIG ROLE.
THE BLONDE-HAIRED, BLUE-EYED, BLOOD-STAINED BOY-NEXT DOOR. THE DEEP THINKER. THE KILLER WITH NIETZSCHE IN ONE HAND, AN AXE IN THE OTHER.

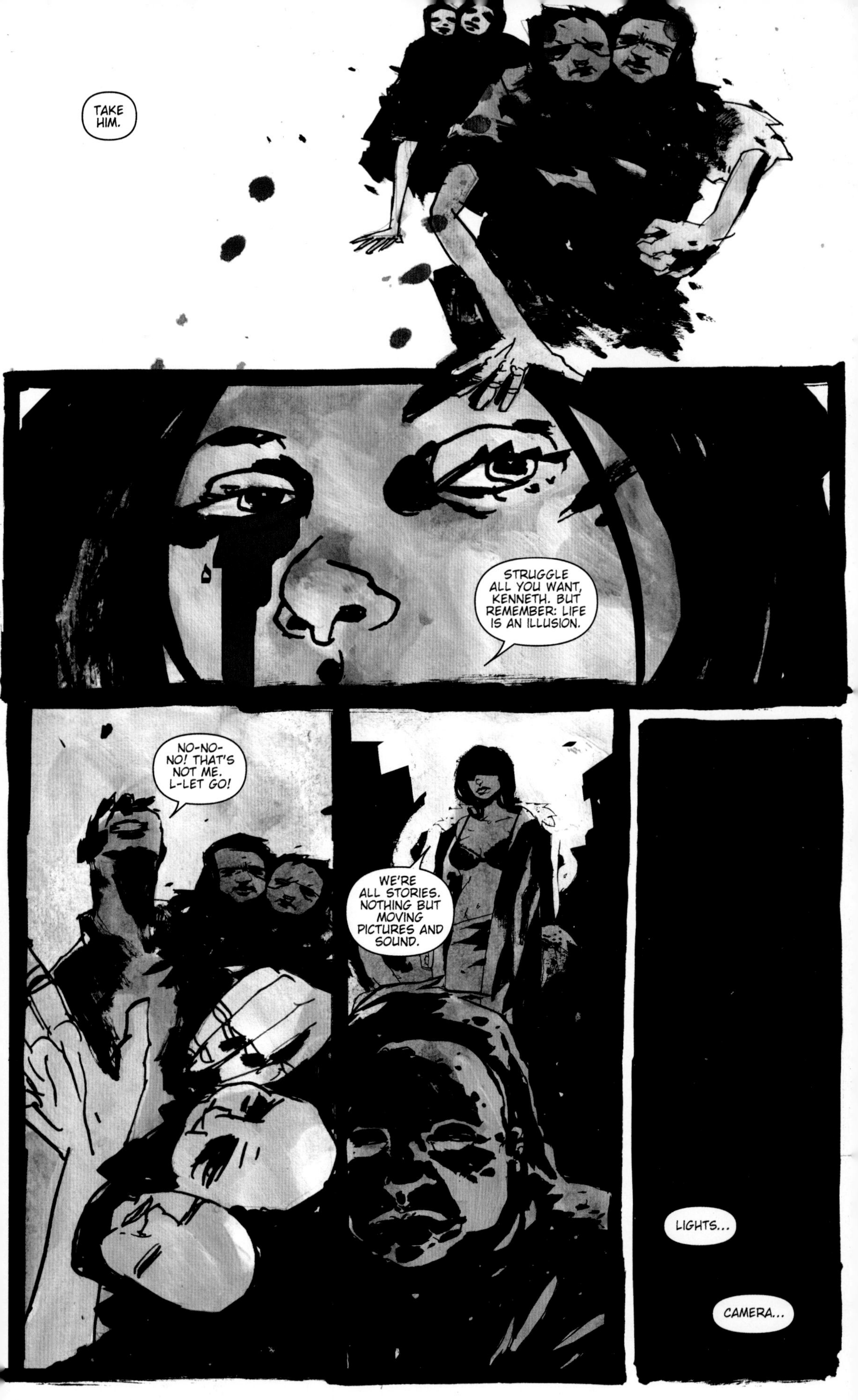
TAKE HIM.
STRUGGLE ALL YOU WANT, KENNETH. BUT REMEMBER: LIFE IS AN ILLUSION.
NO-NO-NO! THAT'S NOT ME. L-LET GO!
WE'RE ALL STORIES. NOTHING BUT MOVING PICTURES AND SOUND.
LIGHTS...
CAMERA...

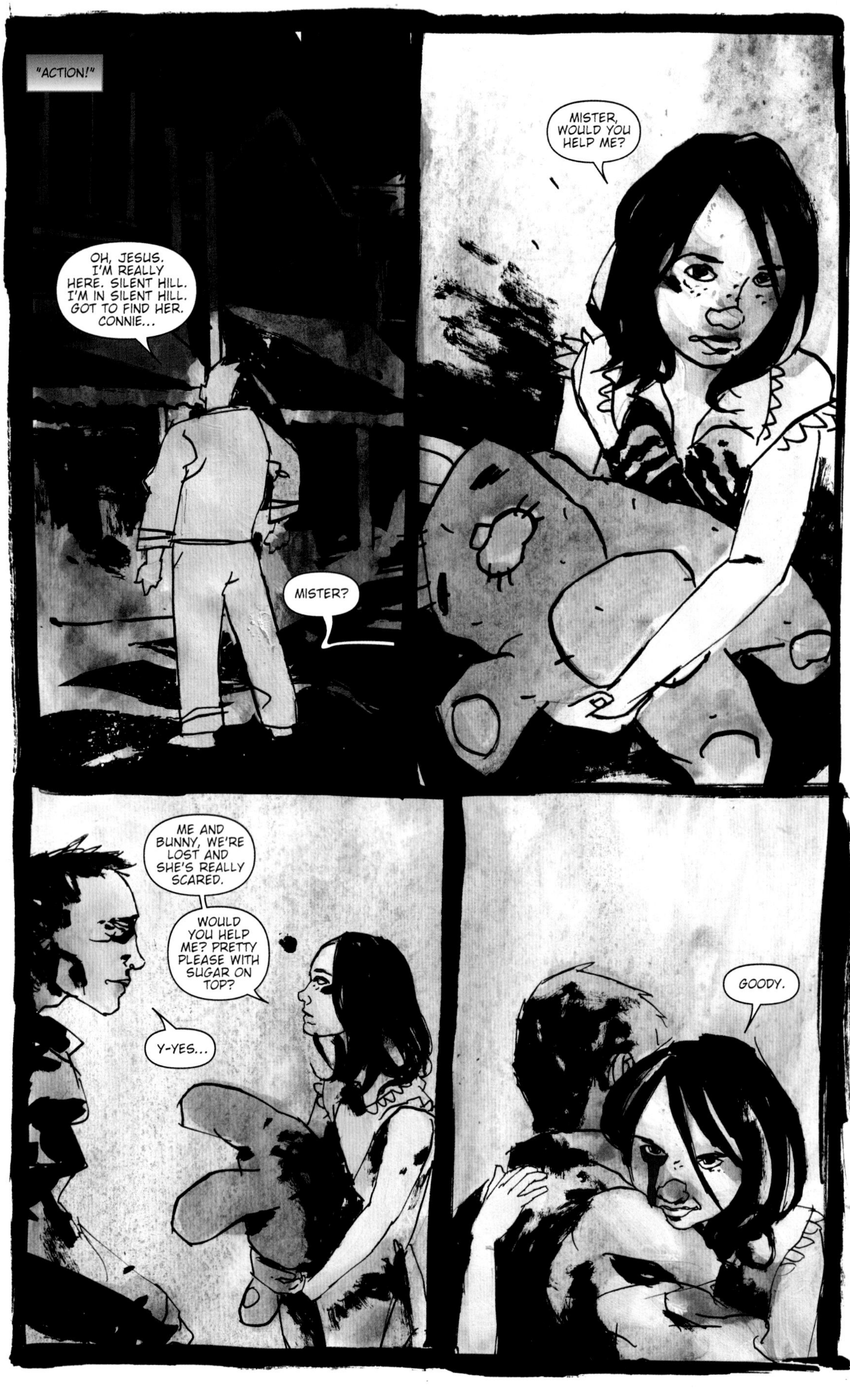
"ACTION!"
OH, JESUS. I'M REALLY HERE. SILENT HILL. I'M IN SILENT HILL. GOT TO FIND HER. CONNIE...
MISTER?
MISTER, WOULD YOU HELP ME?
ME AND BUNNY, WE'RE LOST AND SHE'S REALLY SCARED.
WOULD YOU HELP ME? PRETTY PLEASE WITH SUGAR ON TOP?
Y-YES...
GOODY.

Chapter
2

HERE LIES JESSICA ALDRICH
AN ANNOYING LITTLE WHORE
WHO GOT WHAT SHE DESERVES
I AM COMING
KENNETH WITH BLOOD ON
HIS HANDS   COMING
COMING
WHO'S NEXT?

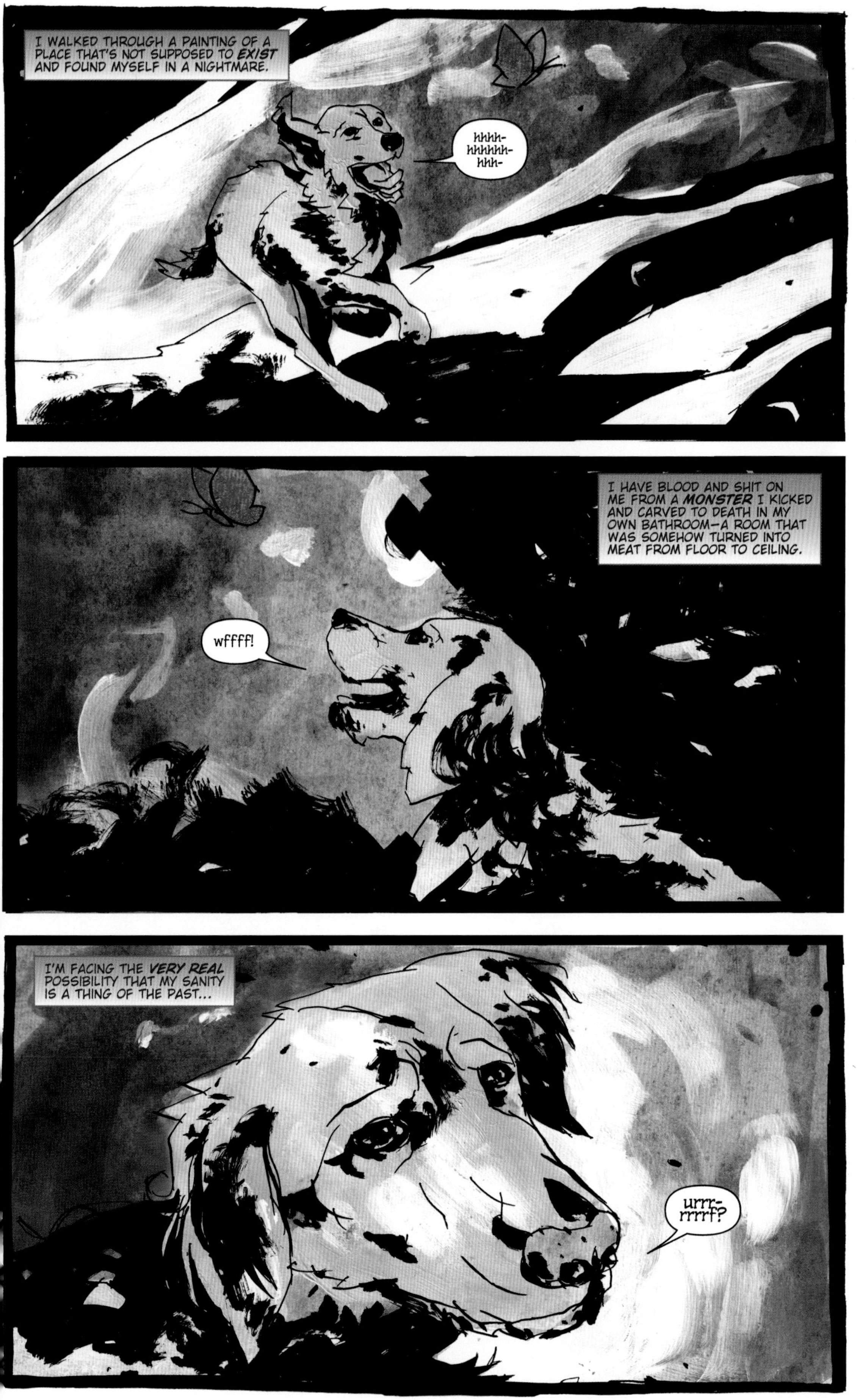
I WALKED THROUGH A PAINTING OF A PLACE THAT'S NOT SUPPOSED TO EXIST AND FOUND MYSELF IN A NIGHTMARE.
hhhh-hhhhhh-hhh-
I HAVE BLOOD AND SHIT ON ME FROM A MONSTER I KICKED AND CARVED TO DEATH IN MY OWN BATHROOM—A ROOM THAT WAS SOMEHOW TURNED INTO MEAT FROM FLOOR TO CEILING.
wffff!
I'M FACING THE VERY REAL POSSIBILITY THAT MY SANITY IS A THING OF THE PAST...
urrr-rrrrf?

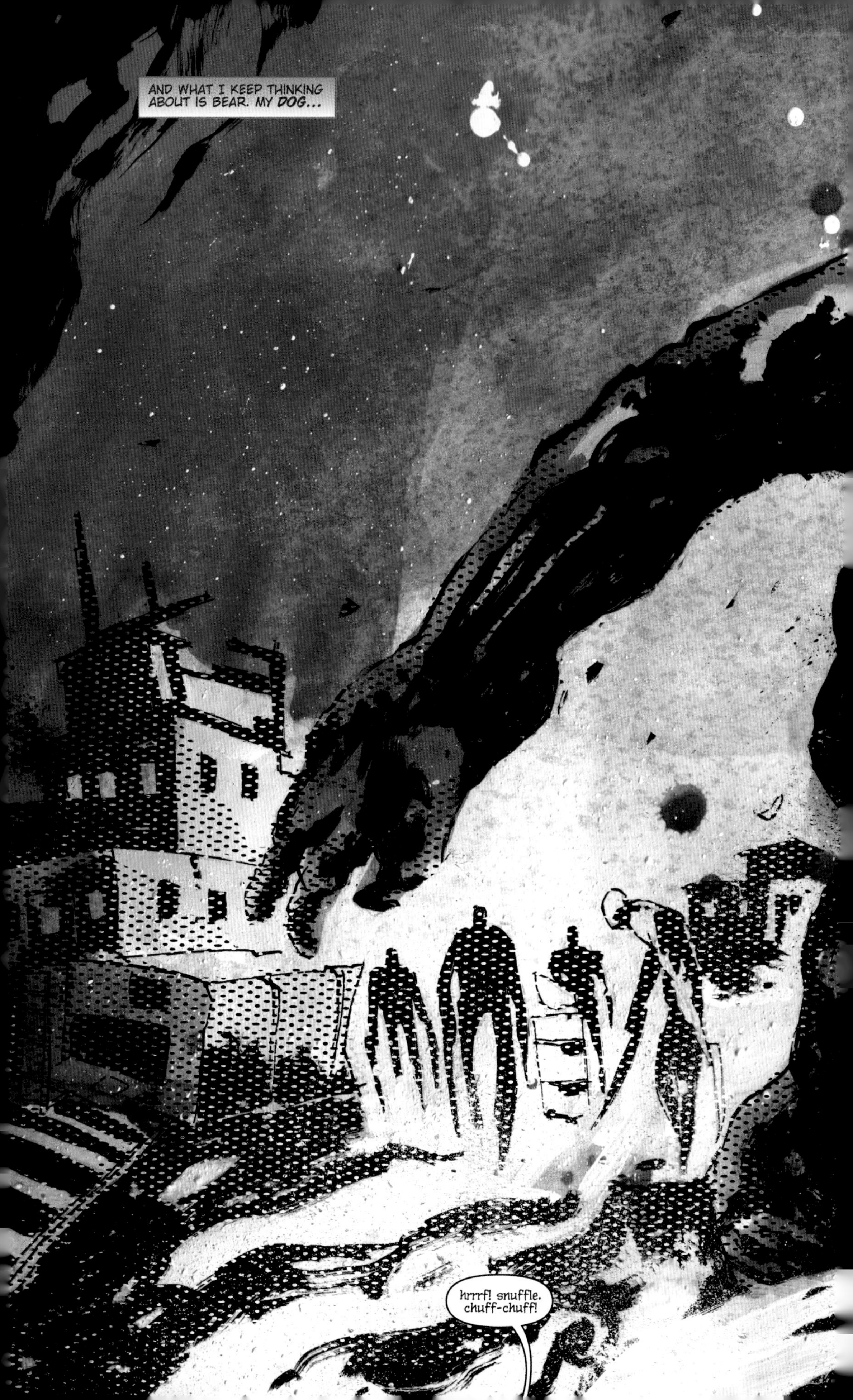
AND WHAT I KEEP THINKING ABOUT IS BEAR. MY *DOG*...
hrrrf! snuffle. chuff-chuff!

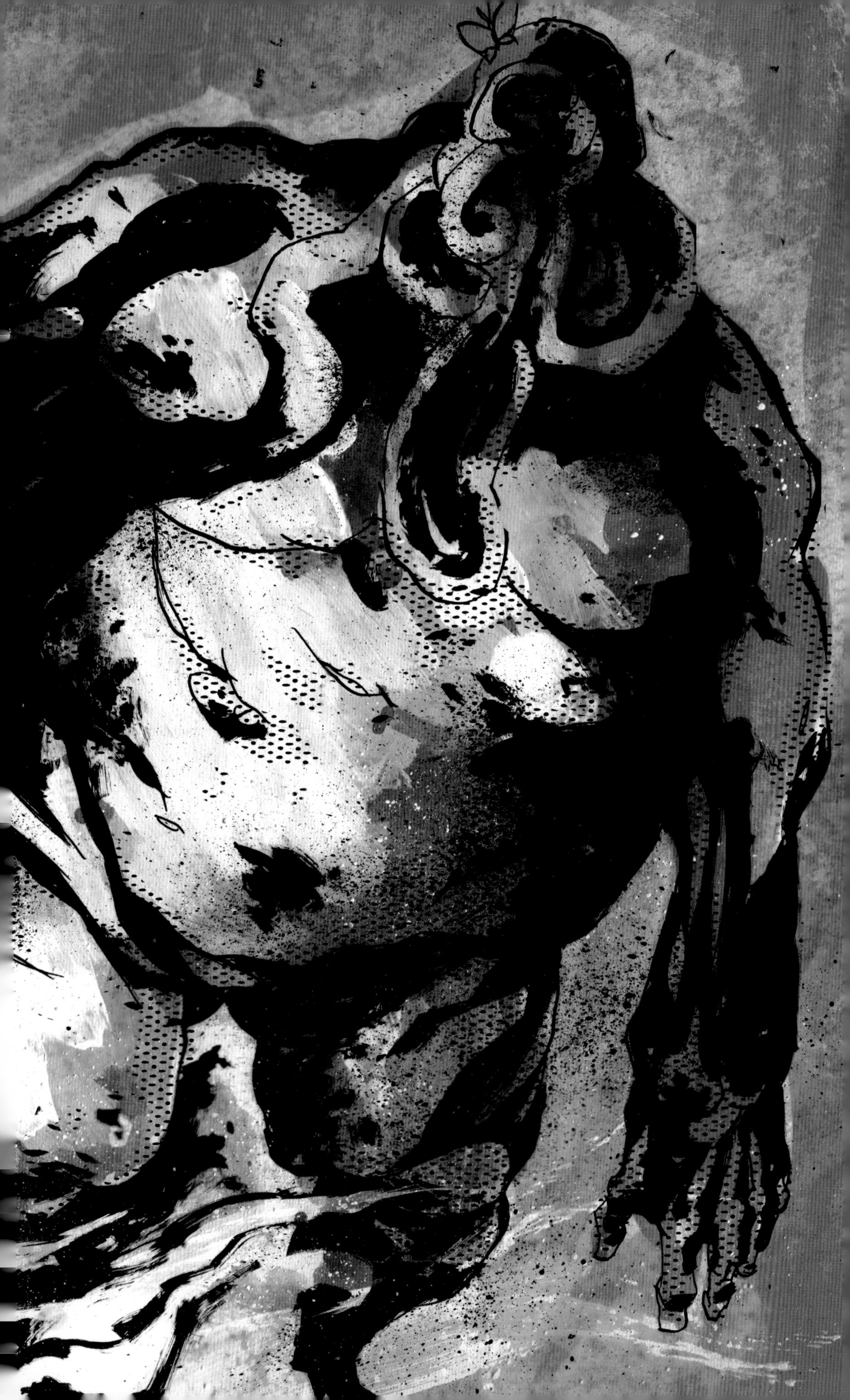

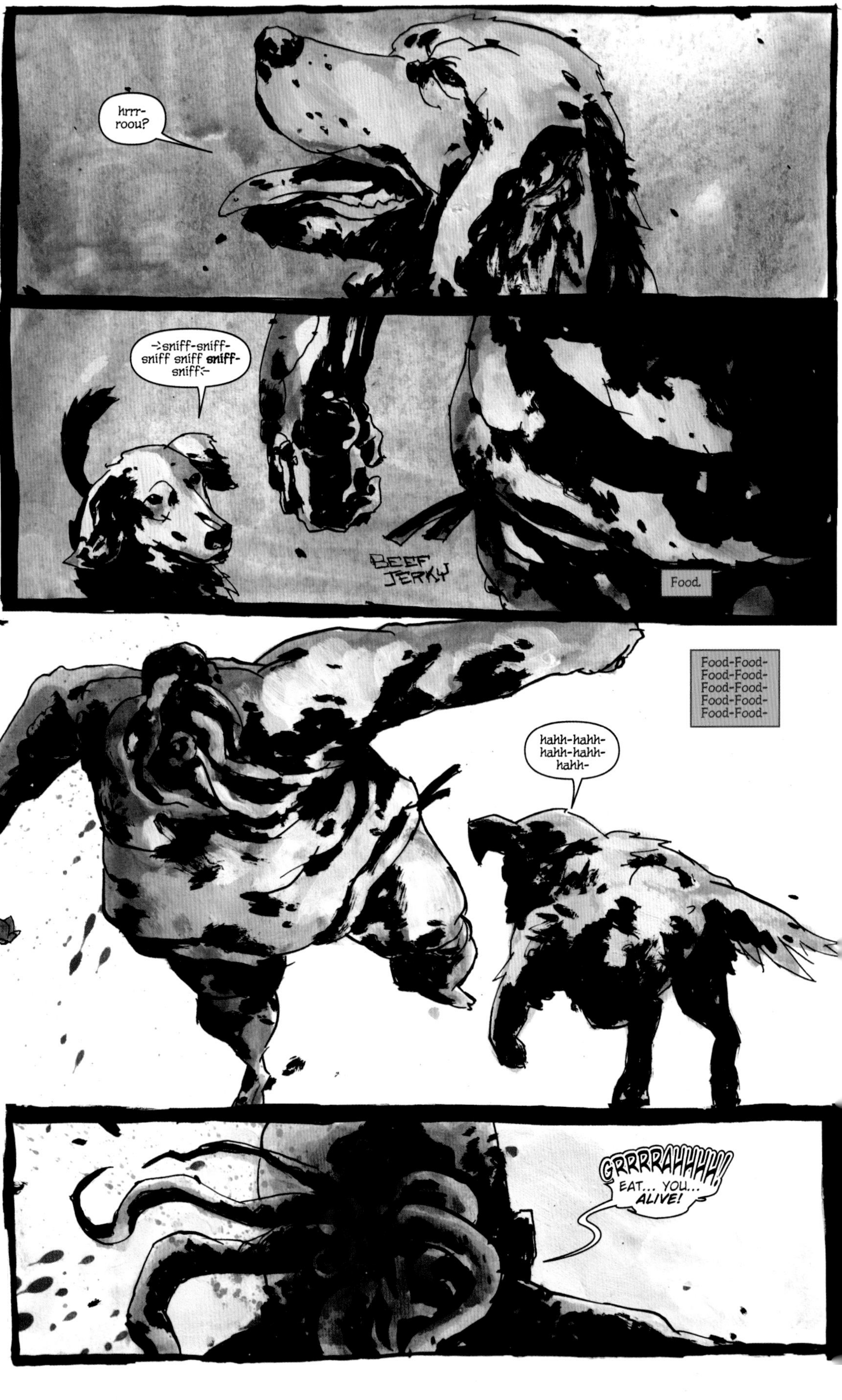
hrrr-
roou?
-sniff-sniff-
sniff sniff sniff-
sniff-
BEEF JERKY
Food.
Food-Food-
Food-Food-
Food-Food-
Food-Food-
Food-Food-
hahh-hahh-
hahh-hahh-
hahh-
GRRRRAHHHH!
EAT... YOU...
ALIVE!

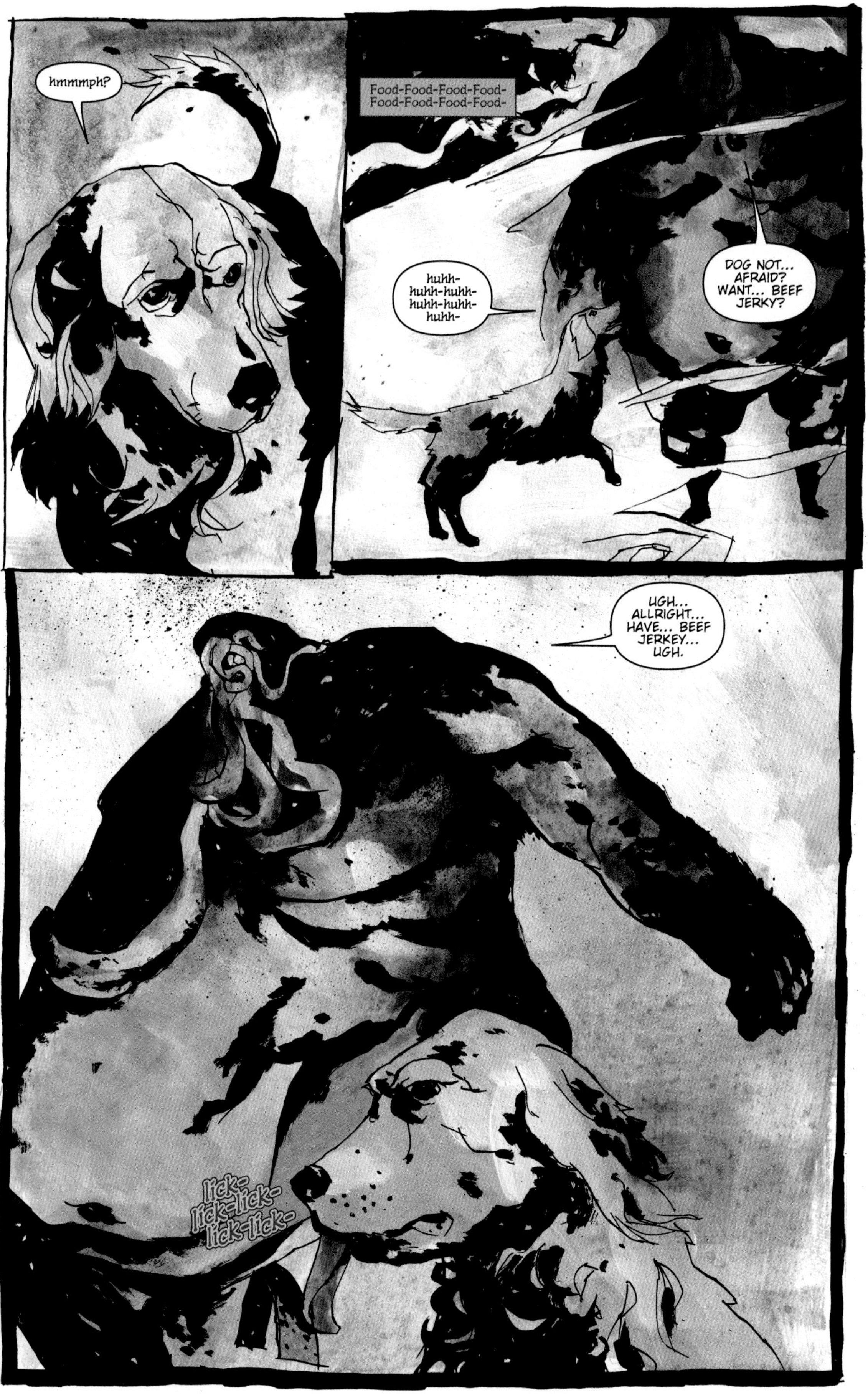
hmmmph?
Food-Food-Food-Food-
Food-Food-Food-Food-
huhh-
huhh-huhh-
huhh-huhh-
huhh-
DOG NOT... AFRAID? WANT... BEEF JERKY?
UGH... ALLRIGHT... HAVE... BEEF JERKEY... UGH.
lick-
lick-lick-
lick-lick-

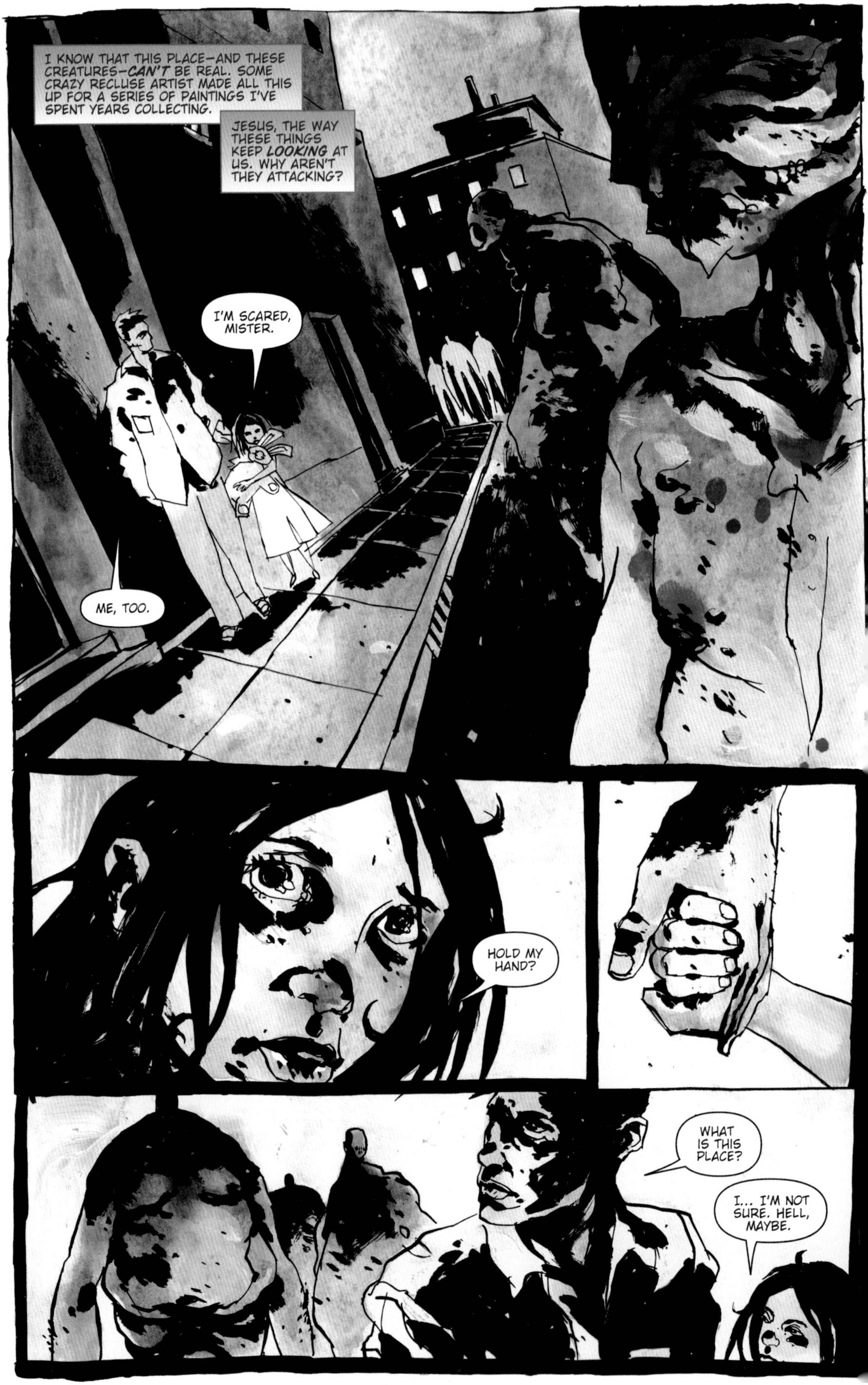
I KNOW THAT THIS PLACE—AND THESE CREATURES—CAN'T BE REAL. SOME CRAZY RECLUSE ARTIST MADE ALL THIS UP FOR A SERIES OF PAINTINGS I'VE SPENT YEARS COLLECTING.
JESUS, THE WAY THESE THINGS KEEP LOOKING AT US. WHY AREN'T THEY ATTACKING?
I'M SCARED, MISTER.
ME, TOO.
HOLD MY HAND?
WHAT IS THIS PLACE?
I... I'M NOT SURE. HELL, MAYBE.

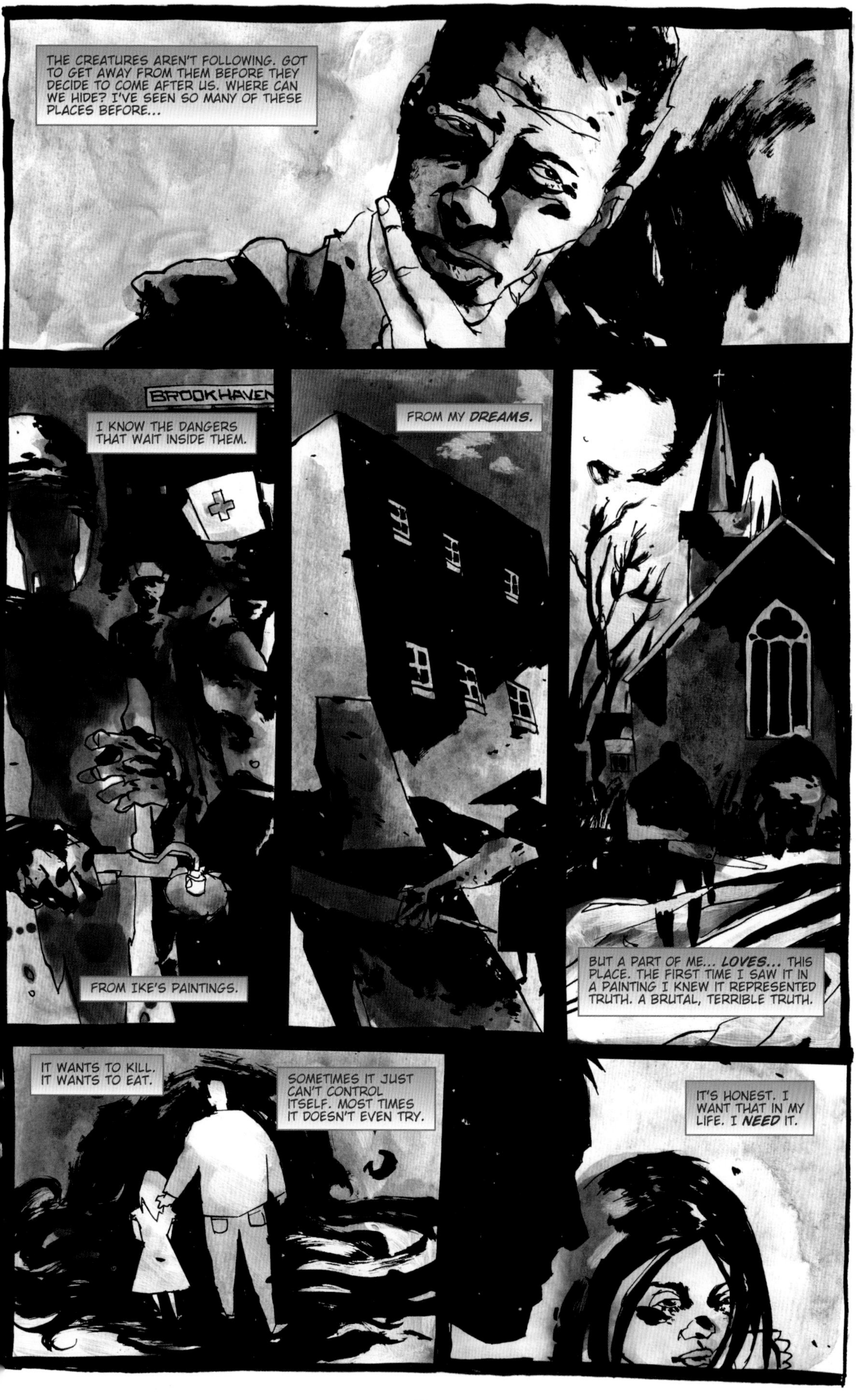

THE CREATURES AREN'T FOLLOWING. GOT TO GET AWAY FROM THEM BEFORE THEY DECIDE TO COME AFTER US. WHERE CAN WE HIDE? I'VE SEEN SO MANY OF THESE PLACES BEFORE...
BROOKHAVEN
I KNOW THE DANGERS THAT WAIT INSIDE THEM.
FROM IKE'S PAINTINGS.
FROM MY DREAMS.
BUT A PART OF ME... LOVES... THIS PLACE. THE FIRST TIME I SAW IT IN A PAINTING I KNEW IT REPRESENTED TRUTH. A BRUTAL, TERRIBLE TRUTH.
IT WANTS TO KILL. IT WANTS TO EAT.
SOMETIMES IT JUST CAN'T CONTROL ITSELF. MOST TIMES IT DOESN'T EVEN TRY.
IT'S HONEST. I WANT THAT IN MY LIFE. I NEED IT.

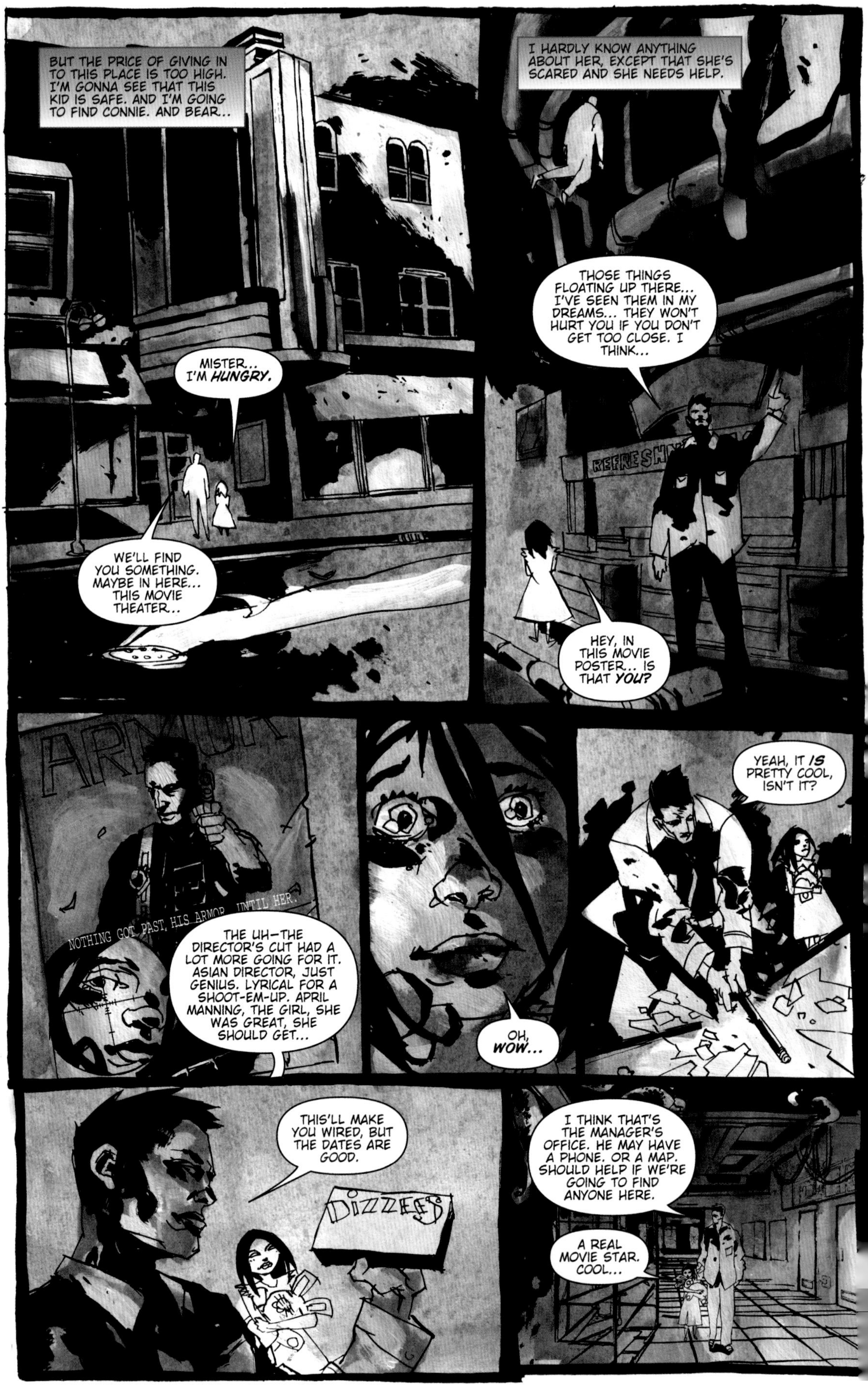
BUT THE PRICE OF GIVING IN TO THIS PLACE IS TOO HIGH. I'M GONNA SEE THAT THIS KID IS SAFE. AND I'M GOING TO FIND CONNIE. AND BEAR...
MISTER... I'M *HUNGRY.*
WE'LL FIND YOU SOMETHING. MAYBE IN HERE... THIS MOVIE THEATER...
I HARDLY KNOW ANYTHING ABOUT HER, EXCEPT THAT SHE'S SCARED AND SHE NEEDS HELP.
THOSE THINGS FLOATING UP THERE... I'VE SEEN THEM IN MY DREAMS... THEY WON'T HURT YOU IF YOU DON'T GET TOO CLOSE. I THINK...
HEY, IN THIS MOVIE POSTER... IS THAT *YOU?*
NOTHING GOT PAST HIS ARMOR. UNTIL HER.
THE UH—THE DIRECTOR'S CUT HAD A LOT MORE GOING FOR IT. ASIAN DIRECTOR, JUST GENIUS. LYRICAL FOR A SHOOT-EM-UP. APRIL MANNING, THE GIRL, SHE WAS GREAT, SHE SHOULD GET...
OH, *WOW...*
YEAH, IT *IS* PRETTY COOL, ISN'T IT?
THIS'LL MAKE YOU WIRED, BUT THE DATES ARE GOOD.
DIZZEES
I THINK THAT'S THE MANAGER'S OFFICE. HE MAY HAVE A PHONE. OR A MAP. SHOULD HELP IF WE'RE GOING TO FIND ANYONE HERE.
A REAL MOVIE STAR. COOL...

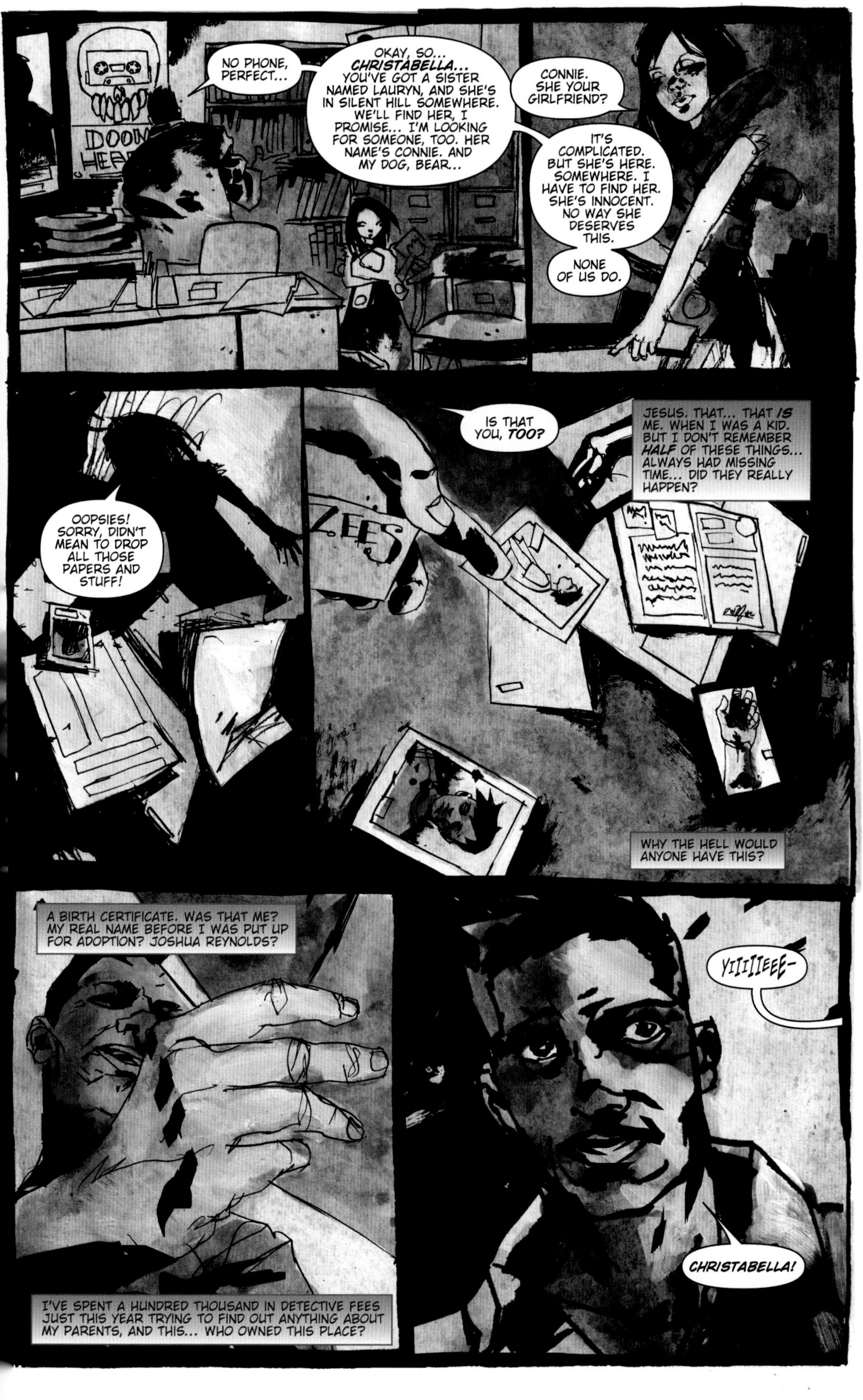
NO PHONE, PERFECT...
OKAY, SO... CHRISTABELLA... YOU'VE GOT A SISTER NAMED LAURYN, AND SHE'S IN SILENT HILL SOMEWHERE. WE'LL FIND HER, I PROMISE... I'M LOOKING FOR SOMEONE, TOO. HER NAME'S CONNIE. AND MY DOG, BEAR...
CONNIE. SHE YOUR GIRLFRIEND?
IT'S COMPLICATED. BUT SHE'S HERE. SOMEWHERE. I HAVE TO FIND HER. SHE'S INNOCENT. NO WAY SHE DESERVES THIS.
NONE OF US DO.
OOPSIES! SORRY, DIDN'T MEAN TO DROP ALL THOSE PAPERS AND STUFF!
IS THAT YOU, TOO?
JESUS. THAT... THAT IS ME. WHEN I WAS A KID. BUT I DON'T REMEMBER HALF OF THESE THINGS... ALWAYS HAD MISSING TIME... DID THEY REALLY HAPPEN?
WHY THE HELL WOULD ANYONE HAVE THIS?
A BIRTH CERTIFICATE. WAS THAT ME? MY REAL NAME BEFORE I WAS PUT UP FOR ADOPTION? JOSHUA REYNOLDS?
I'VE SPENT A HUNDRED THOUSAND IN DETECTIVE FEES JUST THIS YEAR TRYING TO FIND OUT ANYTHING ABOUT MY PARENTS, AND THIS... WHO OWNED THIS PLACE?
YIIIIEEE-
CHRISTABELLA!

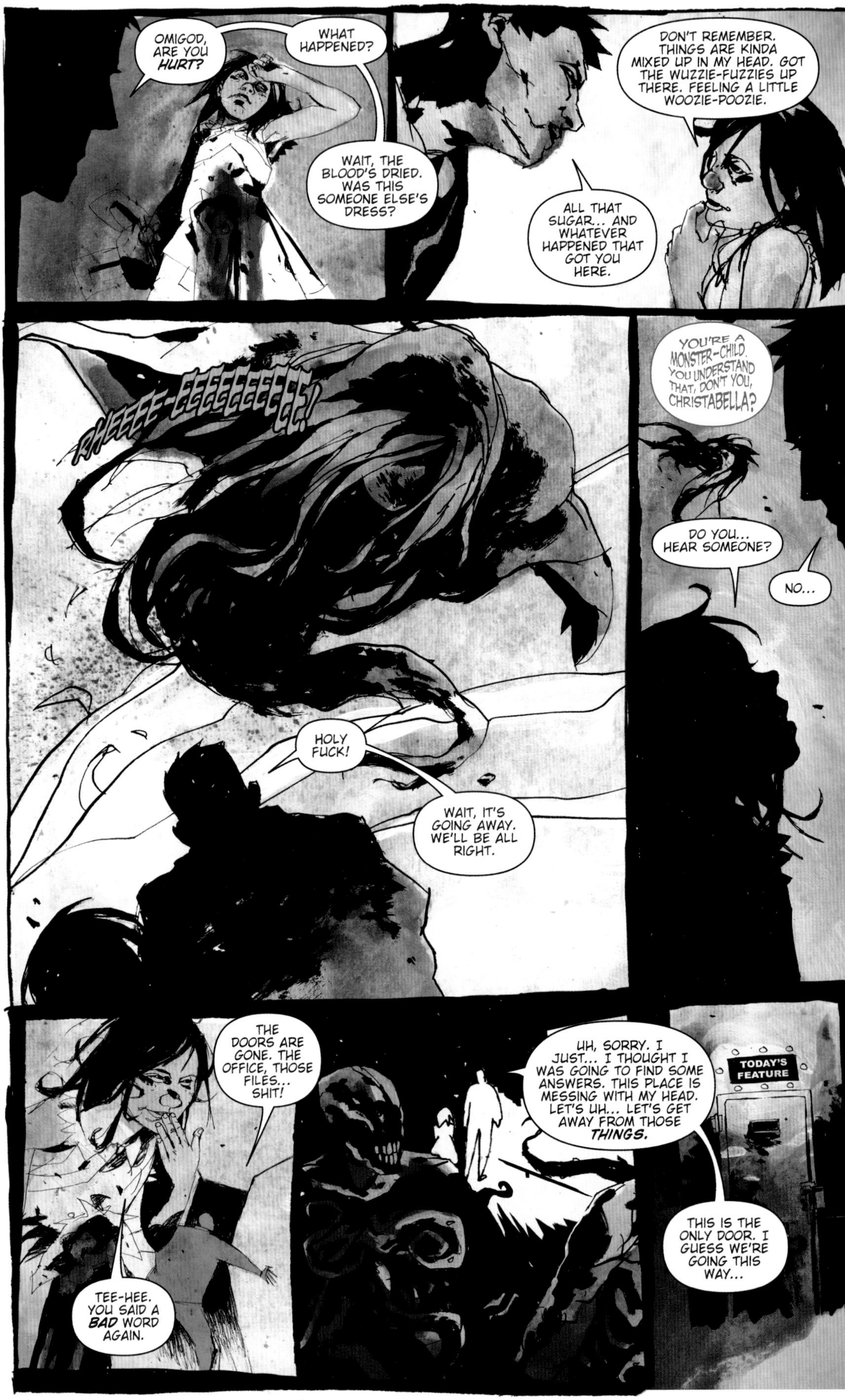

OMIGOD, ARE YOU *HURT?*
WHAT HAPPENED?
WAIT, THE BLOOD'S DRIED. WAS THIS SOMEONE ELSE'S DRESS?
DON'T REMEMBER. THINGS ARE KINDA MIXED UP IN MY HEAD. GOT THE WUZZIE-FUZZIES UP THERE. FEELING A LITTLE WOOZIE-POOZIE.
ALL THAT SUGAR... AND WHATEVER HAPPENED THAT GOT YOU HERE.
RHEEEE-EEEEEEEEEEEE!
HOLY FUCK!
WAIT, IT'S GOING AWAY. WE'LL BE ALL RIGHT.
YOU'RE A MONSTER-CHILD. YOU UNDERSTAND THAT, DON'T YOU, CHRISTABELLA?
DO YOU... HEAR SOMEONE?
NO...
THE DOORS ARE GONE. THE OFFICE, THOSE FILES... SHIT!
TEE-HEE. YOU SAID A *BAD* WORD AGAIN.
UH, SORRY. I JUST... I THOUGHT I WAS GOING TO FIND SOME ANSWERS. THIS PLACE IS MESSING WITH MY HEAD. LET'S UH... LET'S GET AWAY FROM THOSE *THINGS.*
TODAY'S FEATURE
THIS IS THE ONLY DOOR. I GUESS WE'RE GOING THIS WAY...

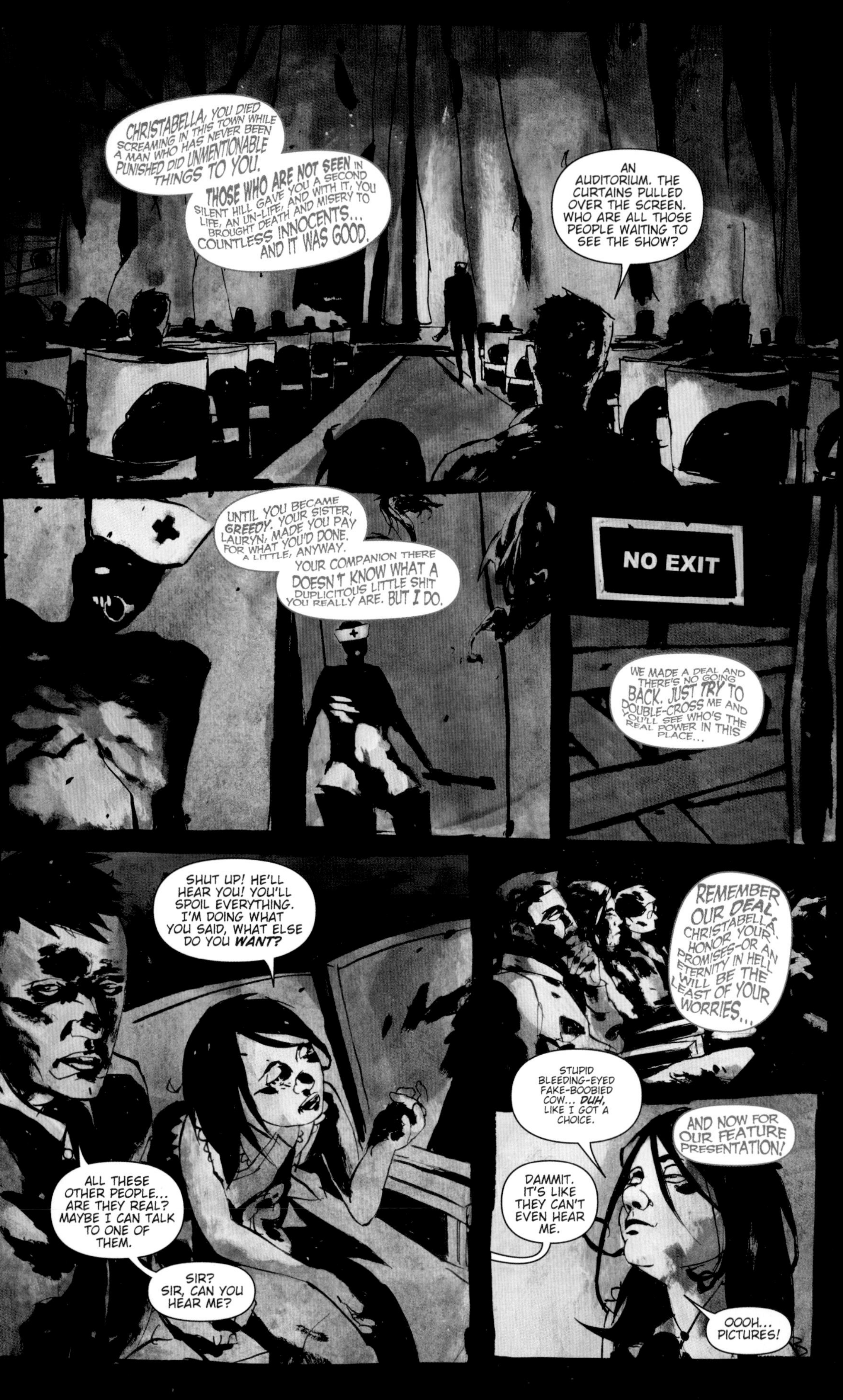

CHRISTABELLA, YOU DIED SCREAMING IN THIS TOWN WHILE A MAN WHO HAS NEVER BEEN PUNISHED DID UNMENTIONABLE THINGS TO YOU.
THOSE WHO ARE NOT SEEN IN SILENT HILL GAVE YOU A SECOND LIFE, AN UN-LIFE, AND WITH IT, YOU BROUGHT DEATH AND MISERY TO COUNTLESS INNOCENTS... AND IT WAS GOOD.
AN AUDITORIUM. THE CURTAINS PULLED OVER THE SCREEN. WHO ARE ALL THOSE PEOPLE WAITING TO SEE THE SHOW?
UNTIL YOU BECAME GREEDY. YOUR SISTER, LAURYN, MADE YOU PAY FOR WHAT YOU'D DONE. A LITTLE, ANYWAY.
YOUR COMPANION THERE DOESN'T KNOW WHAT A DUPLICITOUS LITTLE SHIT YOU REALLY ARE. BUT I DO.
NO EXIT
WE MADE A DEAL AND THERE'S NO GOING BACK. JUST TRY TO DOUBLE-CROSS ME AND YOU'LL SEE WHO'S THE REAL POWER IN THIS PLACE...
SHUT UP! HE'LL HEAR YOU! YOU'LL SPOIL EVERYTHING. I'M DOING WHAT YOU SAID, WHAT ELSE DO YOU WANT?
ALL THESE OTHER PEOPLE... ARE THEY REAL? MAYBE I CAN TALK TO ONE OF THEM.
SIR? SIR, CAN YOU HEAR ME?
REMEMBER OUR DEAL, CHRISTABELLA. HONOR YOUR PROMISES—OR AN ETERNITY IN HELL WILL BE THE LEAST OF YOUR WORRIES...
STUPID BLEEDING-EYED FAKE-BOOBIED COW... DUH, LIKE I GOT A CHOICE.
AND NOW FOR OUR FEATURE PRESENTATION!
DAMMIT. IT'S LIKE THEY CAN'T EVEN HEAR ME.
OOOH... PICTURES!

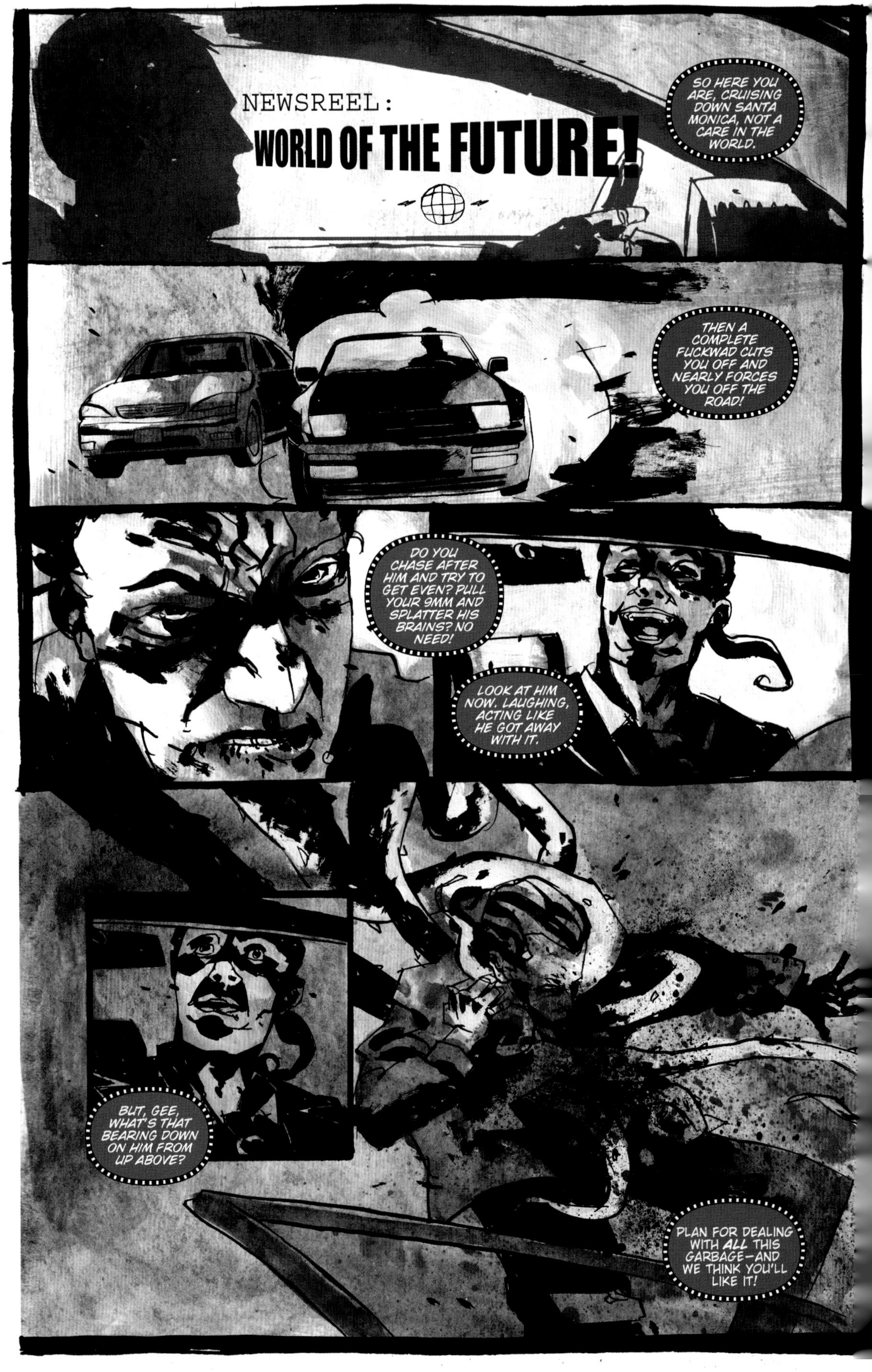
NEWSREEL:
WORLD OF THE FUTURE!
SO HERE YOU ARE, CRUISING DOWN SANTA MONICA, NOT A CARE IN THE WORLD.
THEN A COMPLETE FUCKWAD CUTS YOU OFF AND NEARLY FORCES YOU OFF THE ROAD!
DO YOU CHASE AFTER HIM AND TRY TO GET EVEN? PULL YOUR 9MM AND SPLATTER HIS BRAINS? NO NEED!
LOOK AT HIM NOW. LAUGHING, ACTING LIKE HE GOT AWAY WITH IT.
BUT, GEE, WHAT'S THAT BEARING DOWN ON HIM FROM UP ABOVE?
PLAN FOR DEALING WITH ALL THIS GARBAGE—AND WE THINK YOU'LL LIKE IT!

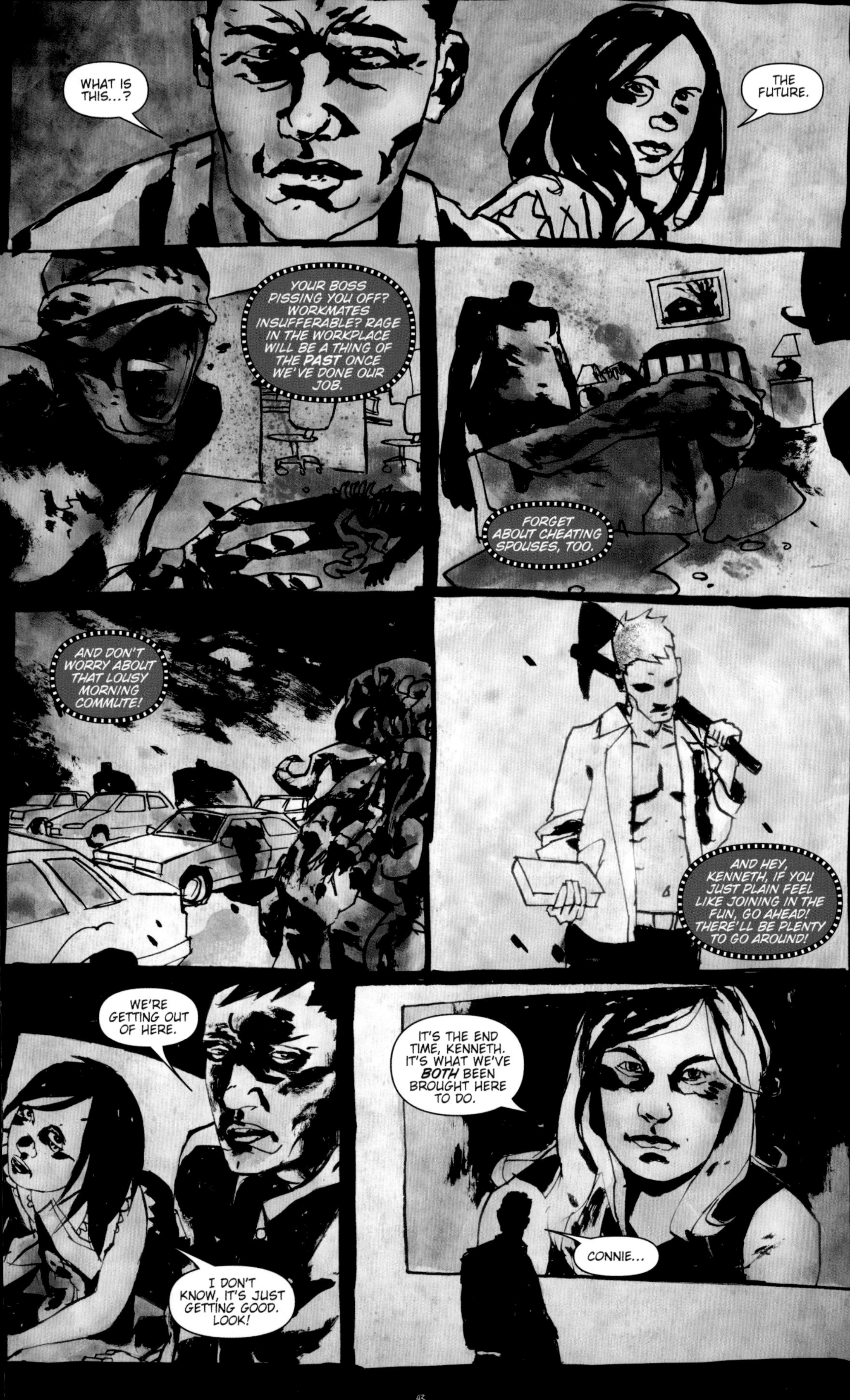
WHAT IS THIS...?
THE FUTURE.
YOUR BOSS PISSING YOU OFF? WORKMATES INSUFFERABLE? RAGE IN THE WORKPLACE WILL BE A THING OF THE PAST ONCE WE'VE DONE OUR JOB.
FORGET ABOUT CHEATING SPOUSES, TOO.
AND DON'T WORRY ABOUT THAT LOUSY MORNING COMMUTE!
AND HEY, KENNETH, IF YOU JUST PLAIN FEEL LIKE JOINING IN THE FUN, GO AHEAD! THERE'LL BE PLENTY TO GO AROUND!
WE'RE GETTING OUT OF HERE.
I DON'T KNOW, IT'S JUST GETTING GOOD. LOOK!
IT'S THE END TIME, KENNETH. IT'S WHAT WE'VE BOTH BEEN BROUGHT HERE TO DO.
CONNIE...

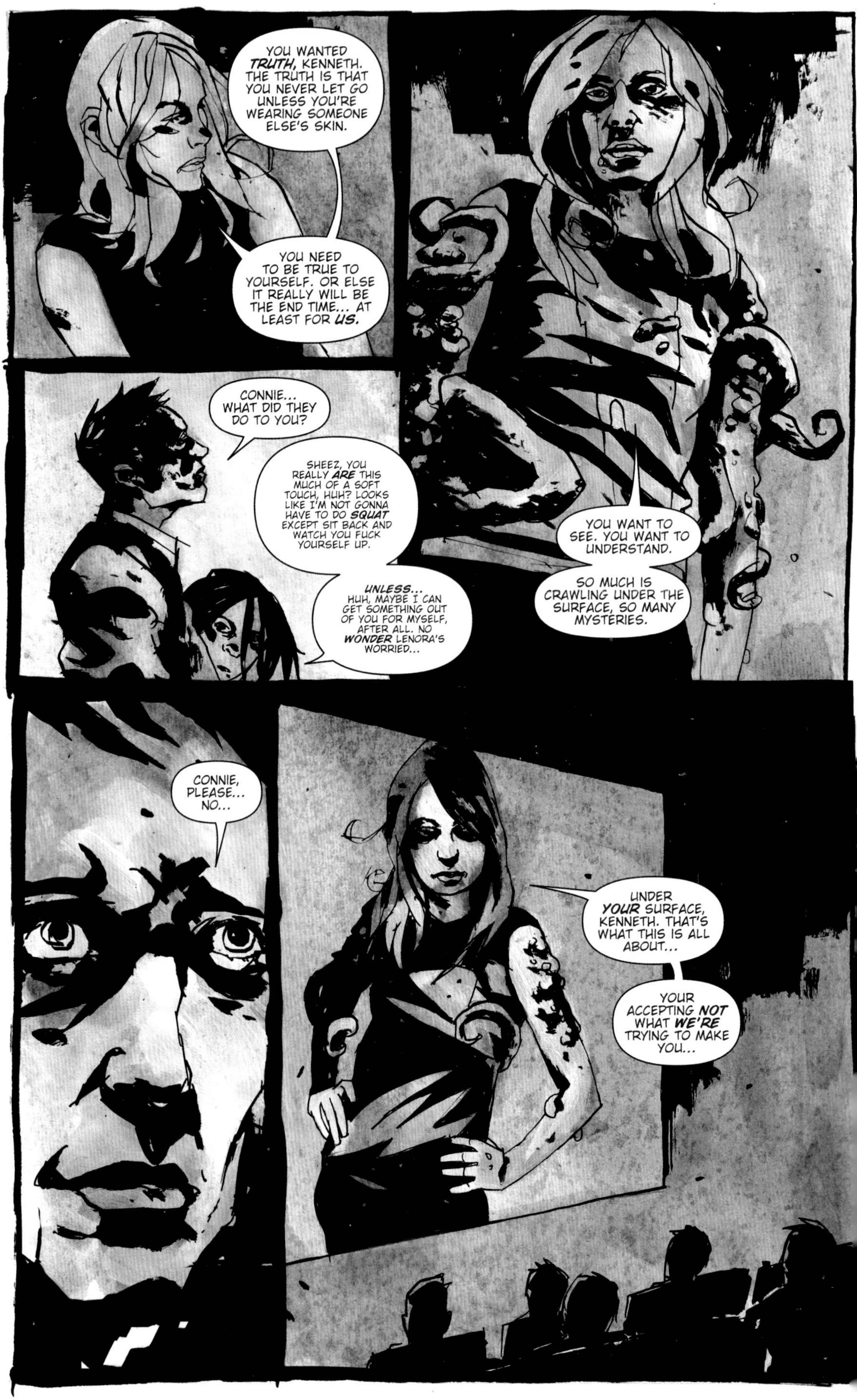
YOU WANTED TRUTH, KENNETH. THE TRUTH IS THAT YOU NEVER LET GO UNLESS YOU'RE WEARING SOMEONE ELSE'S SKIN.
YOU NEED TO BE TRUE TO YOURSELF. OR ELSE IT REALLY WILL BE THE END TIME... AT LEAST FOR US.
CONNIE... WHAT DID THEY DO TO YOU?
SHEEZ, YOU REALLY ARE THIS MUCH OF A SOFT TOUCH, HUH? LOOKS LIKE I'M NOT GONNA HAVE TO DO SQUAT EXCEPT SIT BACK AND WATCH YOU FUCK YOURSELF UP.
UNLESS... HUH, MAYBE I CAN GET SOMETHING OUT OF YOU FOR MYSELF, AFTER ALL. NO WONDER LENORA'S WORRIED...
YOU WANT TO SEE. YOU WANT TO UNDERSTAND.
SO MUCH IS CRAWLING UNDER THE SURFACE, SO MANY MYSTERIES.
CONNIE, PLEASE... NO...
UNDER YOUR SURFACE, KENNETH. THAT'S WHAT THIS IS ALL ABOUT...
YOUR ACCEPTING NOT WHAT WE'RE TRYING TO MAKE YOU...

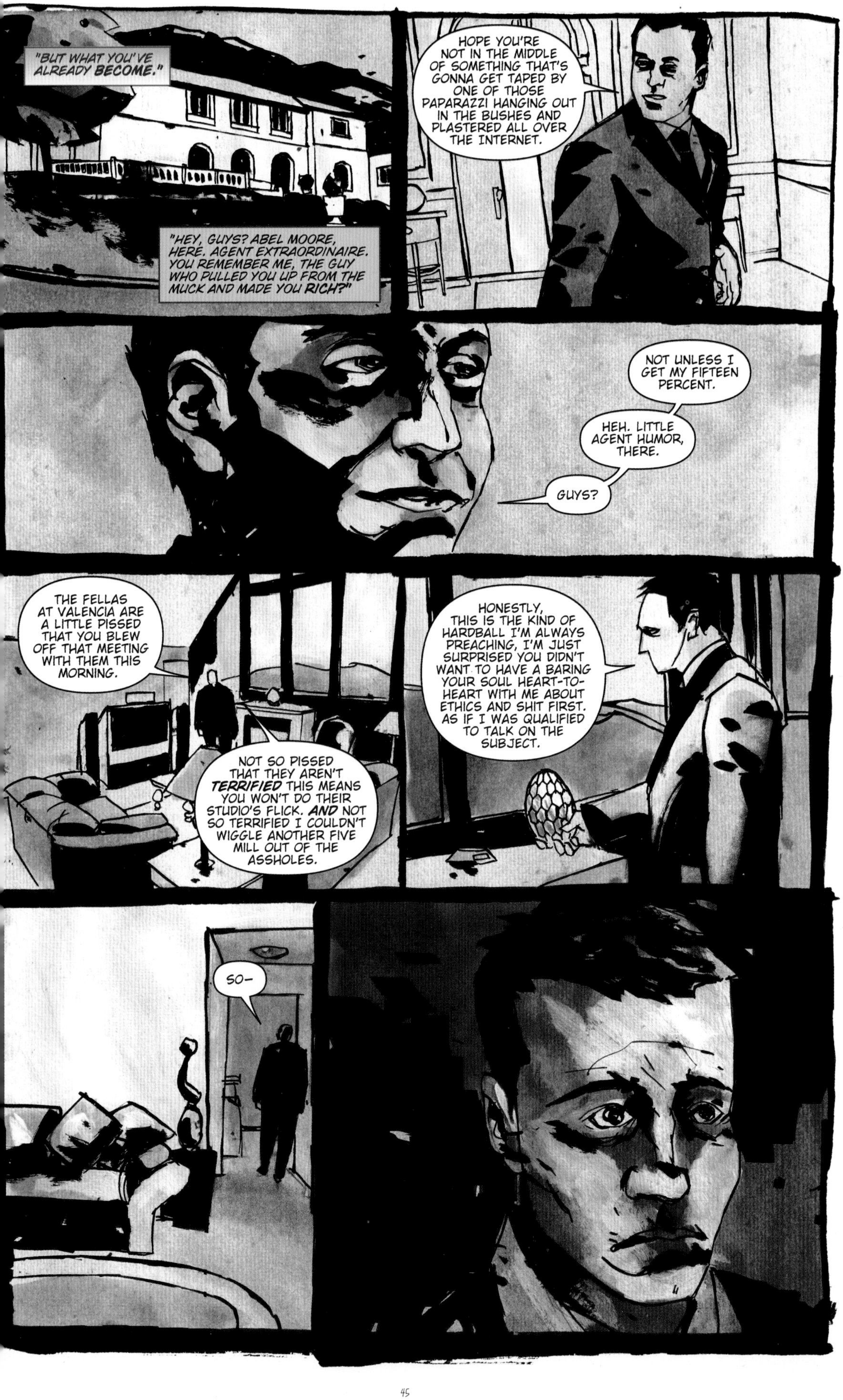
"BUT WHAT YOU'VE ALREADY BECOME."
"HEY, GUYS? ABEL MOORE, HERE. AGENT EXTRAORDINAIRE. YOU REMEMBER ME, THE GUY WHO PULLED YOU UP FROM THE MUCK AND MADE YOU RICH?"
HOPE YOU'RE NOT IN THE MIDDLE OF SOMETHING THAT'S GONNA GET TAPED BY ONE OF THOSE PAPARAZZI HANGING OUT IN THE BUSHES AND PLASTERED ALL OVER THE INTERNET.
NOT UNLESS I GET MY FIFTEEN PERCENT.
HEH. LITTLE AGENT HUMOR, THERE.
GUYS?
THE FELLAS AT VALENCIA ARE A LITTLE PISSED THAT YOU BLEW OFF THAT MEETING WITH THEM THIS MORNING.
NOT SO PISSED THAT THEY AREN'T TERRIFIED THIS MEANS YOU WON'T DO THEIR STUDIO'S FLICK. AND NOT SO TERRIFIED I COULDN'T WIGGLE ANOTHER FIVE MILL OUT OF THE ASSHOLES.
HONESTLY, THIS IS THE KIND OF HARDBALL I'M ALWAYS PREACHING, I'M JUST SURPRISED YOU DIDN'T WANT TO HAVE A BARING YOUR SOUL HEART-TO-HEART WITH ME ABOUT ETHICS AND SHIT FIRST. AS IF I WAS QUALIFIED TO TALK ON THE SUBJECT.
SO–

HERE LIES JESSICA ALDRICH
AN ANNOYING LITTLE WHORE
WHO GOT WHAT SHE DESERVES
I AM COMING
KENNETH WITH BLOOD ON
HIS HANDS COMING
COMING
WHO'S NEXT?

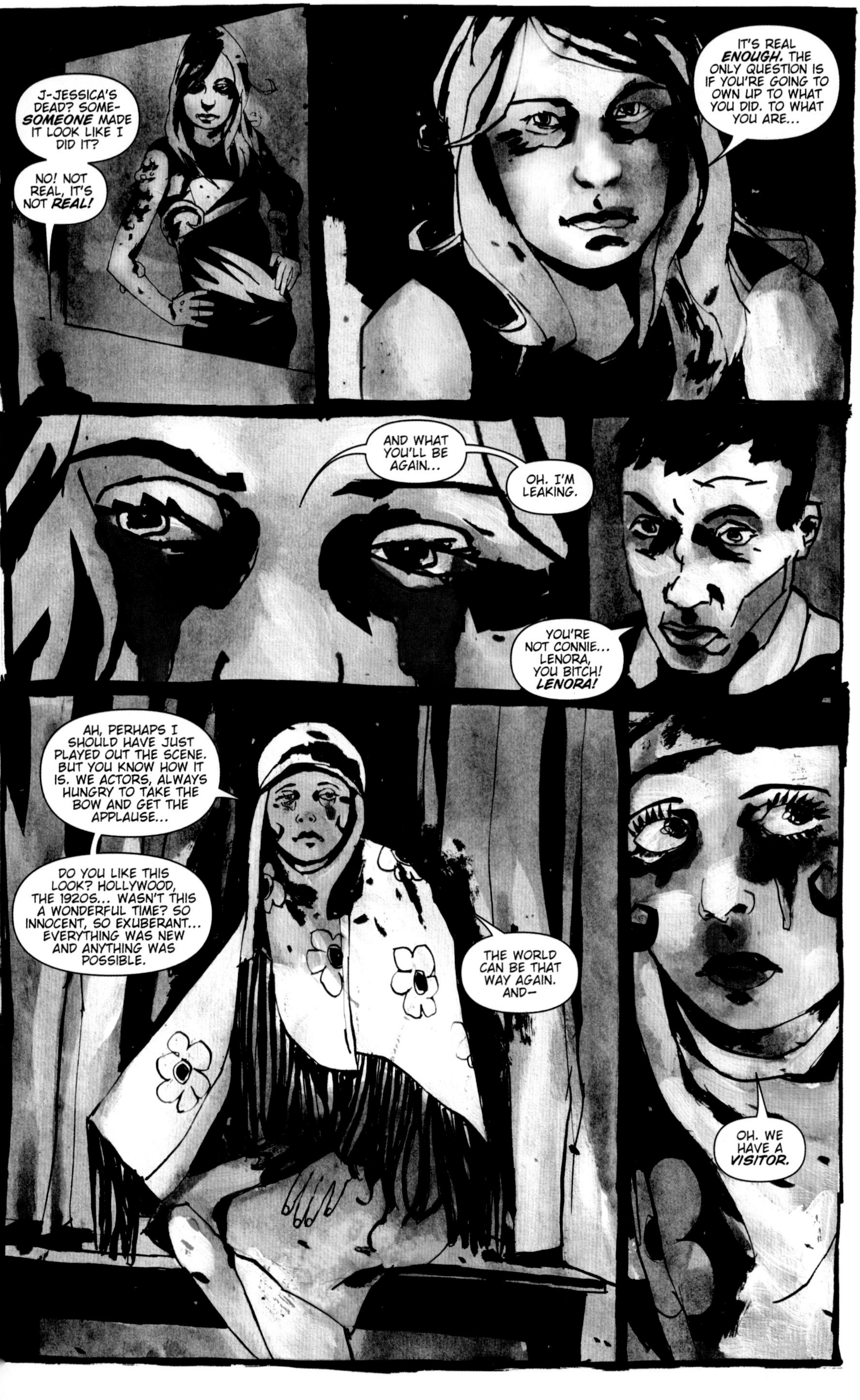
J-JESSICA'S DEAD? SOME-SOMEONE MADE IT LOOK LIKE I DID IT?
NO! NOT REAL, IT'S NOT REAL!
IT'S REAL ENOUGH. THE ONLY QUESTION IS IF YOU'RE GOING TO OWN UP TO WHAT YOU DID. TO WHAT YOU ARE...
AND WHAT YOU'LL BE AGAIN...
OH. I'M LEAKING.
YOU'RE NOT CONNIE... LENORA, YOU BITCH! LENORA!
AH, PERHAPS I SHOULD HAVE JUST PLAYED OUT THE SCENE. BUT YOU KNOW HOW IT IS. WE ACTORS, ALWAYS HUNGRY TO TAKE THE BOW AND GET THE APPLAUSE...
DO YOU LIKE THIS LOOK? HOLLYWOOD, THE 1920S... WASN'T THIS A WONDERFUL TIME? SO INNOCENT, SO EXUBERANT... EVERYTHING WAS NEW AND ANYTHING WAS POSSIBLE.
THE WORLD CAN BE THAT WAY AGAIN. AND—
OH. WE HAVE A VISITOR.

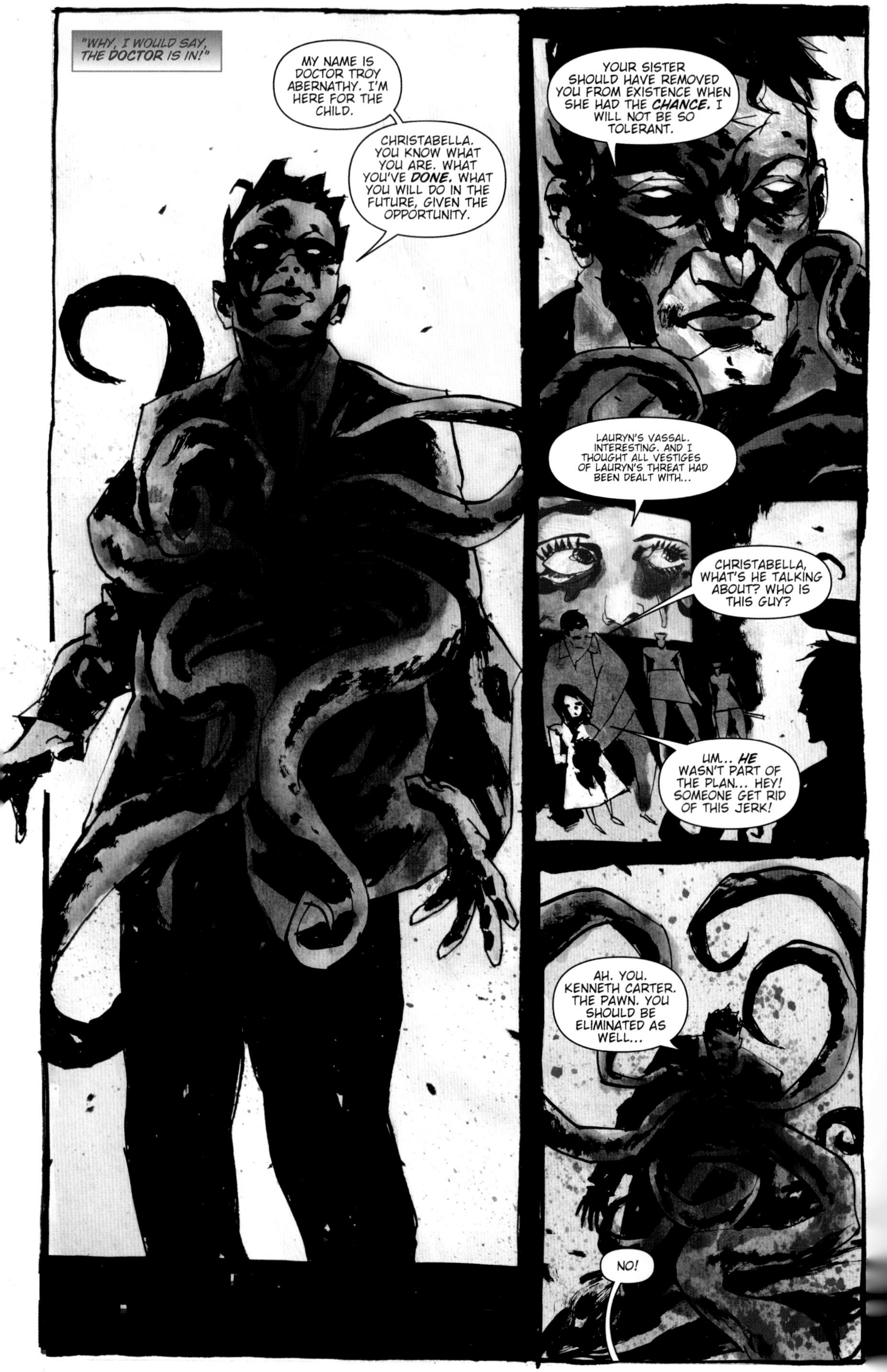
"WHY, I WOULD SAY, THE DOCTOR IS IN!"
MY NAME IS DOCTOR TROY ABERNATHY. I'M HERE FOR THE CHILD.
CHRISTABELLA. YOU KNOW WHAT YOU ARE. WHAT YOU'VE DONE. WHAT YOU WILL DO IN THE FUTURE, GIVEN THE OPPORTUNITY.
YOUR SISTER SHOULD HAVE REMOVED YOU FROM EXISTENCE WHEN SHE HAD THE CHANCE. I WILL NOT BE SO TOLERANT.
LAURYN'S VASSAL. INTERESTING. AND I THOUGHT ALL VESTIGES OF LAURYN'S THREAT HAD BEEN DEALT WITH...
CHRISTABELLA, WHAT'S HE TALKING ABOUT? WHO IS THIS GUY?
UM... HE WASN'T PART OF THE PLAN... HEY! SOMEONE GET RID OF THIS JERK!
AH. YOU. KENNETH CARTER. THE PAWN. YOU SHOULD BE ELIMINATED AS WELL...
NO!

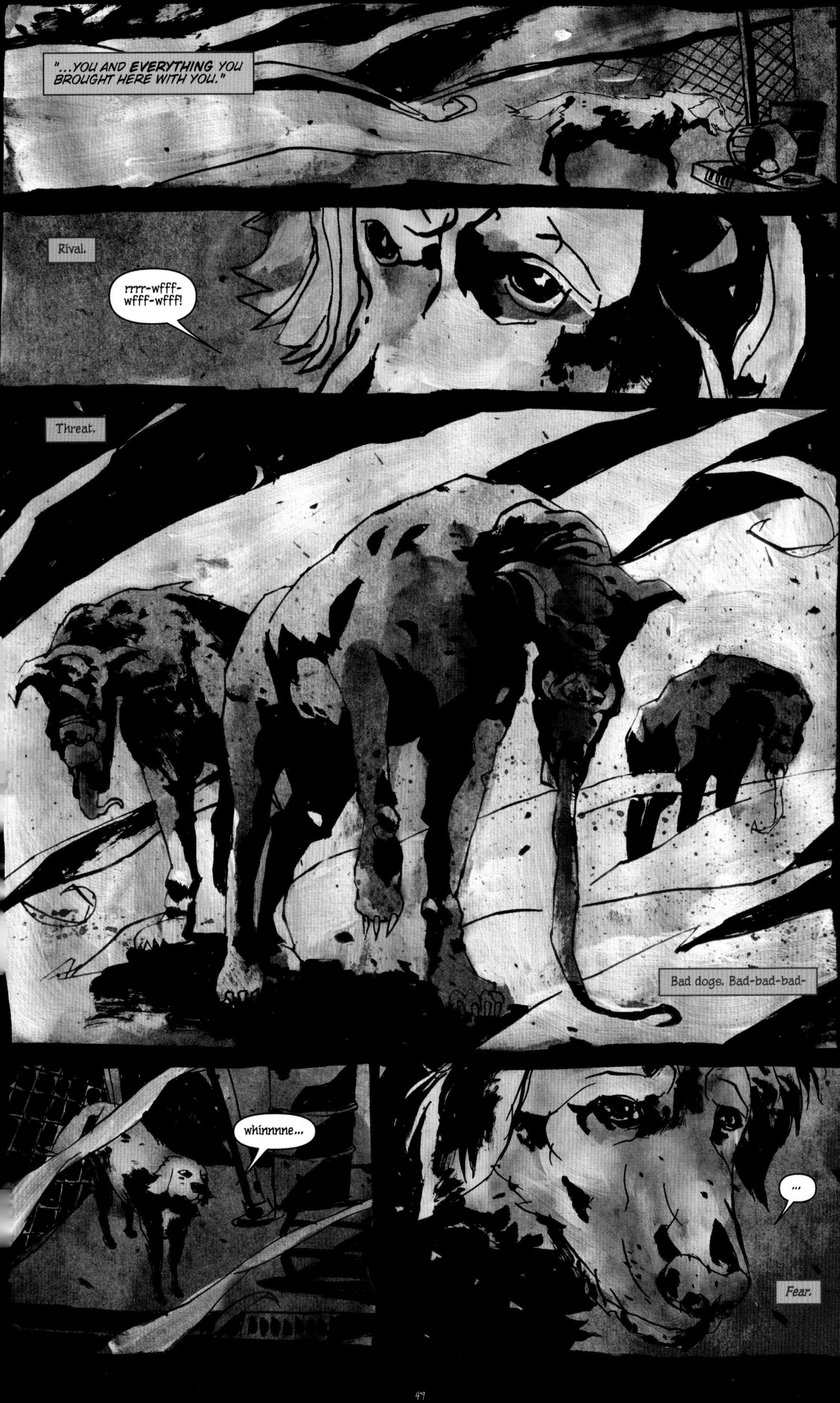
"...YOU AND **EVERYTHING** YOU BROUGHT HERE WITH YOU."
Rival.
rrrr-wfff-wfff-wfff!
Threat.
Bad dogs. Bad-bad-bad-
whinnnne...
...
Fear.

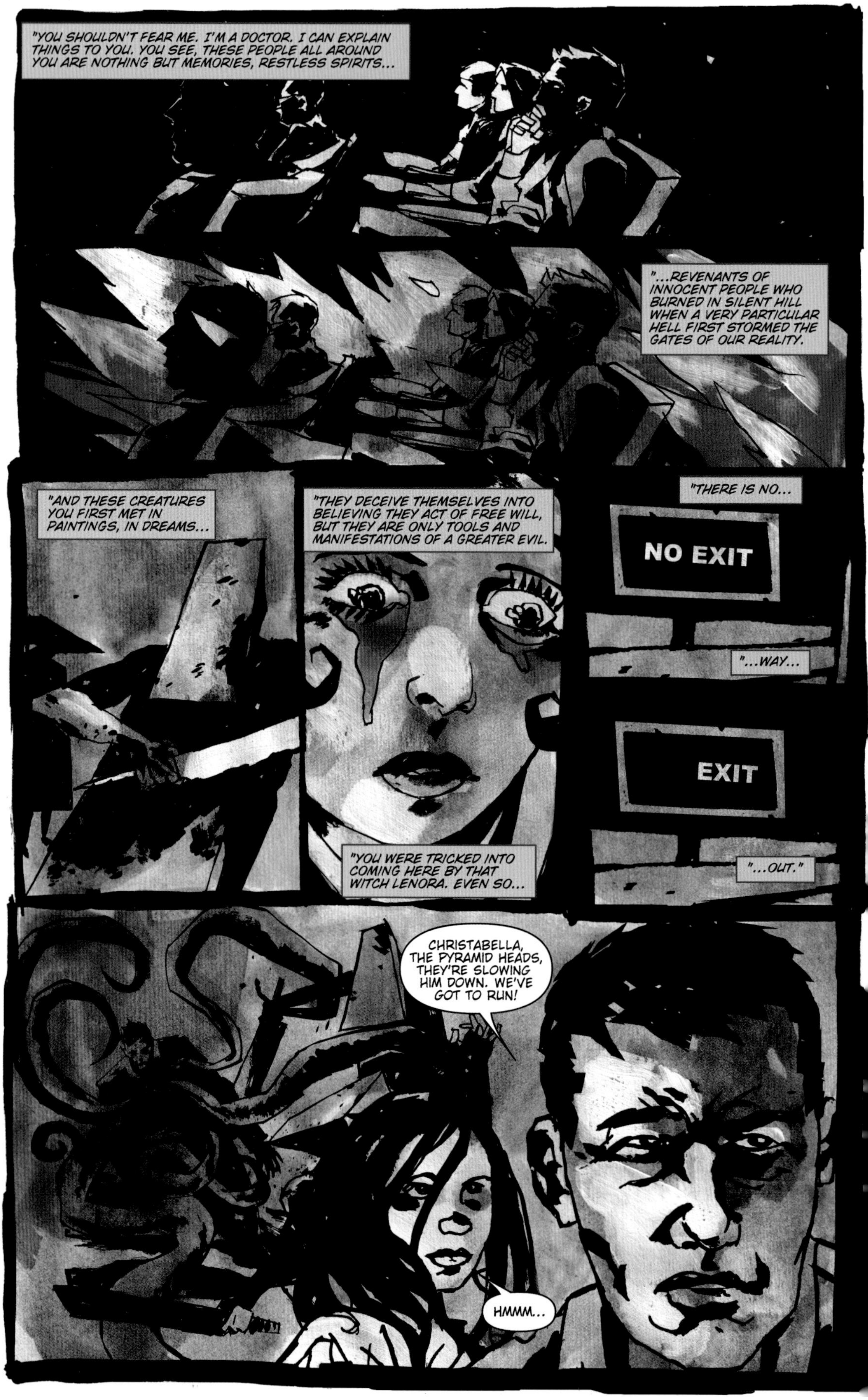
"YOU SHOULDN'T FEAR ME. I'M A DOCTOR. I CAN EXPLAIN THINGS TO YOU. YOU SEE, THESE PEOPLE ALL AROUND YOU ARE NOTHING BUT MEMORIES, RESTLESS SPIRITS...
"...REVENANTS OF INNOCENT PEOPLE WHO BURNED IN SILENT HILL WHEN A VERY PARTICULAR HELL FIRST STORMED THE GATES OF OUR REALITY.
"AND THESE CREATURES YOU FIRST MET IN PAINTINGS, IN DREAMS...
"THEY DECEIVE THEMSELVES INTO BELIEVING THEY ACT OF FREE WILL, BUT THEY ARE ONLY TOOLS AND MANIFESTATIONS OF A GREATER EVIL.
"YOU WERE TRICKED INTO COMING HERE BY THAT WITCH LENORA. EVEN SO...
"THERE IS NO...
NO EXIT
"...WAY...
EXIT
"...OUT."
CHRISTABELLA, THE PYRAMID HEADS, THEY'RE SLOWING HIM DOWN. WE'VE GOT TO RUN!
HMMM...

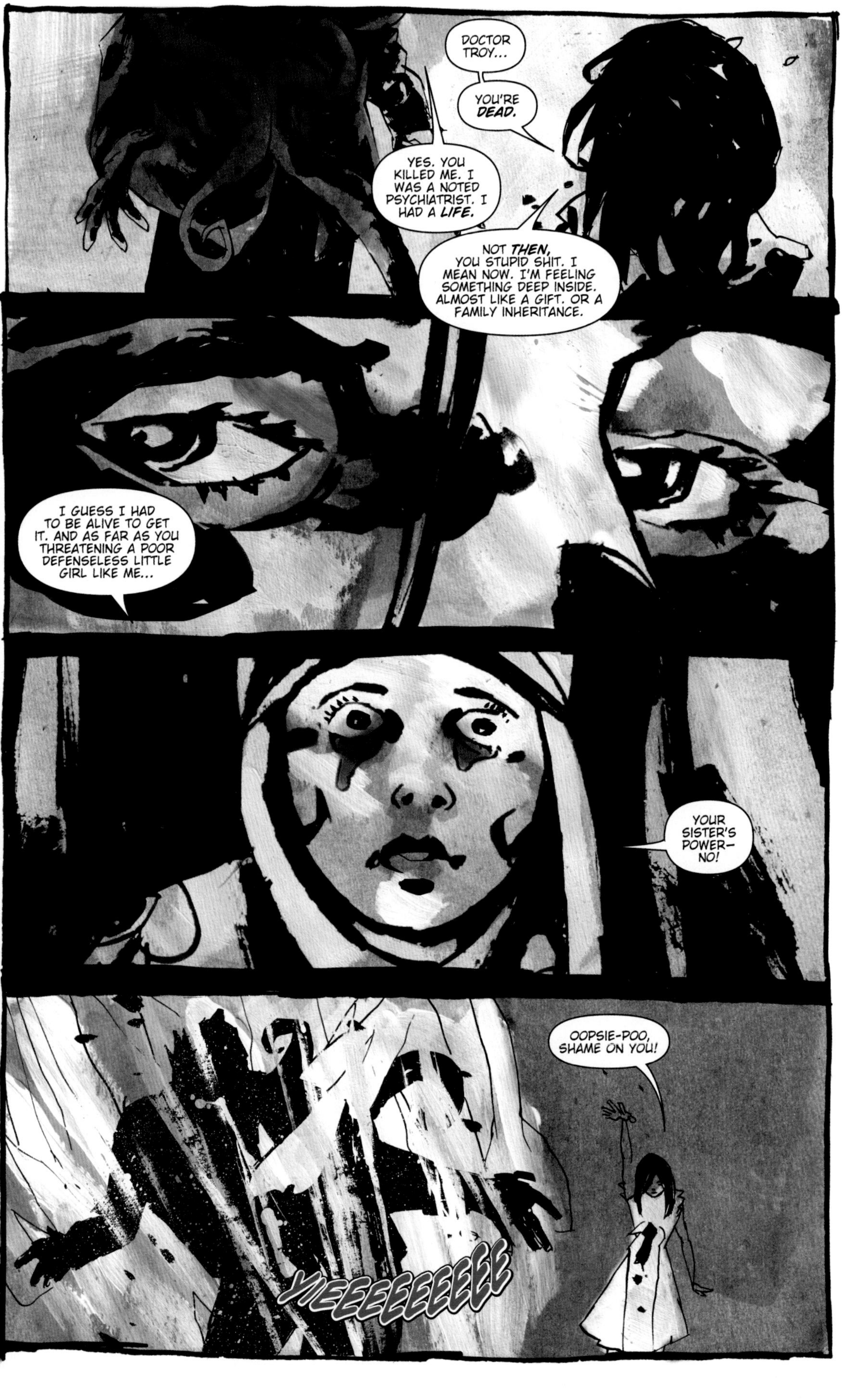
DOCTOR TROY...
YOU'RE DEAD.
YES. YOU KILLED ME. I WAS A NOTED PSYCHIATRIST. I HAD A LIFE.
NOT THEN, YOU STUPID SHIT. I MEAN NOW. I'M FEELING SOMETHING DEEP INSIDE. ALMOST LIKE A GIFT. OR A FAMILY INHERITANCE.
I GUESS I HAD TO BE ALIVE TO GET IT. AND AS FAR AS YOU THREATENING A POOR DEFENSELESS LITTLE GIRL LIKE ME...
YOUR SISTER'S POWER—NO!
OOPSIE-POO, SHAME ON YOU!
YIEEEEEEEEEE

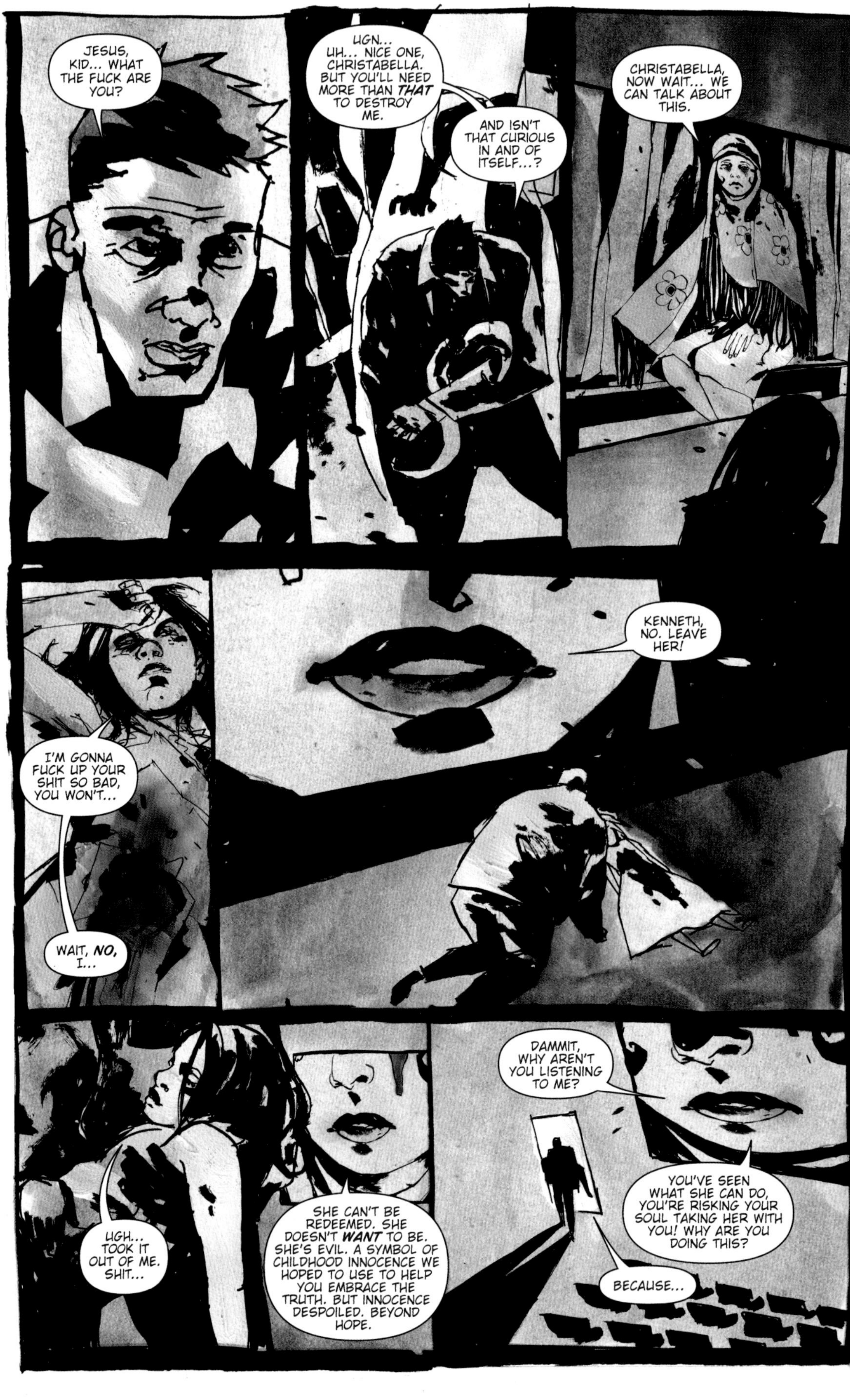
JESUS, KID... WHAT THE FUCK ARE YOU?
UGN... UH... NICE ONE, CHRISTABELLA. BUT YOU'LL NEED MORE THAN THAT TO DESTROY ME.
AND ISN'T THAT CURIOUS IN AND OF ITSELF...?
CHRISTABELLA, NOW WAIT... WE CAN TALK ABOUT THIS.
I'M GONNA FUCK UP YOUR SHIT SO BAD, YOU WON'T...
WAIT, NO, I...
KENNETH, NO. LEAVE HER!
UGH... TOOK IT OUT OF ME. SHIT...
SHE CAN'T BE REDEEMED. SHE DOESN'T WANT TO BE. SHE'S EVIL. A SYMBOL OF CHILDHOOD INNOCENCE WE HOPED TO USE TO HELP YOU EMBRACE THE TRUTH. BUT INNOCENCE DESPOILED. BEYOND HOPE.
DAMMIT, WHY AREN'T YOU LISTENING TO ME?
YOU'VE SEEN WHAT SHE CAN DO, YOU'RE RISKING YOUR SOUL TAKING HER WITH YOU! WHY ARE YOU DOING THIS?
BECAUSE...

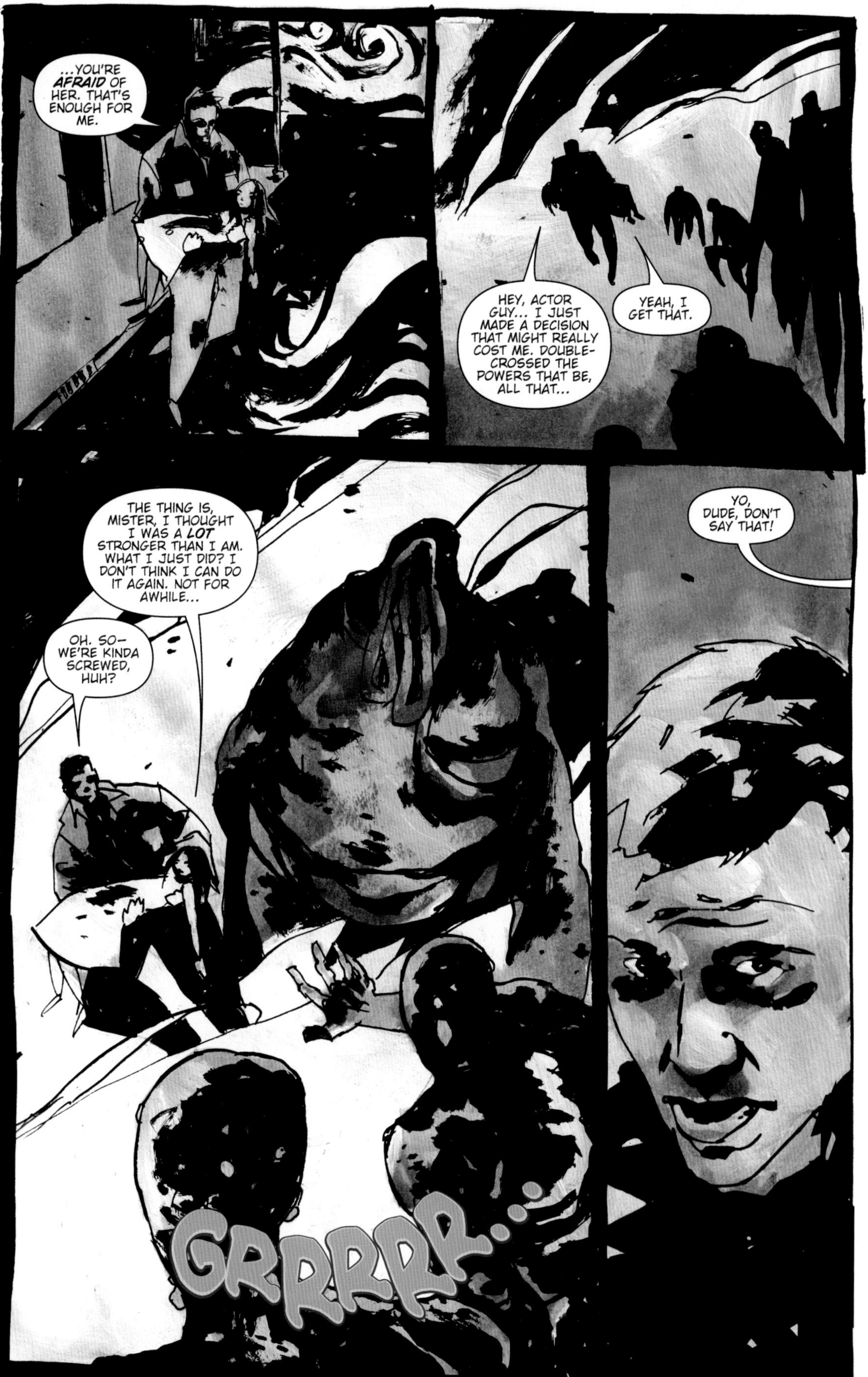
...YOU'RE *AFRAID* OF HER. THAT'S ENOUGH FOR ME.
HEY, ACTOR GUY... I JUST MADE A DECISION THAT MIGHT REALLY COST ME. DOUBLE-CROSSED THE POWERS THAT BE, ALL THAT...
YEAH, I GET THAT.
THE THING IS, MISTER, I THOUGHT I WAS A *LOT* STRONGER THAN I AM. WHAT I JUST DID? I DON'T THINK I CAN DO IT AGAIN. NOT FOR AWHILE...
OH. SO— WE'RE KINDA SCREWED, HUH?
GRRRRR...
YO, DUDE, DON'T SAY THAT!

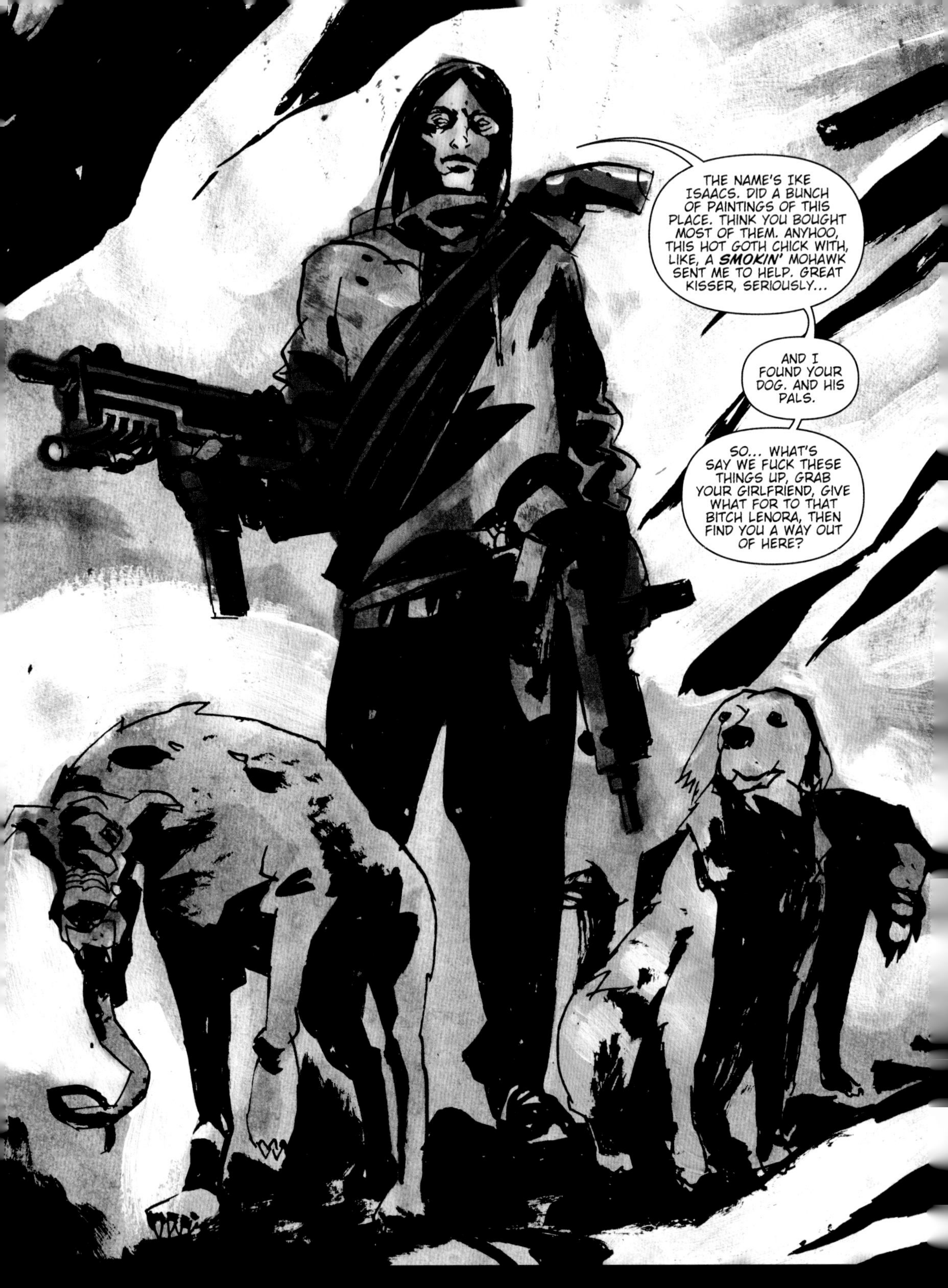
THE NAME'S IKE ISAACS. DID A BUNCH OF PAINTINGS OF THIS PLACE. THINK YOU BOUGHT MOST OF THEM. ANYHOO, THIS HOT GOTH CHICK WITH, LIKE, A SMOKIN' MOHAWK SENT ME TO HELP. GREAT KISSER, SERIOUSLY...
AND I FOUND YOUR DOG. AND HIS PALS.
SO... WHAT'S SAY WE FUCK THESE THINGS UP, GRAB YOUR GIRLFRIEND, GIVE WHAT FOR TO THAT BITCH LENORA, THEN FIND YOU A WAY OUT OF HERE?
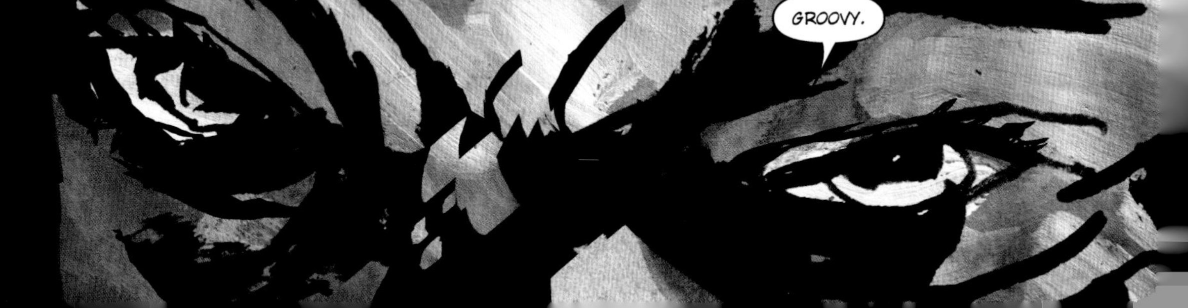
GROOVY.

CHAPTER
3

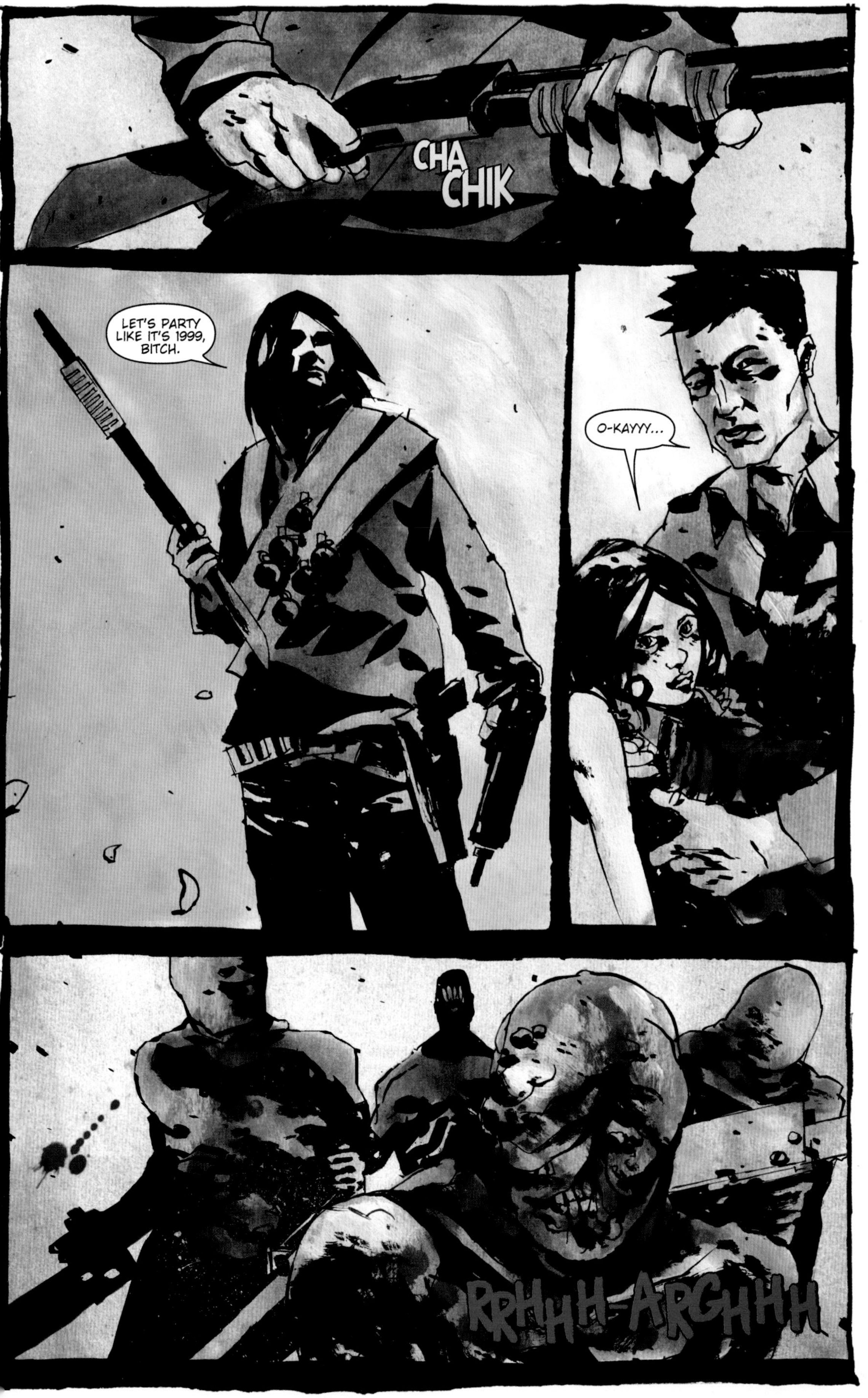
CHA
CHIK
LET'S PARTY LIKE IT'S 1999, BITCH.
O-KAYYY...
RRHHH-ARGHHH

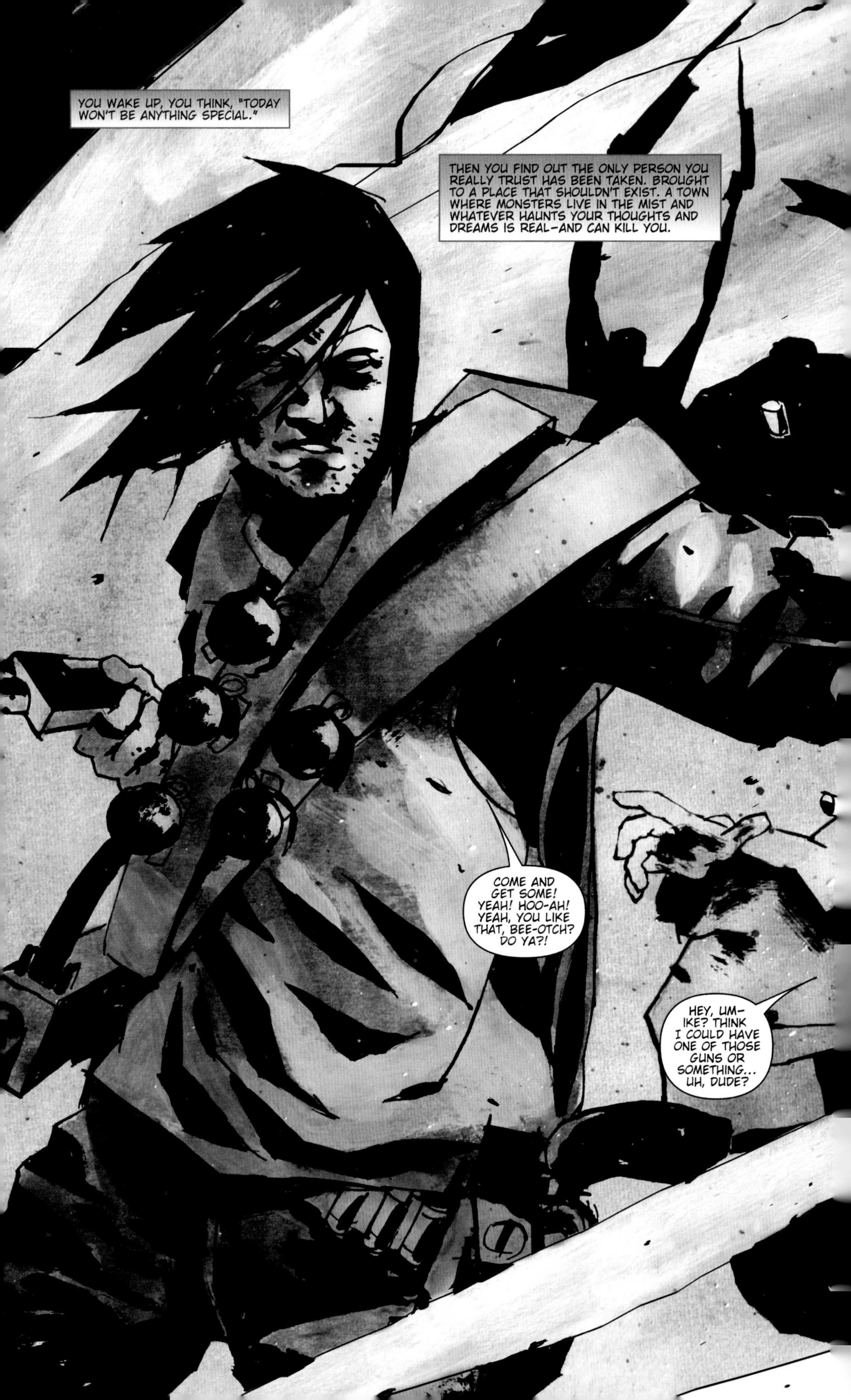
YOU WAKE UP, YOU THINK, "TODAY WON'T BE ANYTHING SPECIAL."
THEN YOU FIND OUT THE ONLY PERSON YOU REALLY TRUST HAS BEEN TAKEN. BROUGHT TO A PLACE THAT SHOULDN'T EXIST. A TOWN WHERE MONSTERS LIVE IN THE MIST AND WHATEVER HAUNTS YOUR THOUGHTS AND DREAMS IS REAL—AND CAN KILL YOU.
COME AND GET SOME! YEAH! HOO-AH! YEAH, YOU LIKE THAT, BEE-OTCH? DO YA?!
HEY, UM--IKE? THINK I COULD HAVE ONE OF THOSE GUNS OR SOMETHING... UH, DUDE?

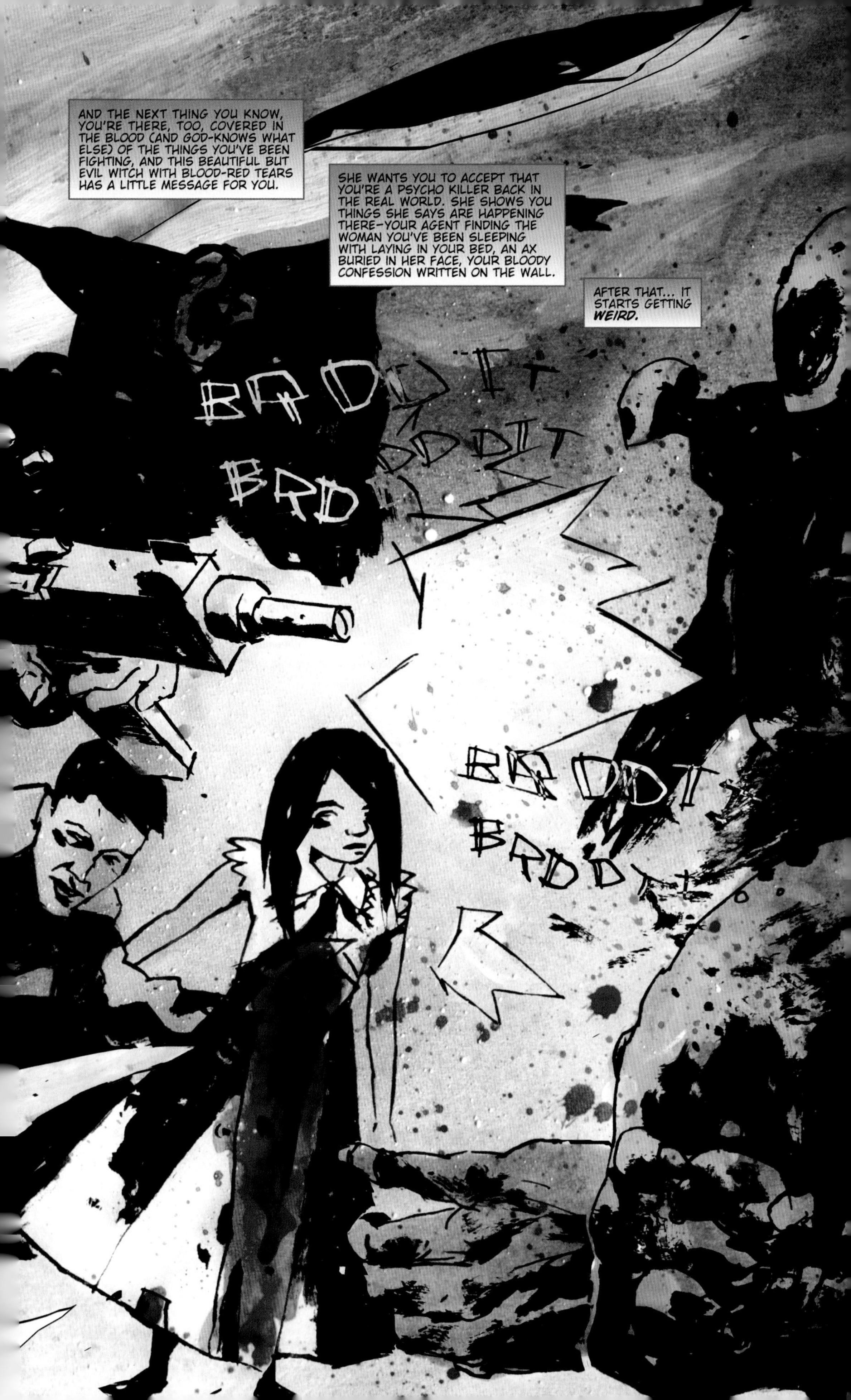
AND THE NEXT THING YOU KNOW, YOU'RE THERE, TOO, COVERED IN THE BLOOD (AND GOD-KNOWS WHAT ELSE) OF THE THINGS YOU'VE BEEN FIGHTING, AND THIS BEAUTIFUL BUT EVIL WITCH WITH BLOOD-RED TEARS HAS A LITTLE MESSAGE FOR YOU.
SHE WANTS YOU TO ACCEPT THAT YOU'RE A PSYCHO KILLER BACK IN THE REAL WORLD. SHE SHOWS YOU THINGS SHE SAYS ARE HAPPENING THERE—YOUR AGENT FINDING THE WOMAN YOU'VE BEEN SLEEPING WITH LAYING IN YOUR BED, AN AX BURIED IN HER FACE, YOUR BLOODY CONFESSION WRITTEN ON THE WALL.
AFTER THAT... IT STARTS GETTING *WEIRD.*

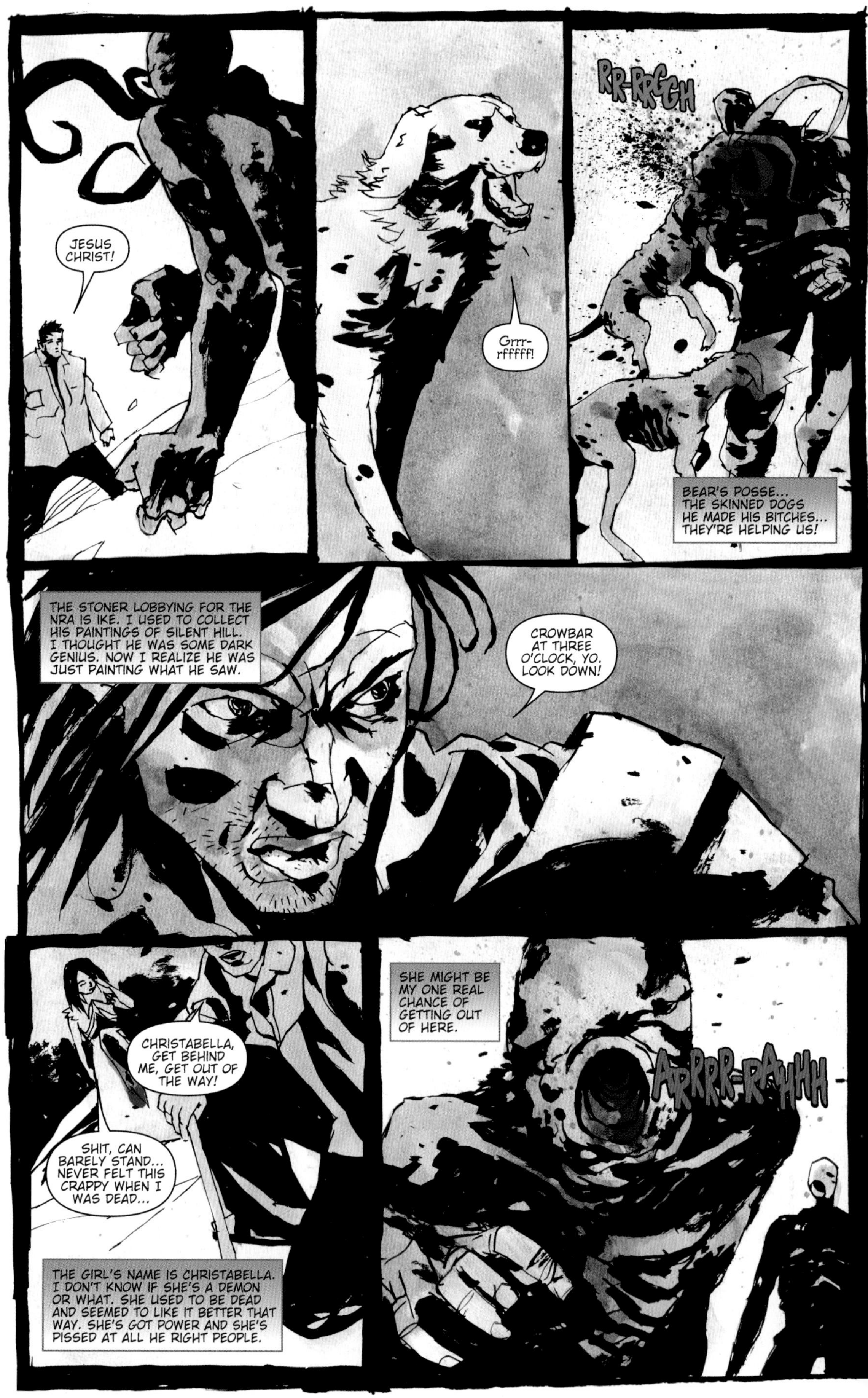

JESUS CHRIST!
Grrr-rfffff!
RR-RRGGH
BEAR'S POSSE... THE SKINNED DOGS HE MADE HIS BITCHES... THEY'RE HELPING US!
THE STONER LOBBYING FOR THE NRA IS IKE. I USED TO COLLECT HIS PAINTINGS OF SILENT HILL. I THOUGHT HE WAS SOME DARK GENIUS. NOW I REALIZE HE WAS JUST PAINTING WHAT HE SAW.
CROWBAR AT THREE O'CLOCK, YO. LOOK DOWN!
CHRISTABELLA, GET BEHIND ME, GET OUT OF THE WAY!
SHIT, CAN BARELY STAND... NEVER FELT THIS CRAPPY WHEN I WAS DEAD...
THE GIRL'S NAME IS CHRISTABELLA. I DON'T KNOW IF SHE'S A DEMON OR WHAT. SHE USED TO BE DEAD AND SEEMED TO LIKE IT BETTER THAT WAY. SHE'S GOT POWER AND SHE'S PISSED AT ALL HE RIGHT PEOPLE.
SHE MIGHT BE MY ONE REAL CHANCE OF GETTING OUT OF HERE.
ARRRR-RAHHH

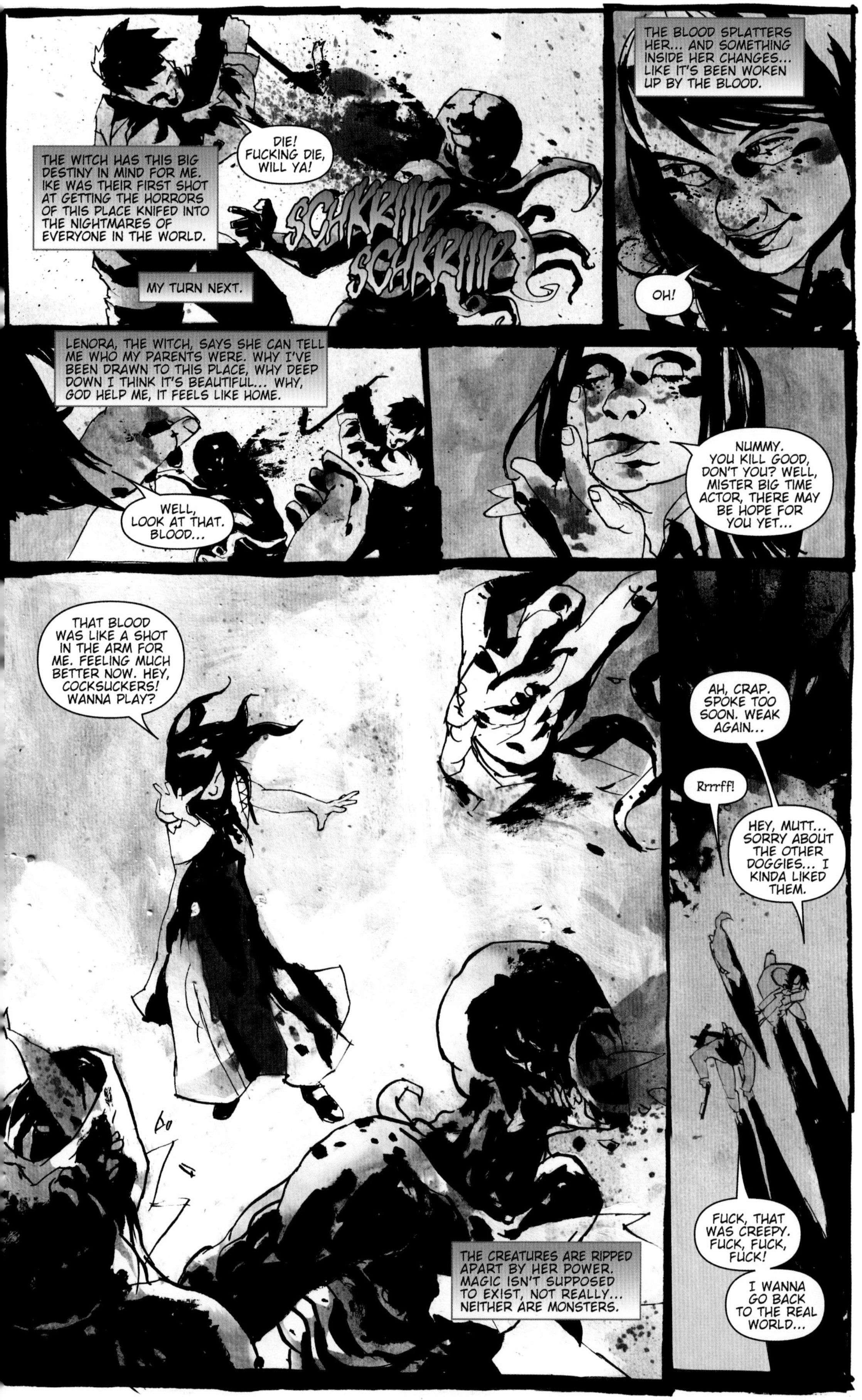
THE WITCH HAS THIS BIG DESTINY IN MIND FOR ME. IKE WAS THEIR FIRST SHOT AT GETTING THE HORRORS OF THIS PLACE KNIFED INTO THE NIGHTMARES OF EVERYONE IN THE WORLD.
MY TURN NEXT.
DIE! FUCKING DIE, WILL YA!
SCHKRIIIP SCHKRIIIP
THE BLOOD SPLATTERS HER... AND SOMETHING INSIDE HER CHANGES... LIKE IT'S BEEN WOKEN UP BY THE BLOOD.
OH!
LENORA, THE WITCH, SAYS SHE CAN TELL ME WHO MY PARENTS WERE. WHY I'VE BEEN DRAWN TO THIS PLACE, WHY DEEP DOWN I THINK IT'S BEAUTIFUL... WHY, GOD HELP ME, IT FEELS LIKE HOME.
WELL, LOOK AT THAT. BLOOD...
NUMMY. YOU KILL GOOD, DON'T YOU? WELL, MISTER BIG TIME ACTOR, THERE MAY BE HOPE FOR YOU YET...
THAT BLOOD WAS LIKE A SHOT IN THE ARM FOR ME. FEELING MUCH BETTER NOW. HEY, COCKSUCKERS! WANNA PLAY?
THE CREATURES ARE RIPPED APART BY HER POWER. MAGIC ISN'T SUPPOSED TO EXIST, NOT REALLY... NEITHER ARE MONSTERS.
AH, CRAP. SPOKE TOO SOON. WEAK AGAIN...
Rrrrff!
HEY, MUTT... SORRY ABOUT THE OTHER DOGGIES... I KINDA LIKED THEM.
FUCK, THAT WAS CREEPY. FUCK, FUCK, FUCK!
I WANNA GO BACK TO THE REAL WORLD...

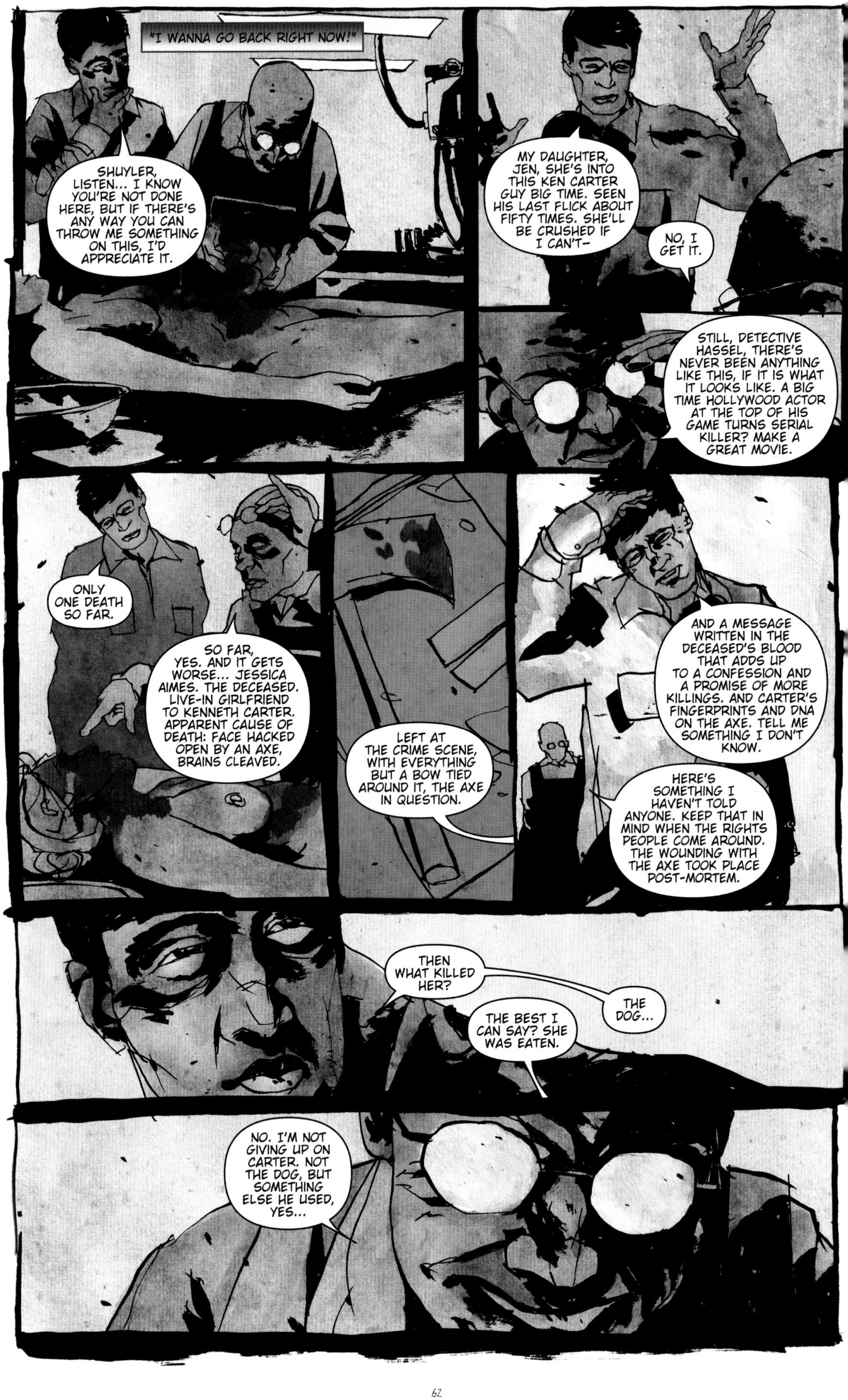
"I WANNA GO BACK RIGHT NOW!"
SHUYLER, LISTEN... I KNOW YOU'RE NOT DONE HERE, BUT IF THERE'S ANY WAY YOU CAN THROW ME SOMETHING ON THIS, I'D APPRECIATE IT.
MY DAUGHTER, JEN, SHE'S INTO THIS KEN CARTER GUY BIG TIME. SEEN HIS LAST FLICK ABOUT FIFTY TIMES. SHE'LL BE CRUSHED IF I CAN'T-
NO, I GET IT.
STILL, DETECTIVE HASSEL, THERE'S NEVER BEEN ANYTHING LIKE THIS, IF IT IS WHAT IT LOOKS LIKE. A BIG TIME HOLLYWOOD ACTOR AT THE TOP OF HIS GAME TURNS SERIAL KILLER? MAKE A GREAT MOVIE.
ONLY ONE DEATH SO FAR.
SO FAR, YES. AND IT GETS WORSE... JESSICA AIMES. THE DECEASED. LIVE-IN GIRLFRIEND TO KENNETH CARTER. APPARENT CAUSE OF DEATH: FACE HACKED OPEN BY AN AXE, BRAINS CLEAVED.
LEFT AT THE CRIME SCENE, WITH EVERYTHING BUT A BOW TIED AROUND IT, THE AXE IN QUESTION.
AND A MESSAGE WRITTEN IN THE DECEASED'S BLOOD THAT ADDS UP TO A CONFESSION AND A PROMISE OF MORE KILLINGS. AND CARTER'S FINGERPRINTS AND DNA ON THE AXE. TELL ME SOMETHING I DON'T KNOW.
HERE'S SOMETHING I HAVEN'T TOLD ANYONE. KEEP THAT IN MIND WHEN THE RIGHTS PEOPLE COME AROUND. THE WOUNDING WITH THE AXE TOOK PLACE POST-MORTEM.
THEN WHAT KILLED HER?
THE DOG...
THE BEST I CAN SAY? SHE WAS EATEN.
NO. I'M NOT GIVING UP ON CARTER. NOT THE DOG, BUT SOMETHING ELSE HE USED, YES...

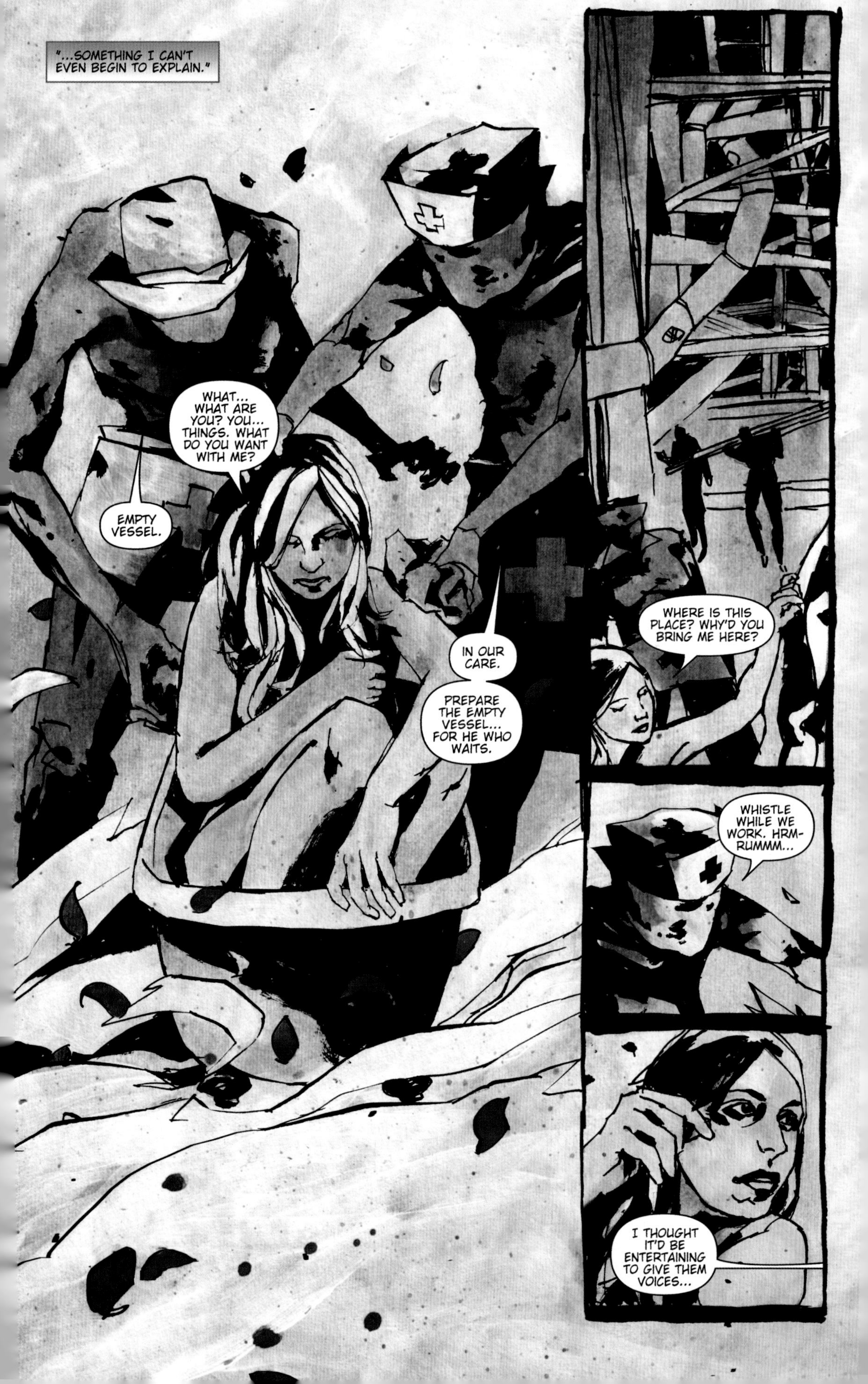
"...SOMETHING I CAN'T EVEN BEGIN TO EXPLAIN."
WHAT... WHAT ARE YOU? YOU... THINGS. WHAT DO YOU WANT WITH ME?
EMPTY VESSEL.
IN OUR CARE.
PREPARE THE EMPTY VESSEL... FOR HE WHO WAITS.
WHERE IS THIS PLACE? WHY'D YOU BRING ME HERE?
WHISTLE WHILE WE WORK. HRM-RUMMM...
I THOUGHT IT'D BE ENTERTAINING TO GIVE THEM VOICES...

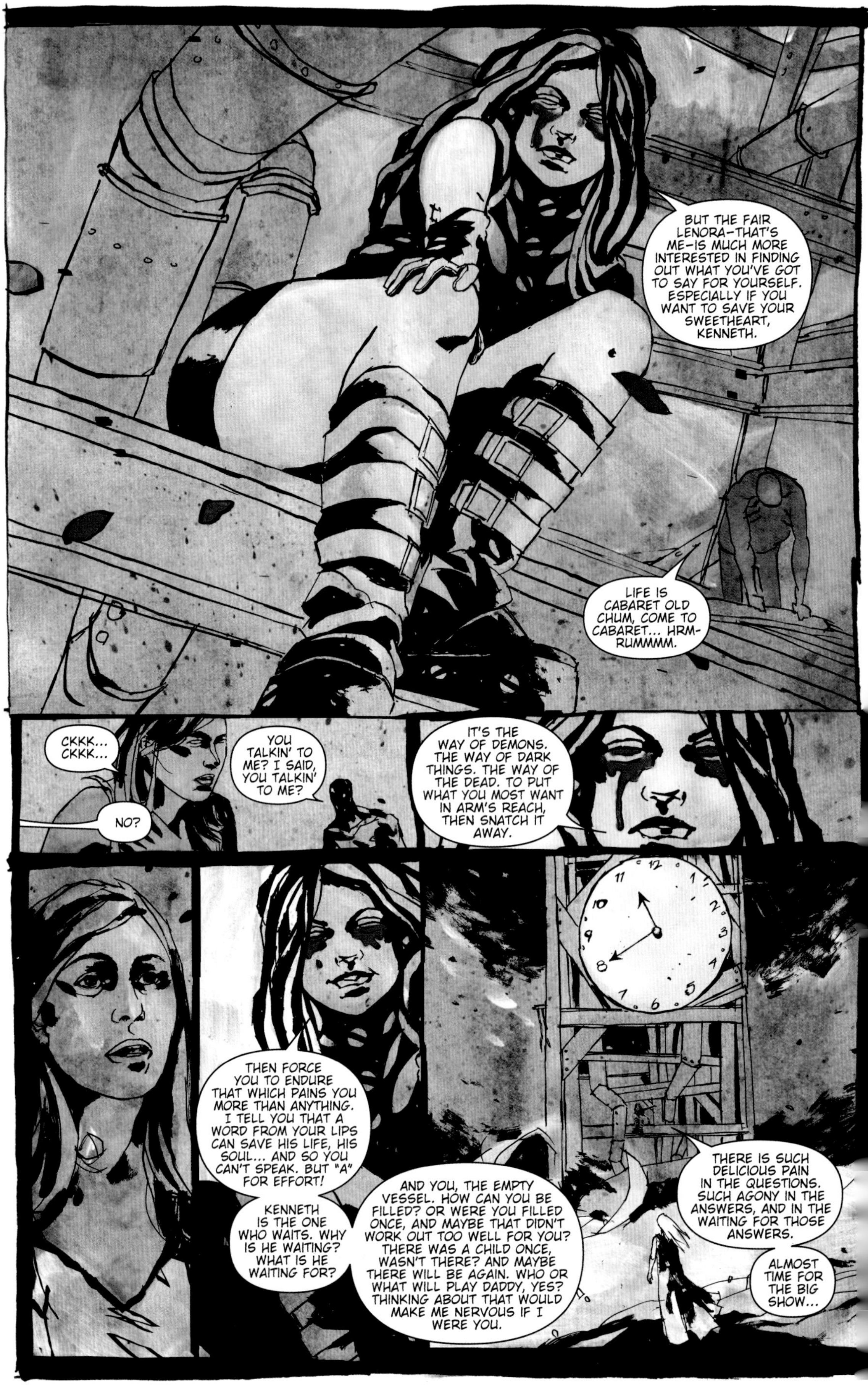

BUT THE FAIR LENORA—THAT'S ME—IS MUCH MORE INTERESTED IN FINDING OUT WHAT YOU'VE GOT TO SAY FOR YOURSELF. ESPECIALLY IF YOU WANT TO SAVE YOUR SWEETHEART, KENNETH.
LIFE IS CABARET OLD CHUM, COME TO CABARET... HRM-RUMMMM.
CKKK... CKKK...
YOU TALKIN' TO ME? I SAID, YOU TALKIN' TO ME?
NO?
IT'S THE WAY OF DEMONS. THE WAY OF DARK THINGS. THE WAY OF THE DEAD. TO PUT WHAT YOU MOST WANT IN ARM'S REACH, THEN SNATCH IT AWAY.
THEN FORCE YOU TO ENDURE THAT WHICH PAINS YOU MORE THAN ANYTHING. I TELL YOU THAT A WORD FROM YOUR LIPS CAN SAVE HIS LIFE, HIS SOUL... AND SO YOU CAN'T SPEAK. BUT "A" FOR EFFORT!
KENNETH IS THE ONE WHO WAITS. WHY IS HE WAITING? WHAT IS HE WAITING FOR?
AND YOU, THE EMPTY VESSEL. HOW CAN YOU BE FILLED? OR WERE YOU FILLED ONCE, AND MAYBE THAT DIDN'T WORK OUT TOO WELL FOR YOU? THERE WAS A CHILD ONCE, WASN'T THERE? AND MAYBE THERE WILL BE AGAIN. WHO OR WHAT WILL PLAY DADDY, YES? THINKING ABOUT THAT WOULD MAKE ME NERVOUS IF I WERE YOU.
THERE IS SUCH DELICIOUS PAIN IN THE QUESTIONS. SUCH AGONY IN THE ANSWERS, AND IN THE WAITING FOR THOSE ANSWERS.
ALMOST TIME FOR THE BIG SHOW...

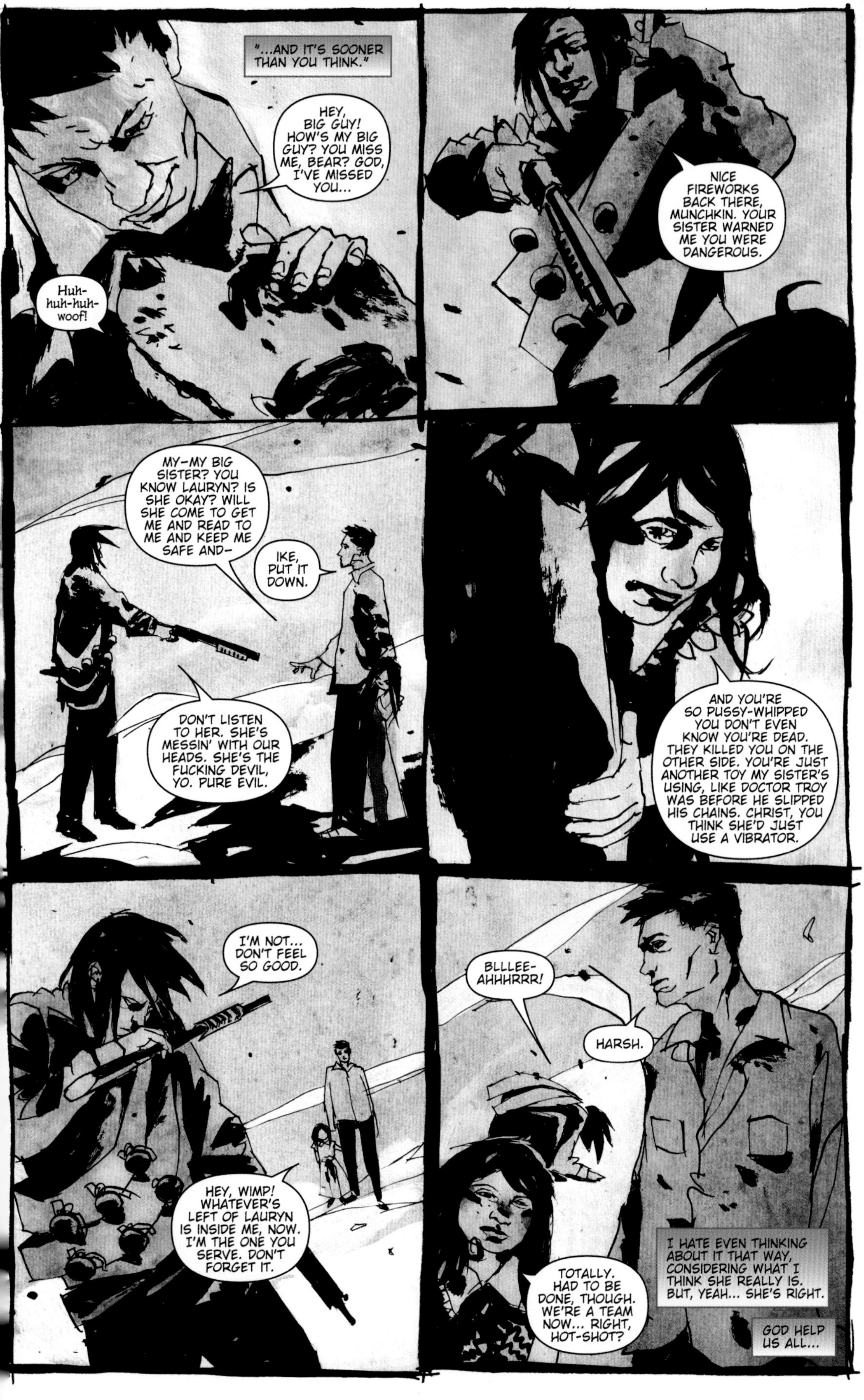
"...AND IT'S SOONER THAN YOU THINK."
HEY, BIG GUY! HOW'S MY BIG GUY? YOU MISS ME, BEAR? GOD, I'VE MISSED YOU...
Huh-huh-huh-woof!
NICE FIREWORKS BACK THERE, MUNCHKIN. YOUR SISTER WARNED ME YOU WERE DANGEROUS.
MY-MY BIG SISTER? YOU KNOW LAURYN? IS SHE OKAY? WILL SHE COME TO GET ME AND READ TO ME AND KEEP ME SAFE AND-
IKE, PUT IT DOWN.
DON'T LISTEN TO HER. SHE'S MESSIN' WITH OUR HEADS. SHE'S THE FUCKING DEVIL, YO. PURE EVIL.
AND YOU'RE SO PUSSY-WHIPPED YOU DON'T EVEN KNOW YOU'RE DEAD. THEY KILLED YOU ON THE OTHER SIDE. YOU'RE JUST ANOTHER TOY MY SISTER'S USING, LIKE DOCTOR TROY WAS BEFORE HE SLIPPED HIS CHAINS. CHRIST, YOU THINK SHE'D JUST USE A VIBRATOR.
I'M NOT... DON'T FEEL SO GOOD.
HEY, WIMP! WHATEVER'S LEFT OF LAURYN IS INSIDE ME, NOW. I'M THE ONE YOU SERVE. DON'T FORGET IT.
BLLLEE-AHHHRRR!
HARSH.
TOTALLY. HAD TO BE DONE, THOUGH. WE'RE A TEAM NOW... RIGHT, HOT-SHOT?
I HATE EVEN THINKING ABOUT IT THAT WAY, CONSIDERING WHAT I THINK SHE REALLY IS. BUT, YEAH... SHE'S RIGHT.
GOD HELP US ALL...

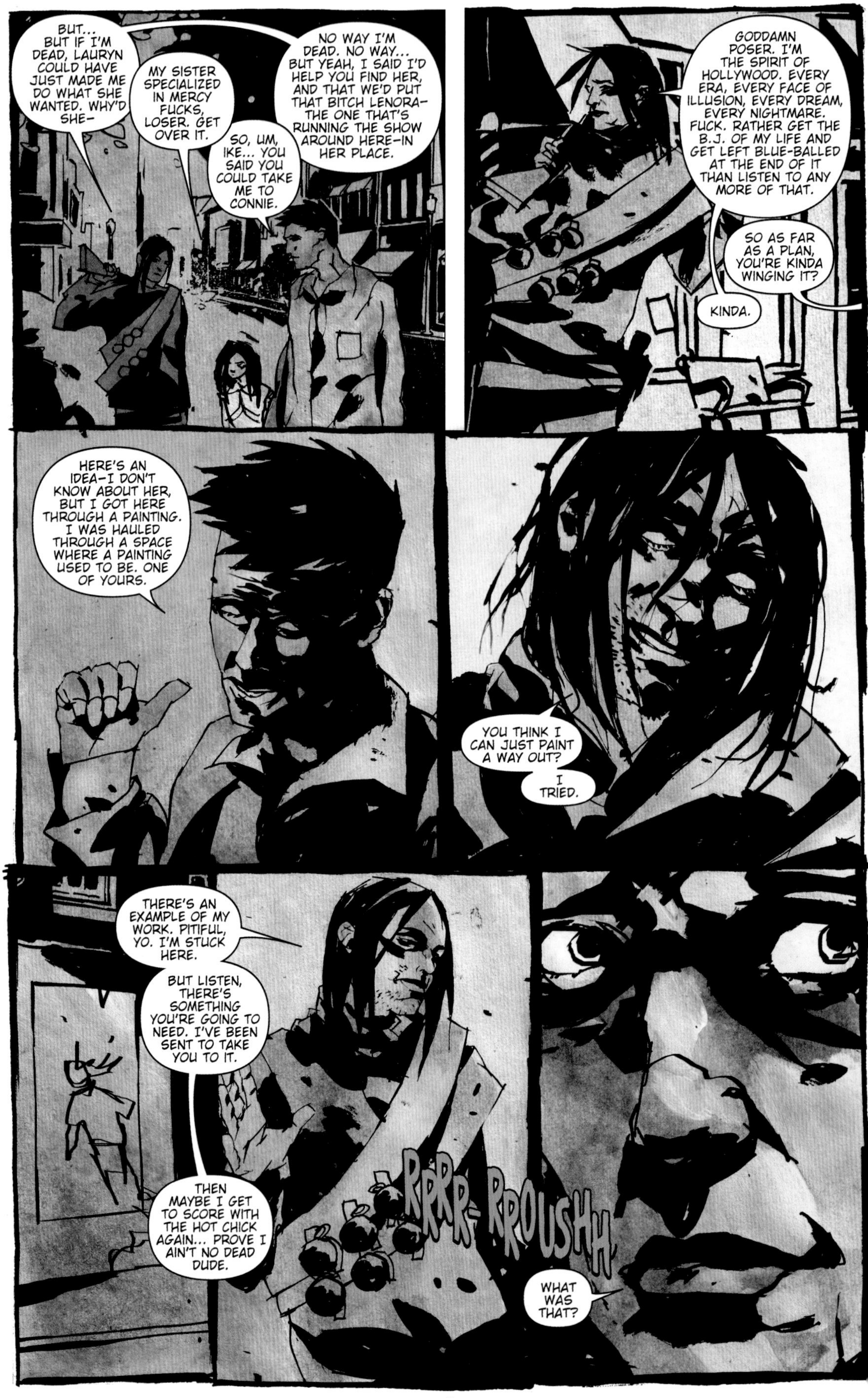

BUT... BUT IF I'M DEAD, LAURYN COULD HAVE JUST MADE ME DO WHAT SHE WANTED. WHY'D SHE-
MY SISTER SPECIALIZED IN MERCY FUCKS, LOSER. GET OVER IT.
NO WAY I'M DEAD. NO WAY... BUT YEAH, I SAID I'D HELP YOU FIND HER, AND THAT WE'D PUT THAT BITCH LENORA-THE ONE THAT'S RUNNING THE SHOW AROUND HERE-IN HER PLACE.
SO, UM, IKE... YOU SAID YOU COULD TAKE ME TO CONNIE.
GODDAMN POSER. I'M THE SPIRIT OF HOLLYWOOD. EVERY ERA, EVERY FACE OF ILLUSION, EVERY DREAM, EVERY NIGHTMARE. FUCK. RATHER GET THE B.J. OF MY LIFE AND GET LEFT BLUE-BALLED AT THE END OF IT THAN LISTEN TO ANY MORE OF THAT.
SO AS FAR AS A PLAN, YOU'RE KINDA WINGING IT?
KINDA.
HERE'S AN IDEA-I DON'T KNOW ABOUT HER, BUT I GOT HERE THROUGH A PAINTING. I WAS HAULED THROUGH A SPACE WHERE A PAINTING USED TO BE. ONE OF YOURS.
YOU THINK I CAN JUST PAINT A WAY OUT?
I TRIED.
THERE'S AN EXAMPLE OF MY WORK. PITIFUL, YO. I'M STUCK HERE.
BUT LISTEN, THERE'S SOMETHING YOU'RE GOING TO NEED. I'VE BEEN SENT TO TAKE YOU TO IT.
THEN MAYBE I GET TO SCORE WITH THE HOT CHICK AGAIN... PROVE I AIN'T NO DEAD DUDE.
RRRR-RROUSHH
WHAT WAS THAT?

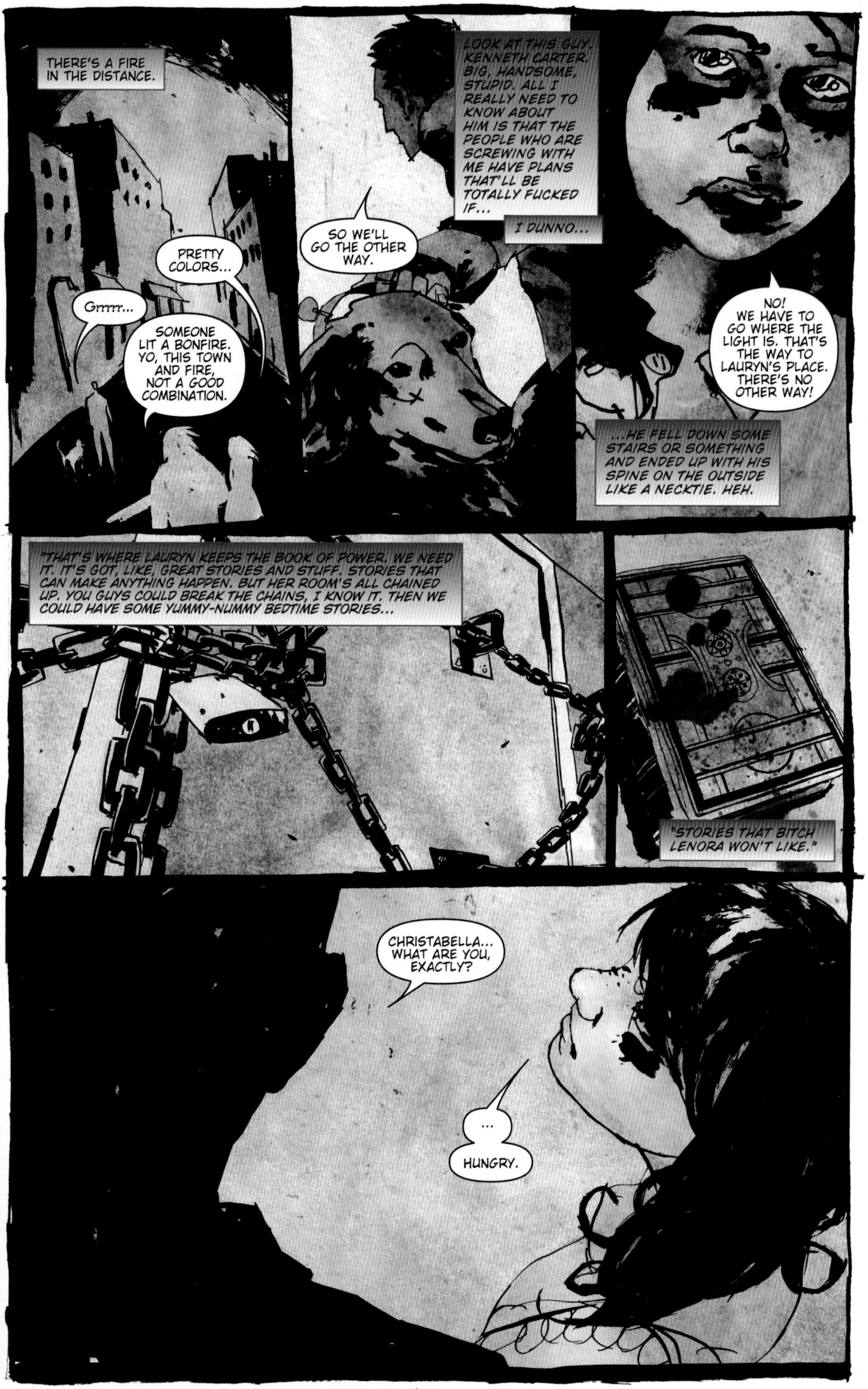

THERE'S A FIRE IN THE DISTANCE.
PRETTY COLORS...
Grrrrr...
SOMEONE LIT A BONFIRE. YO, THIS TOWN AND FIRE, NOT A GOOD COMBINATION.
LOOK AT THIS GUY. KENNETH CARTER. BIG, HANDSOME, STUPID. ALL I REALLY NEED TO KNOW ABOUT HIM IS THAT THE PEOPLE WHO ARE SCREWING WITH ME HAVE PLANS THAT'LL BE TOTALLY FUCKED IF...
I DUNNO...
SO WE'LL GO THE OTHER WAY.
NO! WE HAVE TO GO WHERE THE LIGHT IS. THAT'S THE WAY TO LAURYN'S PLACE. THERE'S NO OTHER WAY!
...HE FELL DOWN SOME STAIRS OR SOMETHING AND ENDED UP WITH HIS SPINE ON THE OUTSIDE LIKE A NECKTIE. HEH.
"THAT'S WHERE LAURYN KEEPS THE BOOK OF POWER. WE NEED IT. IT'S GOT, LIKE, GREAT STORIES AND STUFF. STORIES THAT CAN MAKE ANYTHING HAPPEN. BUT HER ROOM'S ALL CHAINED UP. YOU GUYS COULD BREAK THE CHAINS, I KNOW IT. THEN WE COULD HAVE SOME YUMMY-NUMMY BEDTIME STORIES...
"STORIES THAT BITCH LENORA WON'T LIKE."
CHRISTABELLA... WHAT ARE YOU, EXACTLY?
...
HUNGRY.

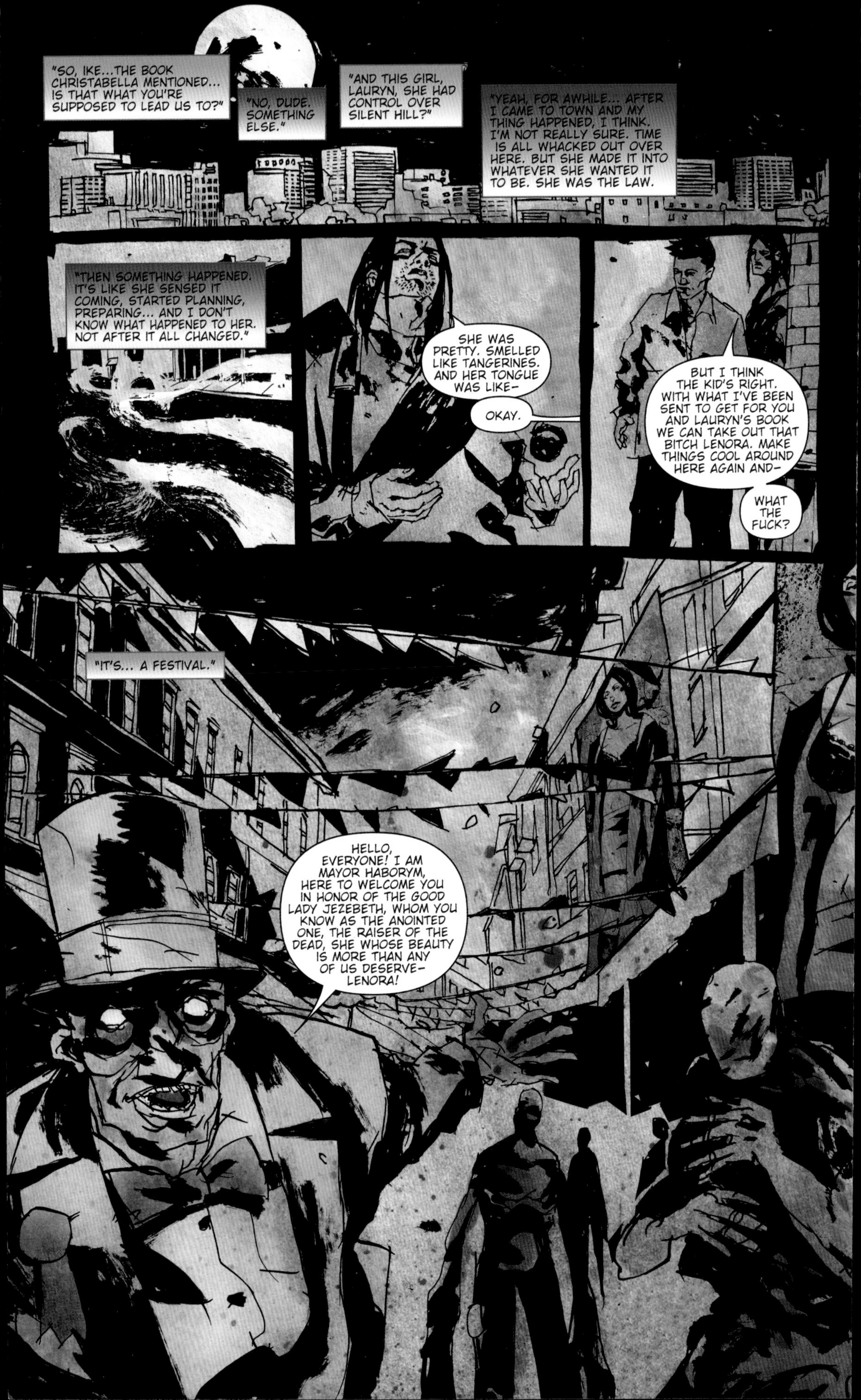
"SO, IKE... THE BOOK CHRISTABELLA MENTIONED... IS THAT WHAT YOU'RE SUPPOSED TO LEAD US TO?"
"NO, DUDE. SOMETHING ELSE."
"AND THIS GIRL, LAURYN, SHE HAD CONTROL OVER SILENT HILL?"
"YEAH, FOR AWHILE... AFTER I CAME TO TOWN AND MY THING HAPPENED, I THINK. I'M NOT REALLY SURE. TIME IS ALL WHACKED OUT OVER HERE. BUT SHE MADE IT INTO WHATEVER SHE WANTED IT TO BE. SHE WAS THE LAW.
"THEN SOMETHING HAPPENED. IT'S LIKE SHE SENSED IT COMING, STARTED PLANNING, PREPARING... AND I DON'T KNOW WHAT HAPPENED TO HER. NOT AFTER IT ALL CHANGED."
SHE WAS PRETTY. SMELLED LIKE TANGERINES. AND HER TONGUE WAS LIKE-
OKAY.
BUT I THINK THE KID'S RIGHT. WITH WHAT I'VE BEEN SENT TO GET FOR YOU AND LAURYN'S BOOK WE CAN TAKE OUT THAT BITCH LENORA. MAKE THINGS COOL AROUND HERE AGAIN AND-
WHAT THE FUCK?
"IT'S... A FESTIVAL."
HELLO, EVERYONE! I AM MAYOR HABORYM, HERE TO WELCOME YOU IN HONOR OF THE GOOD LADY JEZEBETH, WHOM YOU KNOW AS THE ANOINTED ONE, THE RAISER OF THE DEAD, SHE WHOSE BEAUTY IS MORE THAN ANY OF US DESERVE- LENORA!

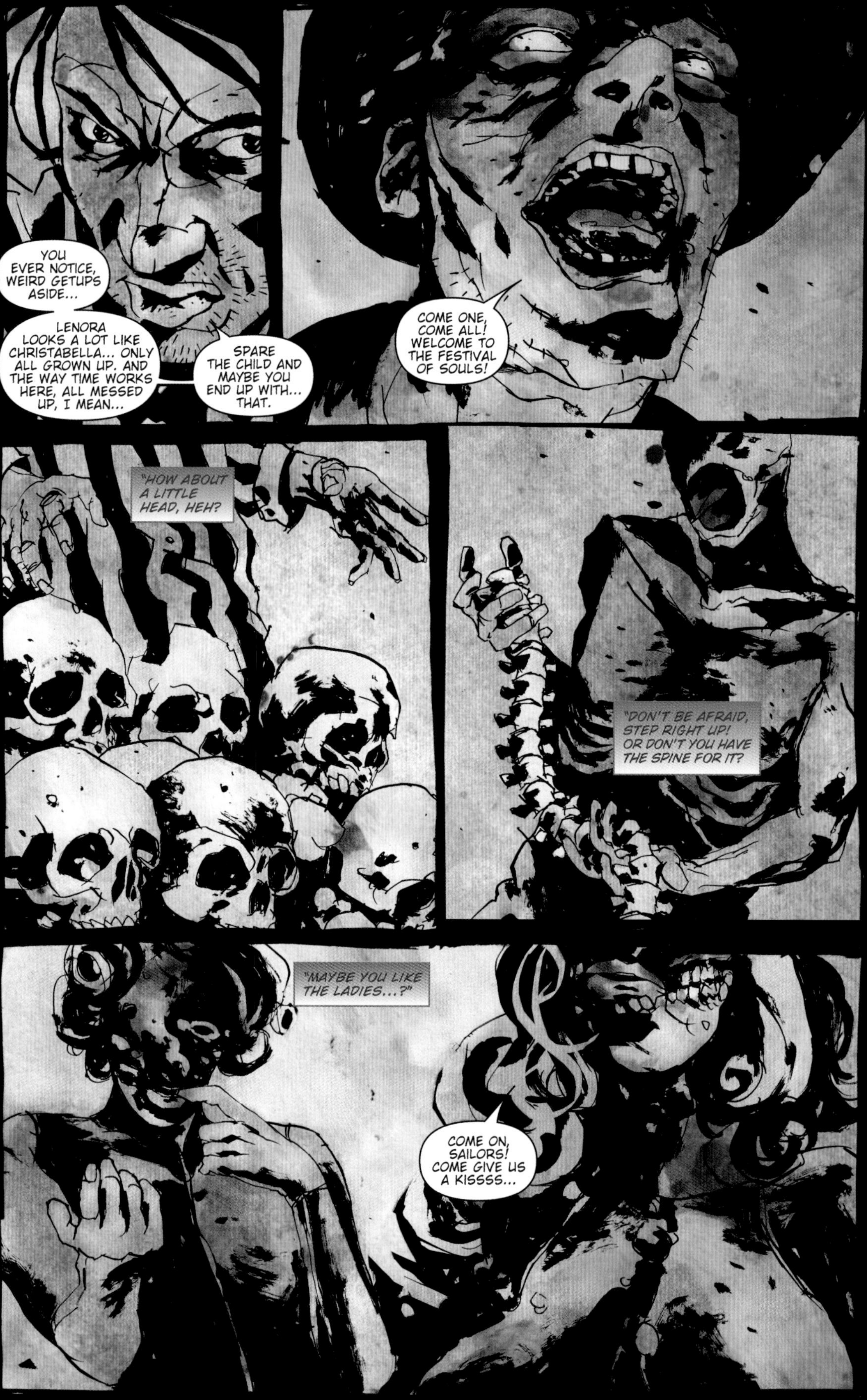

YOU EVER NOTICE, WEIRD GETUPS ASIDE...
LENORA LOOKS A LOT LIKE CHRISTABELLA... ONLY ALL GROWN UP. AND THE WAY TIME WORKS HERE, ALL MESSED UP, I MEAN...
SPARE THE CHILD AND MAYBE YOU END UP WITH... THAT.
COME ONE, COME ALL! WELCOME TO THE FESTIVAL OF SOULS!
"HOW ABOUT A LITTLE HEAD, HEH?
"DON'T BE AFRAID, STEP RIGHT UP! OR DON'T YOU HAVE THE SPINE FOR IT?
"MAYBE YOU LIKE THE LADIES...?"
COME ON, SAILORS! COME GIVE US A KISSSS...

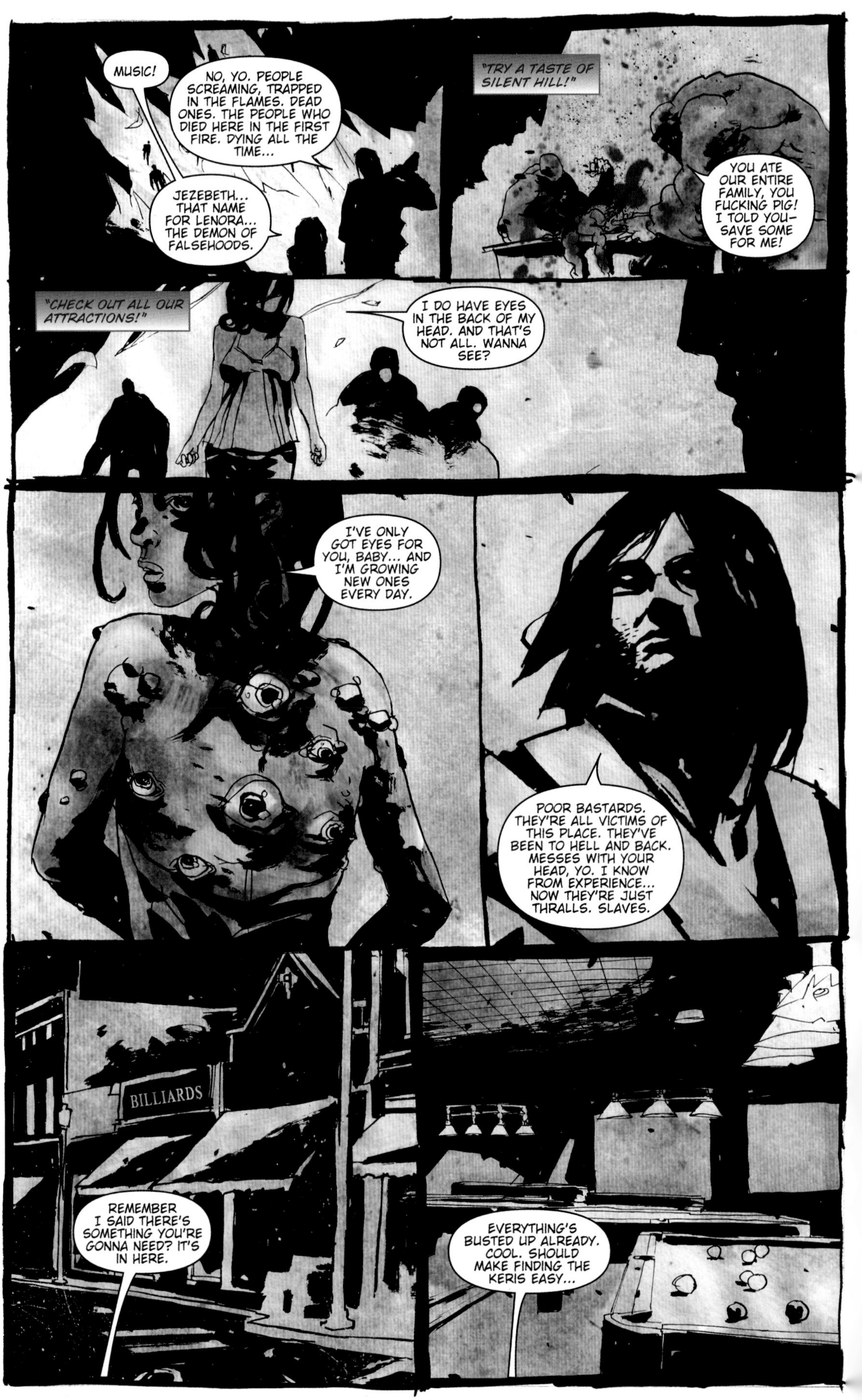
MUSIC!
NO, YO. PEOPLE SCREAMING, TRAPPED IN THE FLAMES. DEAD ONES. THE PEOPLE WHO DIED HERE IN THE FIRST FIRE. DYING ALL THE TIME...
JEZEBETH... THAT NAME FOR LENORA... THE DEMON OF FALSEHOODS.
"TRY A TASTE OF SILENT HILL!"
YOU ATE OUR ENTIRE FAMILY, YOU FUCKING PIG! I TOLD YOU-SAVE SOME FOR ME!
"CHECK OUT ALL OUR ATTRACTIONS!"
I DO HAVE EYES IN THE BACK OF MY HEAD. AND THAT'S NOT ALL. WANNA SEE?
I'VE ONLY GOT EYES FOR YOU, BABY... AND I'M GROWING NEW ONES EVERY DAY.
POOR BASTARDS. THEY'RE ALL VICTIMS OF THIS PLACE. THEY'VE BEEN TO HELL AND BACK. MESSES WITH YOUR HEAD, YO. I KNOW FROM EXPERIENCE... NOW THEY'RE JUST THRALLS. SLAVES.
BILLIARDS
REMEMBER I SAID THERE'S SOMETHING YOU'RE GONNA NEED? IT'S IN HERE.
EVERYTHING'S BUSTED UP ALREADY. COOL. SHOULD MAKE FINDING THE KERIS EASY...

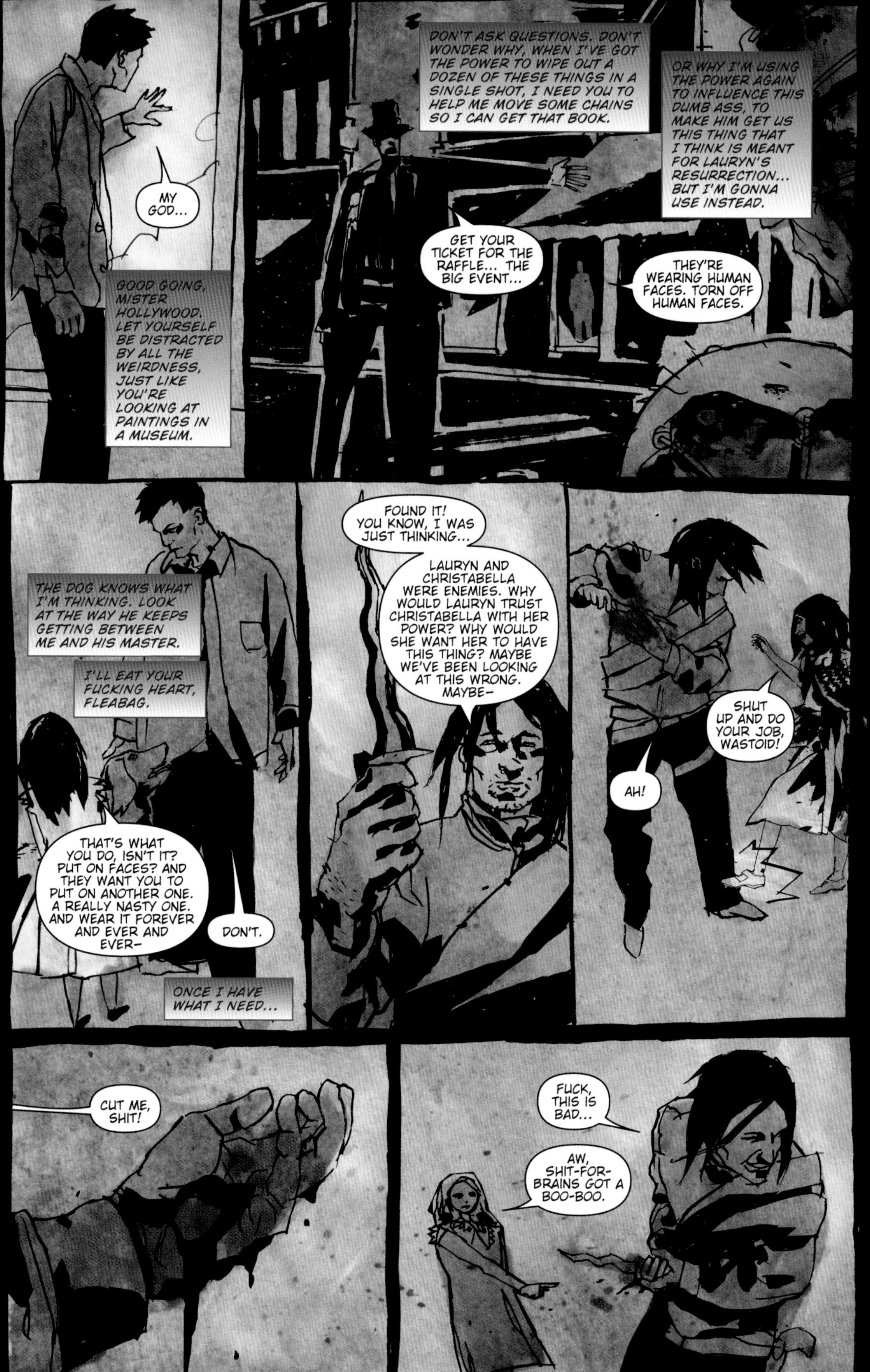
MY GOD...
GOOD GOING, MISTER HOLLYWOOD. LET YOURSELF BE DISTRACTED BY ALL THE WEIRDNESS, JUST LIKE YOU'RE LOOKING AT PAINTINGS IN A MUSEUM.
DON'T ASK QUESTIONS. DON'T WONDER WHY, WHEN I'VE GOT THE POWER TO WIPE OUT A DOZEN OF THESE THINGS IN A SINGLE SHOT, I NEED YOU TO HELP ME MOVE SOME CHAINS SO I CAN GET THAT BOOK.
OR WHY I'M USING THE POWER AGAIN TO INFLUENCE THIS DUMB ASS, TO MAKE HIM GET US THIS THING THAT I THINK IS MEANT FOR LAURYN'S RESURRECTION... BUT I'M GONNA USE INSTEAD.
GET YOUR TICKET FOR THE RAFFLE... THE BIG EVENT...
THEY'RE WEARING HUMAN FACES. TORN OFF HUMAN FACES.
THE DOG KNOWS WHAT I'M THINKING. LOOK AT THE WAY HE KEEPS GETTING BETWEEN ME AND HIS MASTER.
I'LL EAT YOUR FUCKING HEART, FLEABAG.
THAT'S WHAT YOU DO, ISN'T IT? PUT ON FACES? AND THEY WANT YOU TO PUT ON ANOTHER ONE. A REALLY NASTY ONE. AND WEAR IT FOREVER AND EVER AND EVER–
DON'T.
ONCE I HAVE WHAT I NEED...
FOUND IT! YOU KNOW, I WAS JUST THINKING...
LAURYN AND CHRISTABELLA WERE ENEMIES. WHY WOULD LAURYN TRUST CHRISTABELLA WITH HER POWER? WHY WOULD SHE WANT HER TO HAVE THIS THING? MAYBE WE'VE BEEN LOOKING AT THIS WRONG. MAYBE–
SHUT UP AND DO YOUR JOB, WASTOID!
AH!
CUT ME, SHIT!
FUCK, THIS IS BAD...
AW, SHIT-FOR-BRAINS GOT A BOO-BOO.

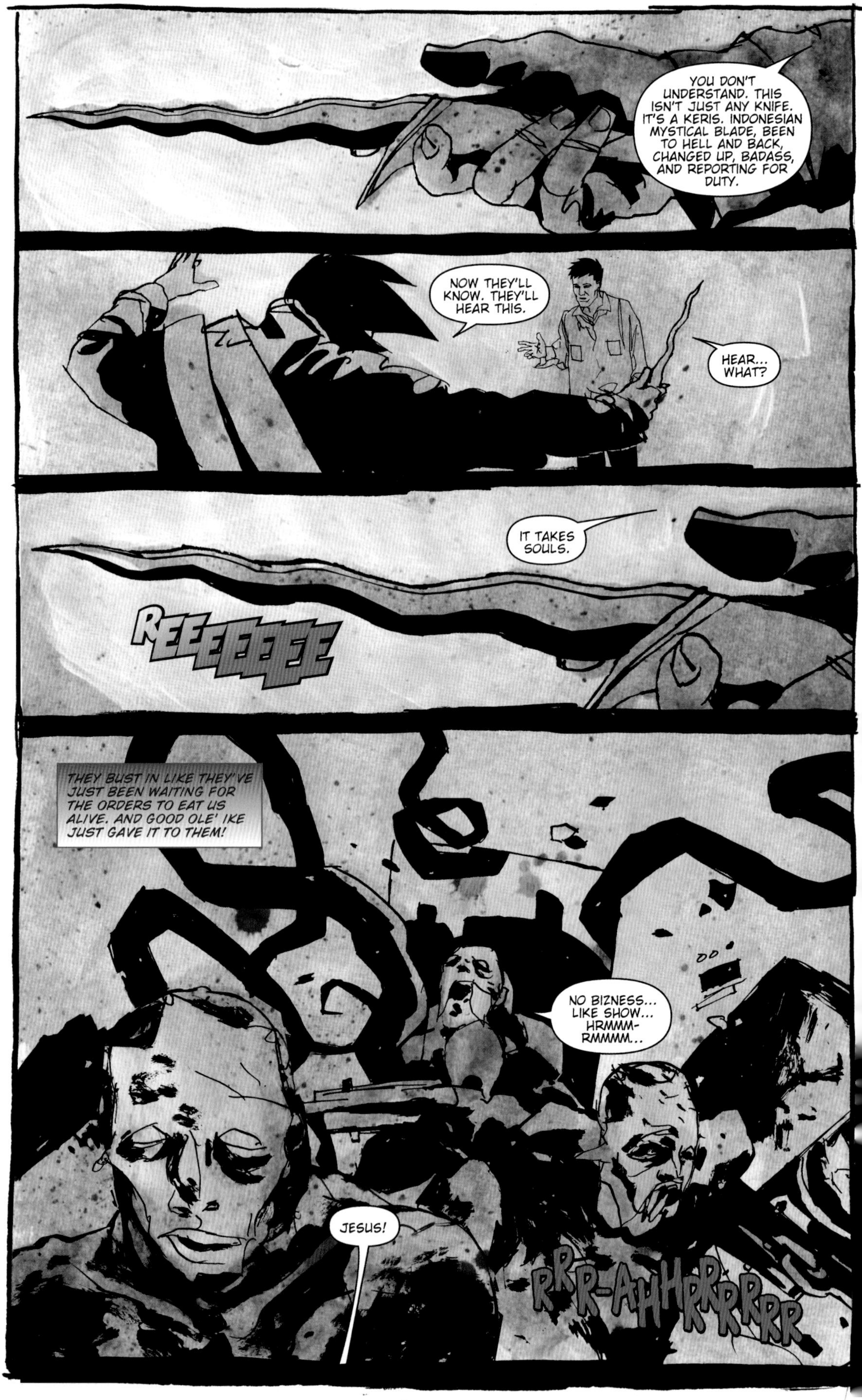

YOU DON'T UNDERSTAND. THIS ISN'T JUST ANY KNIFE. IT'S A KERIS. INDONESIAN MYSTICAL BLADE, BEEN TO HELL AND BACK, CHANGED UP, BADASS, AND REPORTING FOR DUTY.
NOW THEY'LL KNOW. THEY'LL HEAR THIS.
HEAR... WHAT?
IT TAKES SOULS.
REEEEEEE
THEY BUST IN LIKE THEY'VE JUST BEEN WAITING FOR THE ORDERS TO EAT US ALIVE. AND GOOD OLE' IKE JUST GAVE IT TO THEM!
NO BIZNESS... LIKE SHOW... HRMMM-RMMMM...
JESUS!
RRR-AHHRRRRRRR

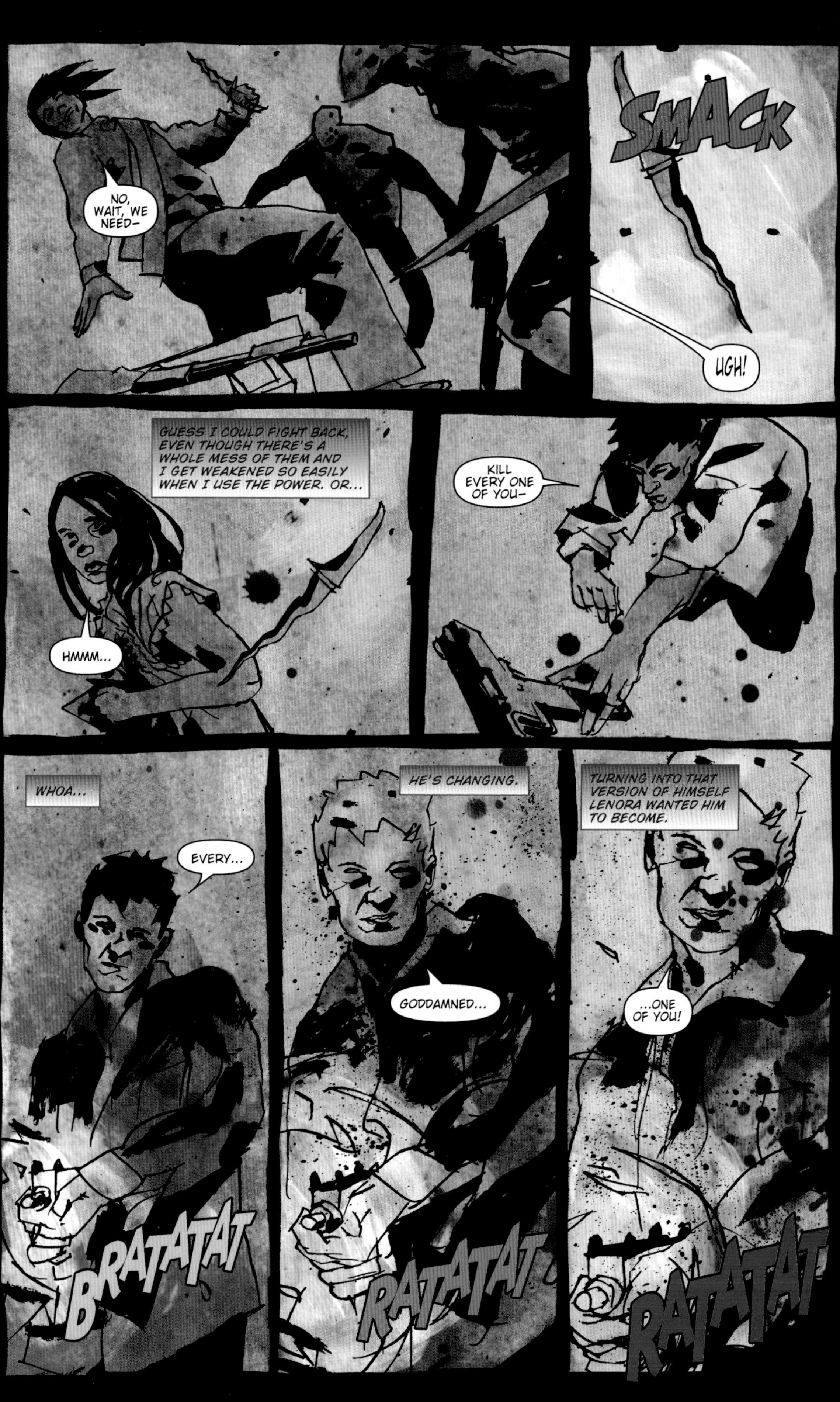
NO, WAIT, WE NEED–
SMACK
UGH!
GUESS I COULD FIGHT BACK, EVEN THOUGH THERE'S A WHOLE MESS OF THEM AND I GET WEAKENED SO EASILY WHEN I USE THE POWER. OR...
HMMM...
KILL EVERY ONE OF YOU–
WHOA...
EVERY...
BRATATAT
HE'S CHANGING.
GODDAMNED...
RATATAT
TURNING INTO THAT VERSION OF HIMSELF LENORA WANTED HIM TO BECOME.
...ONE OF YOU!
RATATAT

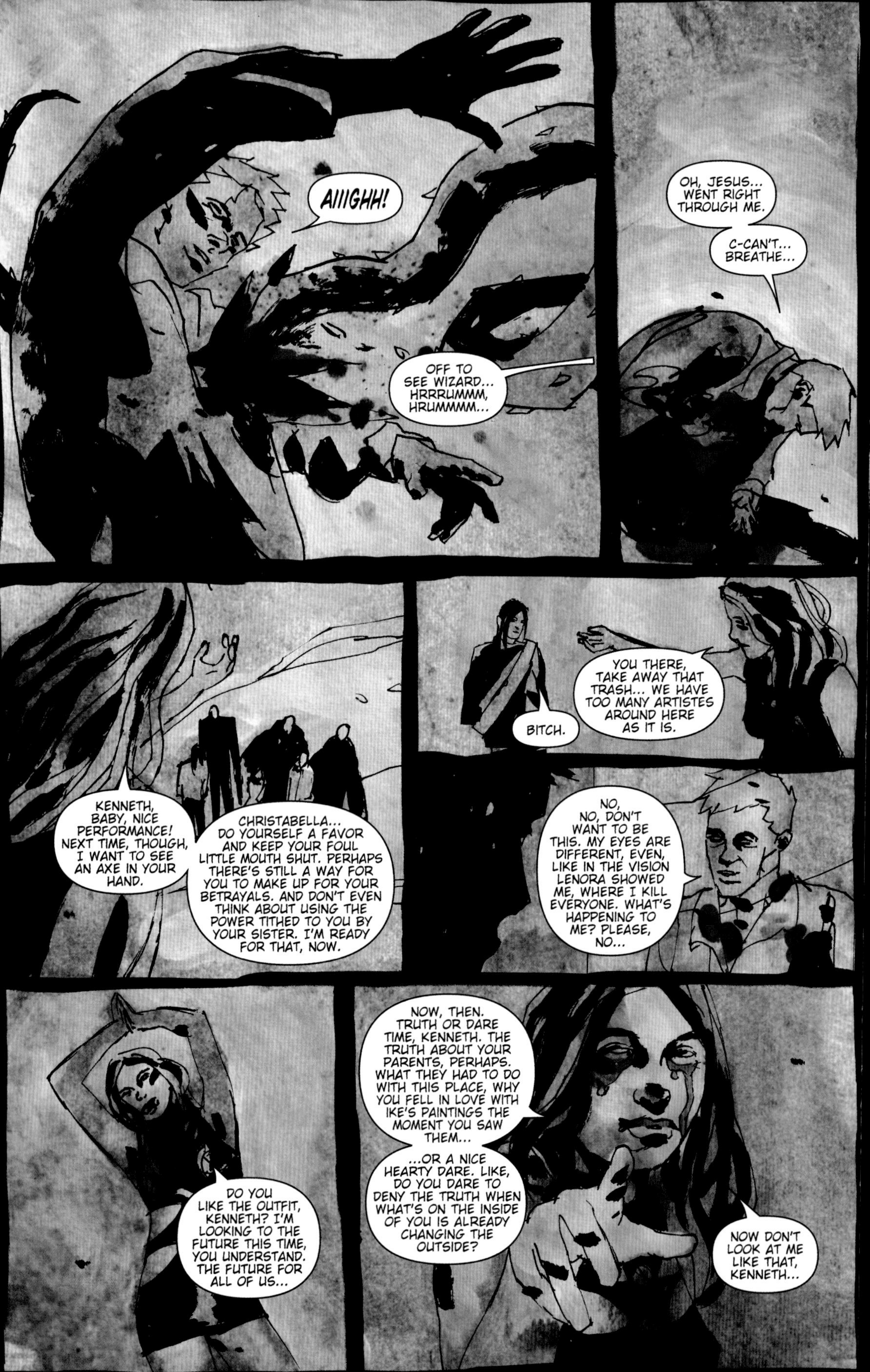
AIIIGHH!
OFF TO SEE WIZARD... HRRRUMMM, HRUMMMM...
OH, JESUS... WENT RIGHT THROUGH ME.
C-CAN'T... BREATHE...
KENNETH, BABY, NICE PERFORMANCE! NEXT TIME, THOUGH, I WANT TO SEE AN AXE IN YOUR HAND.
CHRISTABELLA... DO YOURSELF A FAVOR AND KEEP YOUR FOUL LITTLE MOUTH SHUT. PERHAPS THERE'S STILL A WAY FOR YOU TO MAKE UP FOR YOUR BETRAYALS. AND DON'T EVEN THINK ABOUT USING THE POWER TITHED TO YOU BY YOUR SISTER. I'M READY FOR THAT, NOW.
YOU THERE, TAKE AWAY THAT TRASH... WE HAVE TOO MANY ARTISTES AROUND HERE AS IT IS.
BITCH.
NO, NO, DON'T WANT TO BE THIS. MY EYES ARE DIFFERENT, EVEN, LIKE IN THE VISION LENORA SHOWED ME, WHERE I KILL EVERYONE. WHAT'S HAPPENING TO ME? PLEASE, NO...
DO YOU LIKE THE OUTFIT, KENNETH? I'M LOOKING TO THE FUTURE THIS TIME, YOU UNDERSTAND. THE FUTURE FOR ALL OF US...
NOW, THEN. TRUTH OR DARE TIME, KENNETH. THE TRUTH ABOUT YOUR PARENTS, PERHAPS. WHAT THEY HAD TO DO WITH THIS PLACE, WHY YOU FELL IN LOVE WITH IKE'S PAINTINGS THE MOMENT YOU SAW THEM...
...OR A NICE HEARTY DARE. LIKE, DO YOU DARE TO DENY THE TRUTH WHEN WHAT'S ON THE INSIDE OF YOU IS ALREADY CHANGING THE OUTSIDE?
NOW DON'T LOOK AT ME LIKE THAT, KENNETH...

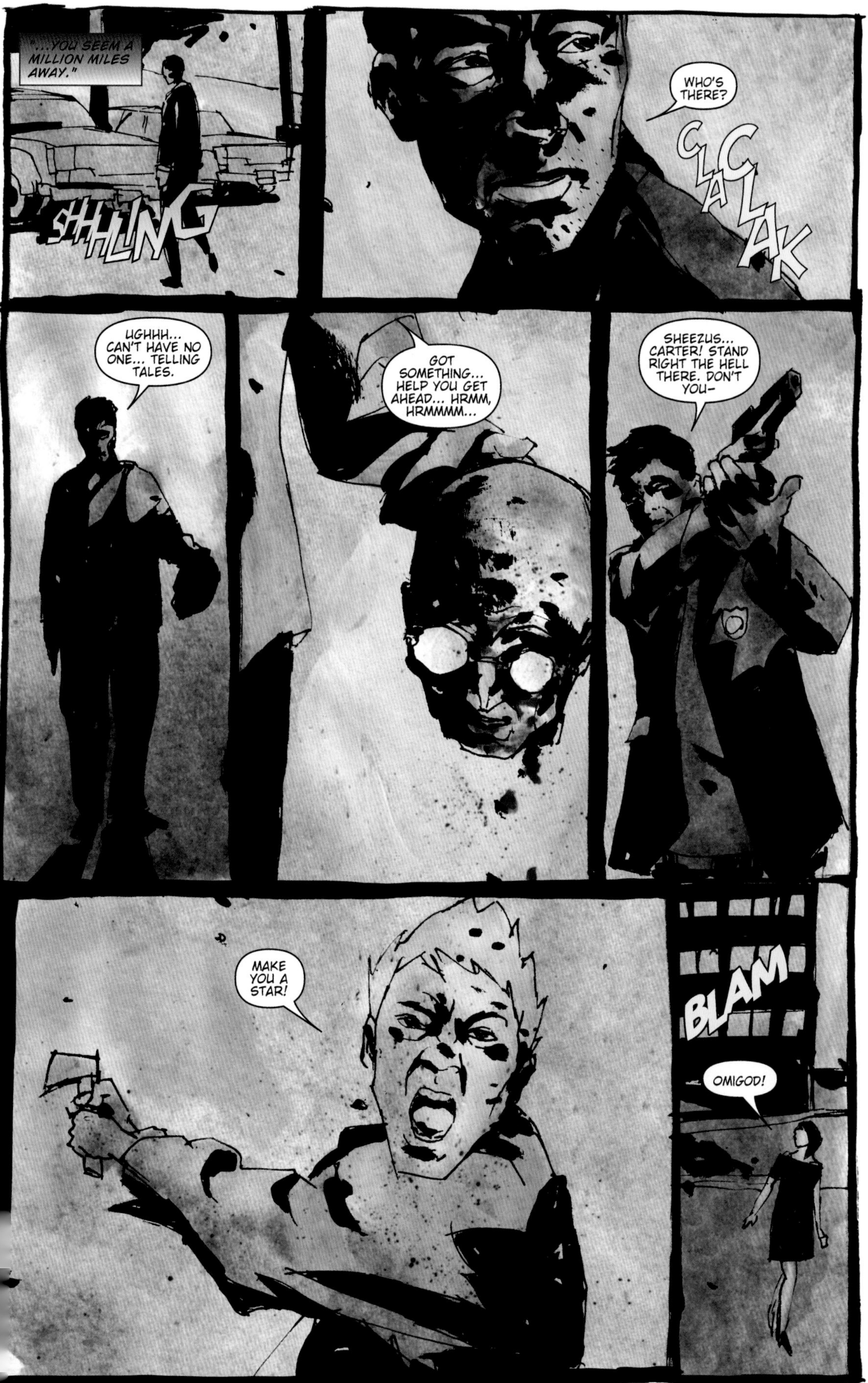
"...YOU SEEM A MILLION MILES AWAY."
SHHHLING
WHO'S THERE?
CLACLAK
UGHHH... CAN'T HAVE NO ONE... TELLING TALES.
GOT SOMETHING... HELP YOU GET AHEAD... HRMM, HRMMMM...
SHEEZUS... CARTER! STAND RIGHT THE HELL THERE. DON'T YOU-
MAKE YOU A STAR!
BLAM
OMIGOD!

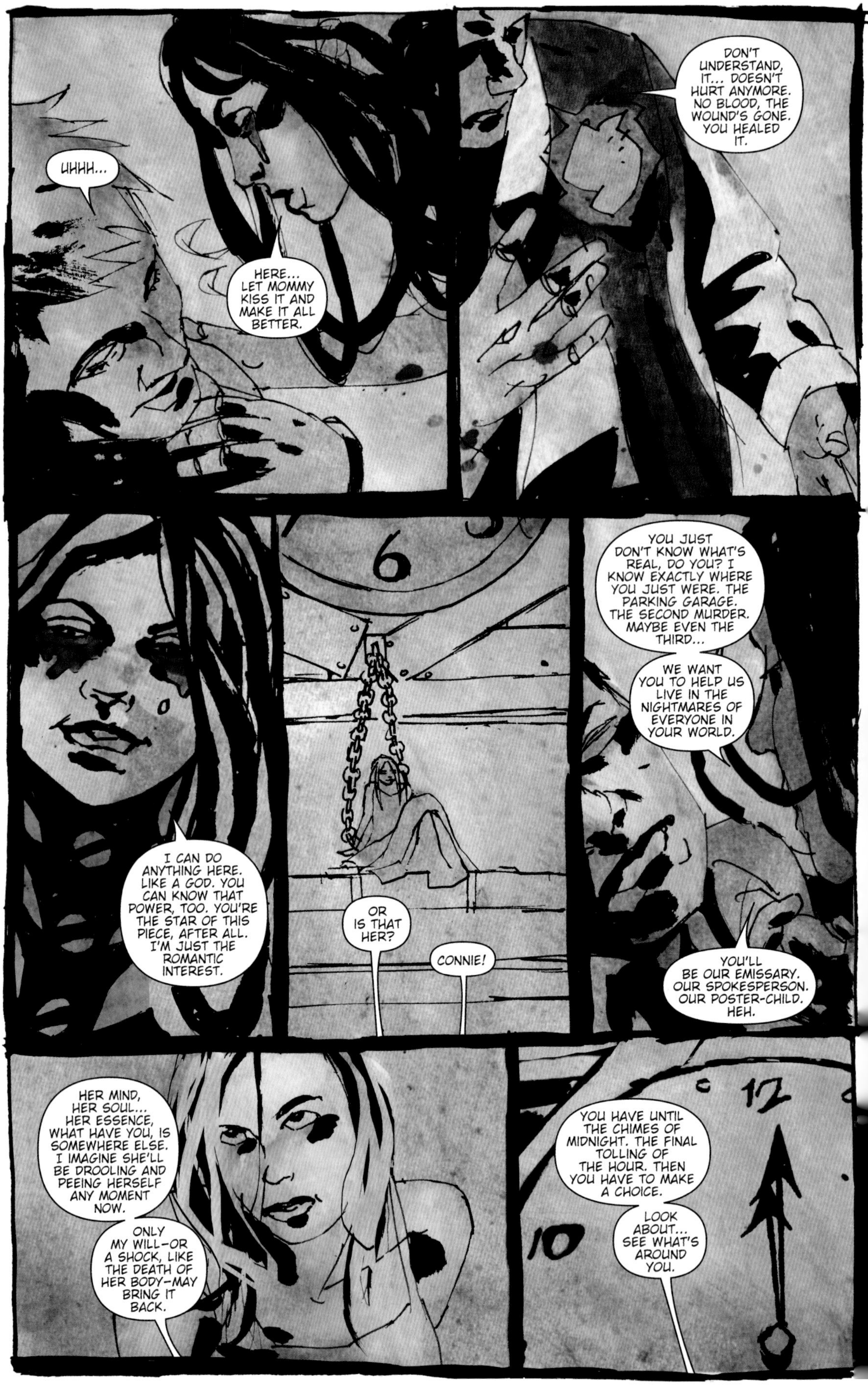
UHHH...
HERE... LET MOMMY KISS IT AND MAKE IT ALL BETTER.
DON'T UNDERSTAND, IT... DOESN'T HURT ANYMORE. NO BLOOD, THE WOUND'S GONE. YOU HEALED IT.
I CAN DO ANYTHING HERE. LIKE A GOD. YOU CAN KNOW THAT POWER, TOO. YOU'RE THE STAR OF THIS PIECE, AFTER ALL. I'M JUST THE ROMANTIC INTEREST.
OR IS THAT HER?
CONNIE!
YOU JUST DON'T KNOW WHAT'S REAL, DO YOU? I KNOW EXACTLY WHERE YOU JUST WERE. THE PARKING GARAGE. THE SECOND MURDER. MAYBE EVEN THE THIRD...
WE WANT YOU TO HELP US LIVE IN THE NIGHTMARES OF EVERYONE IN YOUR WORLD.
YOU'LL BE OUR EMISSARY. OUR SPOKESPERSON. OUR POSTER-CHILD. HEH.
HER MIND, HER SOUL... HER ESSENCE, WHAT HAVE YOU, IS SOMEWHERE ELSE. I IMAGINE SHE'LL BE DROOLING AND PEEING HERSELF ANY MOMENT NOW.
ONLY MY WILL—OR A SHOCK, LIKE THE DEATH OF HER BODY—MAY BRING IT BACK.
YOU HAVE UNTIL THE CHIMES OF MIDNIGHT. THE FINAL TOLLING OF THE HOUR. THEN YOU HAVE TO MAKE A CHOICE.
LOOK ABOUT... SEE WHAT'S AROUND YOU.

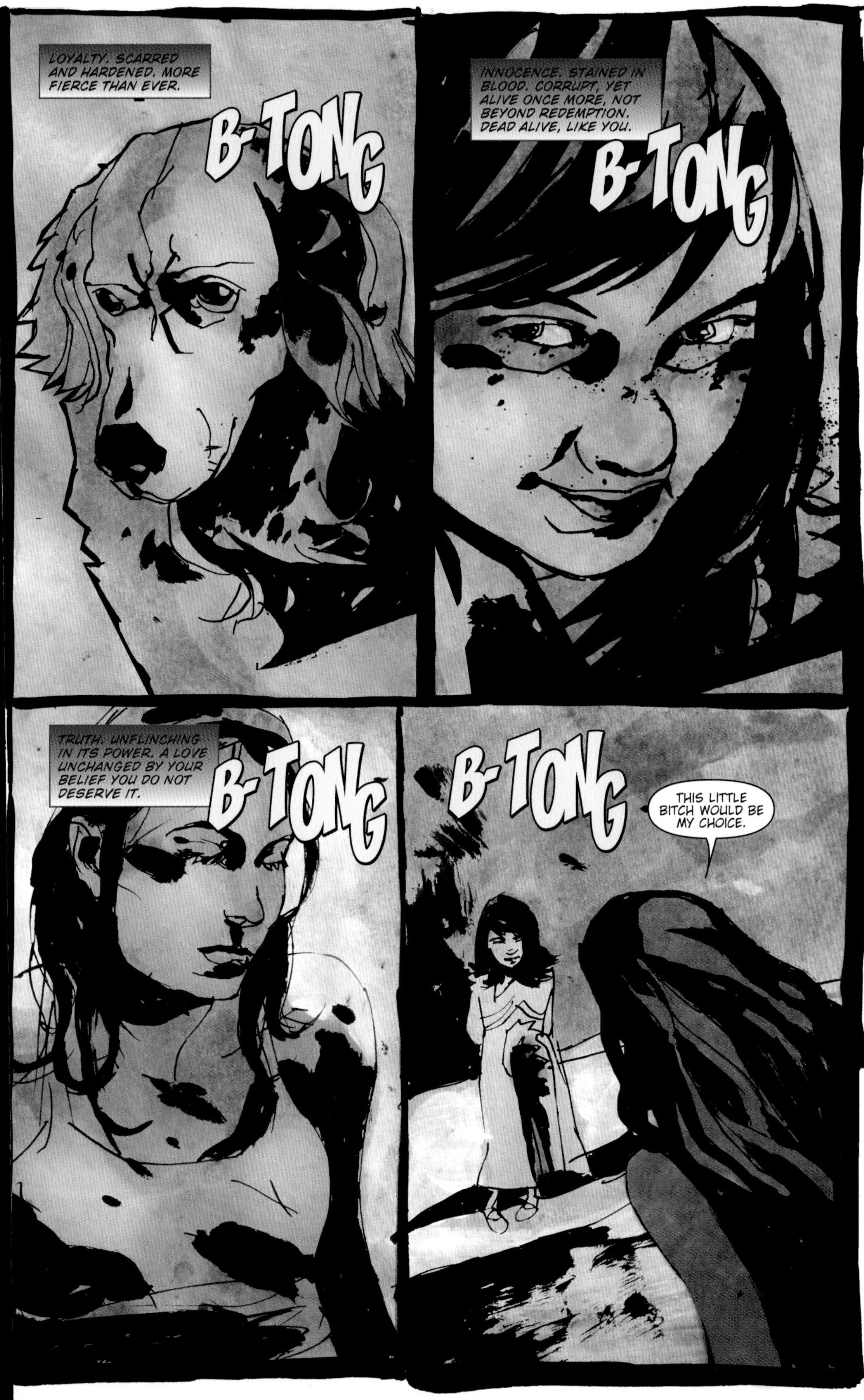
LOYALTY. SCARRED AND HARDENED. MORE FIERCE THAN EVER.
B-TONG
INNOCENCE. STAINED IN BLOOD. CORRUPT, YET ALIVE ONCE MORE, NOT BEYOND REDEMPTION. DEAD ALIVE, LIKE YOU.
B-TONG
TRUTH. UNFLINCHING IN ITS POWER. A LOVE UNCHANGED BY YOUR BELIEF YOU DO NOT DESERVE IT.
B-TONG
B-TONG
THIS LITTLE BITCH WOULD BE MY CHOICE.

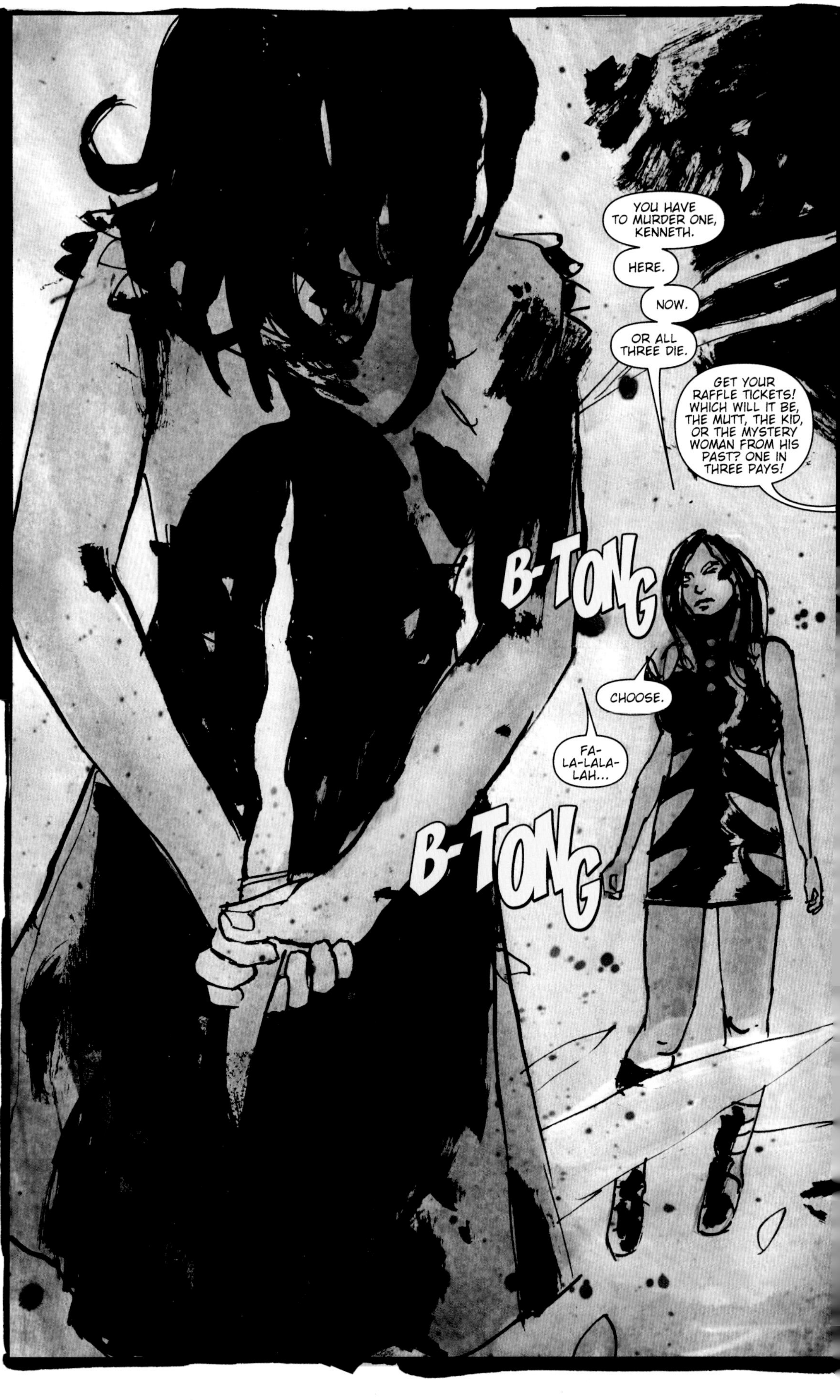
YOU HAVE TO MURDER ONE, KENNETH.
HERE.
NOW.
OR ALL THREE DIE.
GET YOUR RAFFLE TICKETS! WHICH WILL IT BE, THE MUTT, THE KID, OR THE MYSTERY WOMAN FROM HIS PAST? ONE IN THREE PAYS!
B-TONG
CHOOSE.
FA-LA-LALA-LAH...
B-TONG

CHAPTER
4

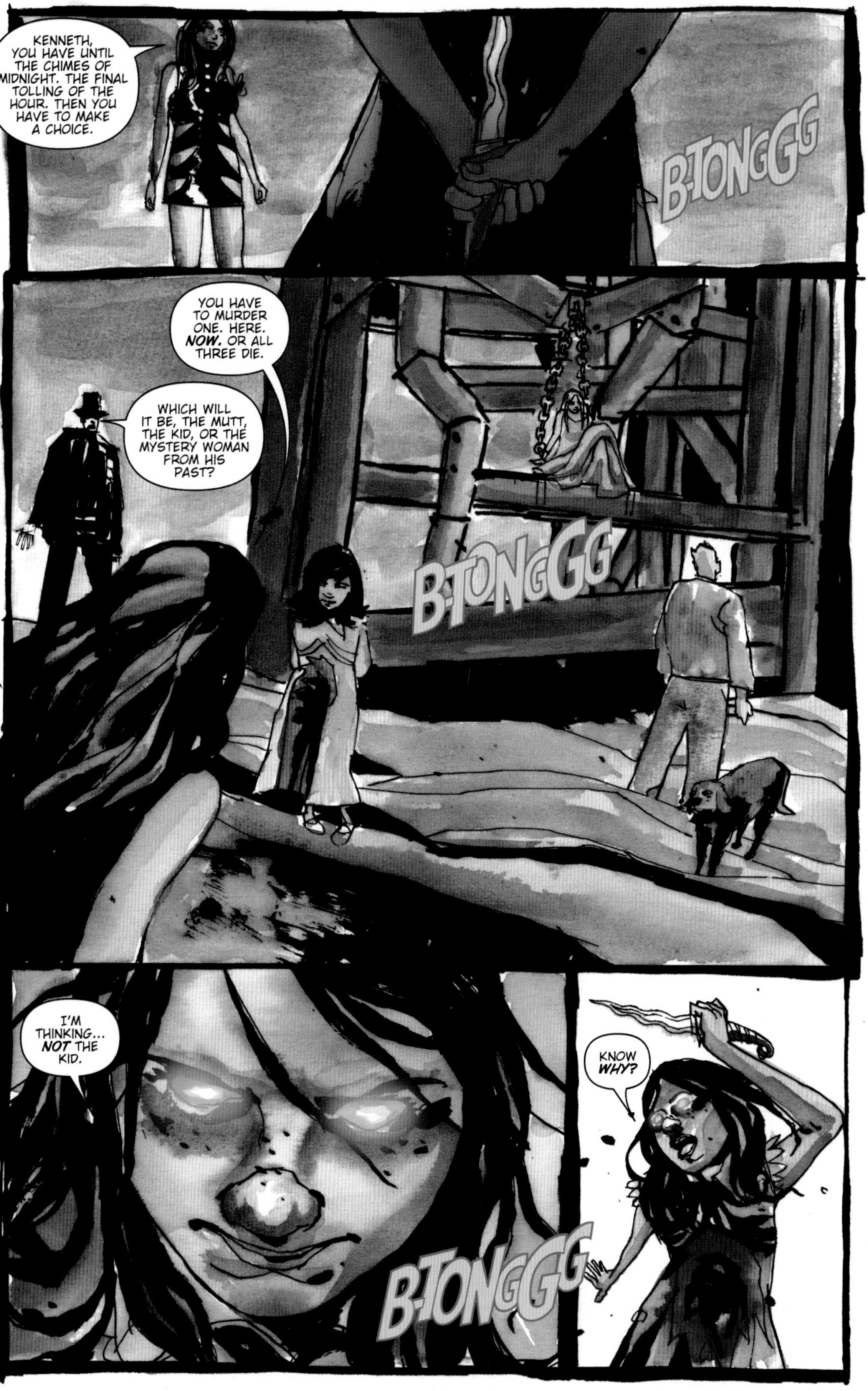
KENNETH, YOU HAVE UNTIL THE CHIMES OF MIDNIGHT. THE FINAL TOLLING OF THE HOUR. THEN YOU HAVE TO MAKE A CHOICE.
B-TONGGG
YOU HAVE TO MURDER ONE. HERE. **NOW.** OR ALL THREE DIE.
WHICH WILL IT BE, THE MUTT, THE KID, OR THE MYSTERY WOMAN FROM HIS PAST?
B-TONGGG
I'M THINKING... **NOT** THE KID.
B-TONGGG
KNOW **WHY?**

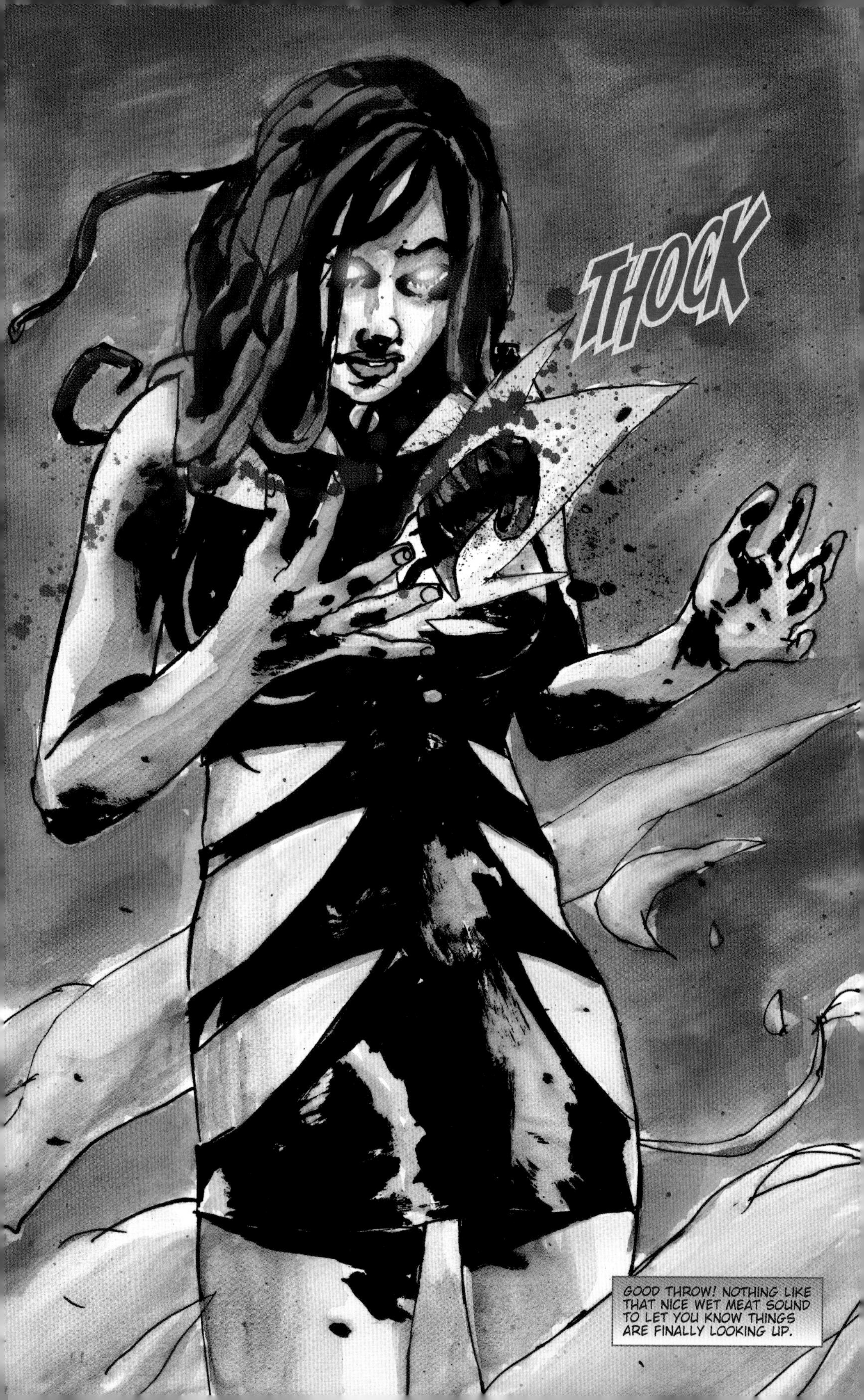
THOCK
GOOD THROW! NOTHING LIKE THAT NICE WET MEAT SOUND TO LET YOU KNOW THINGS ARE FINALLY LOOKING UP.

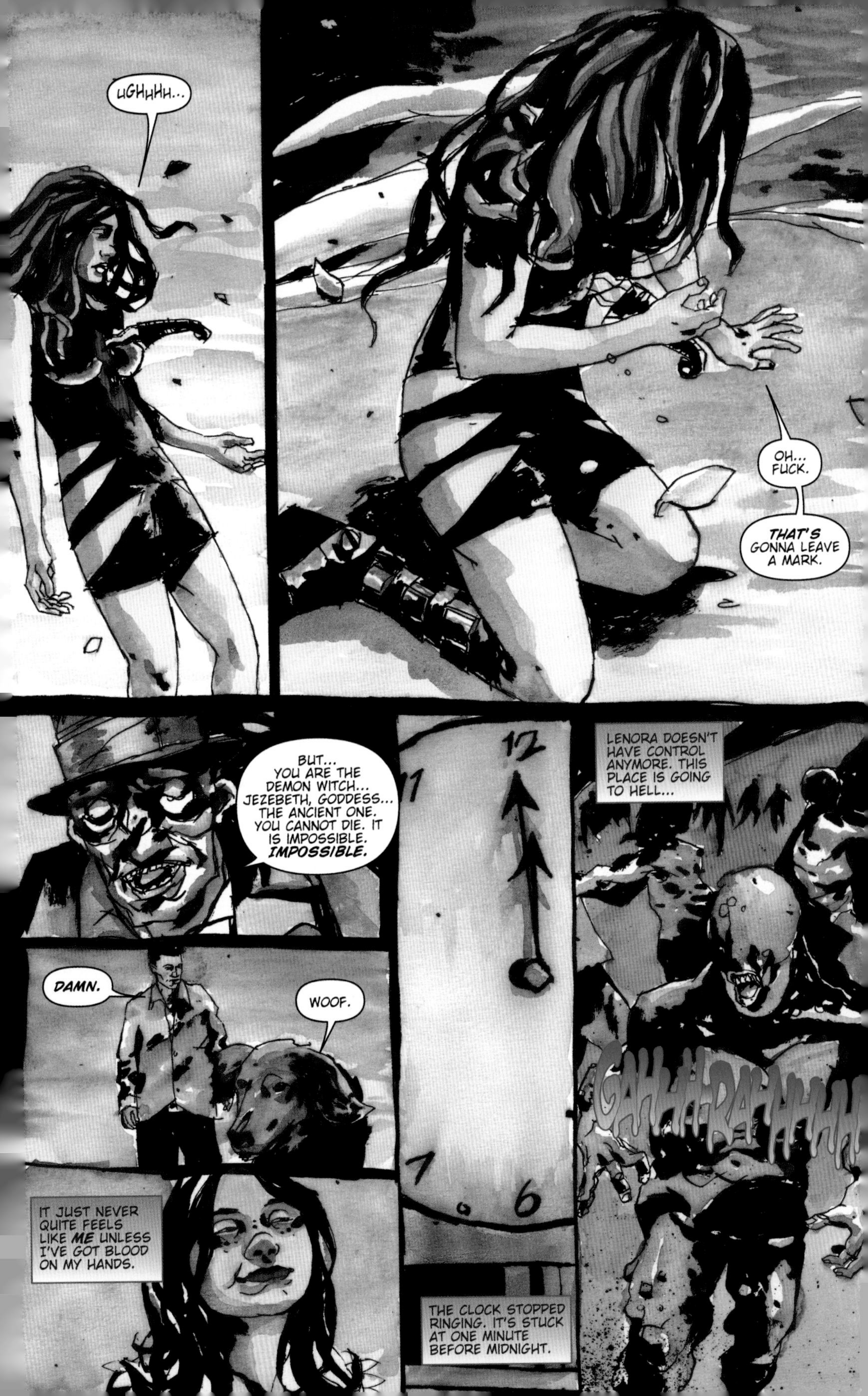

UGHHHH...
OH... FUCK.
THAT'S GONNA LEAVE A MARK.
BUT... YOU ARE THE DEMON WITCH... JEZEBETH, GODDESS... THE ANCIENT ONE. YOU CANNOT DIE. IT IS IMPOSSIBLE. IMPOSSIBLE.
DAMN.
WOOF.
IT JUST NEVER QUITE FEELS LIKE ME UNLESS I'VE GOT BLOOD ON MY HANDS.
THE CLOCK STOPPED RINGING. IT'S STUCK AT ONE MINUTE BEFORE MIDNIGHT.
LENORA DOESN'T HAVE CONTROL ANYMORE. THIS PLACE IS GOING TO HELL...
GAHHH-RAHHHHH

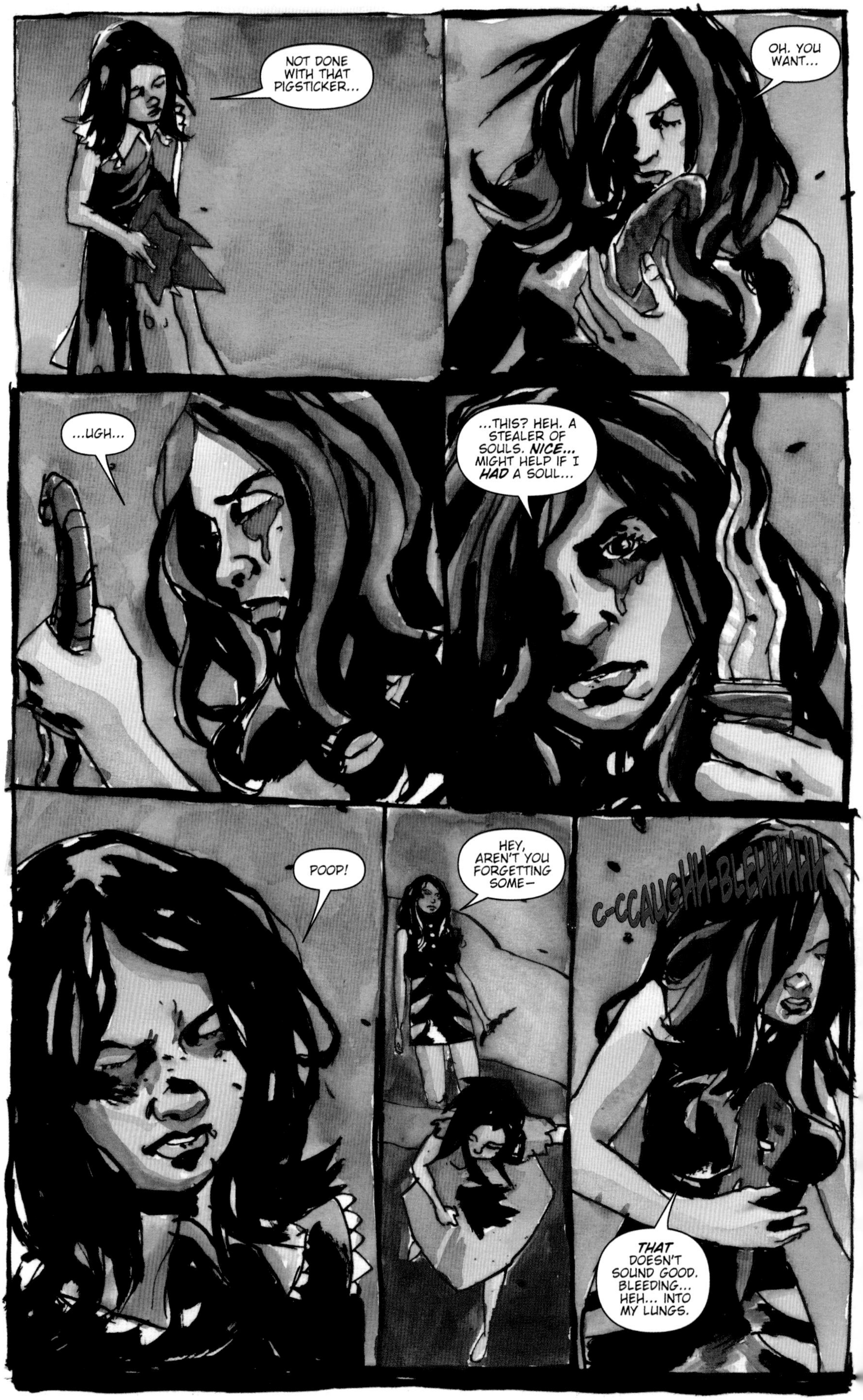
NOT DONE WITH THAT PIGSTICKER...
OH. YOU WANT...
...UGH...
...THIS? HEH. A STEALER OF SOULS. NICE... MIGHT HELP IF I HAD A SOUL...
POOP!
HEY, AREN'T YOU FORGETTING SOME–
C-CCAUGHH-BLEHHHHH
THAT DOESN'T SOUND GOOD. BLEEDING... HEH... INTO MY LUNGS.

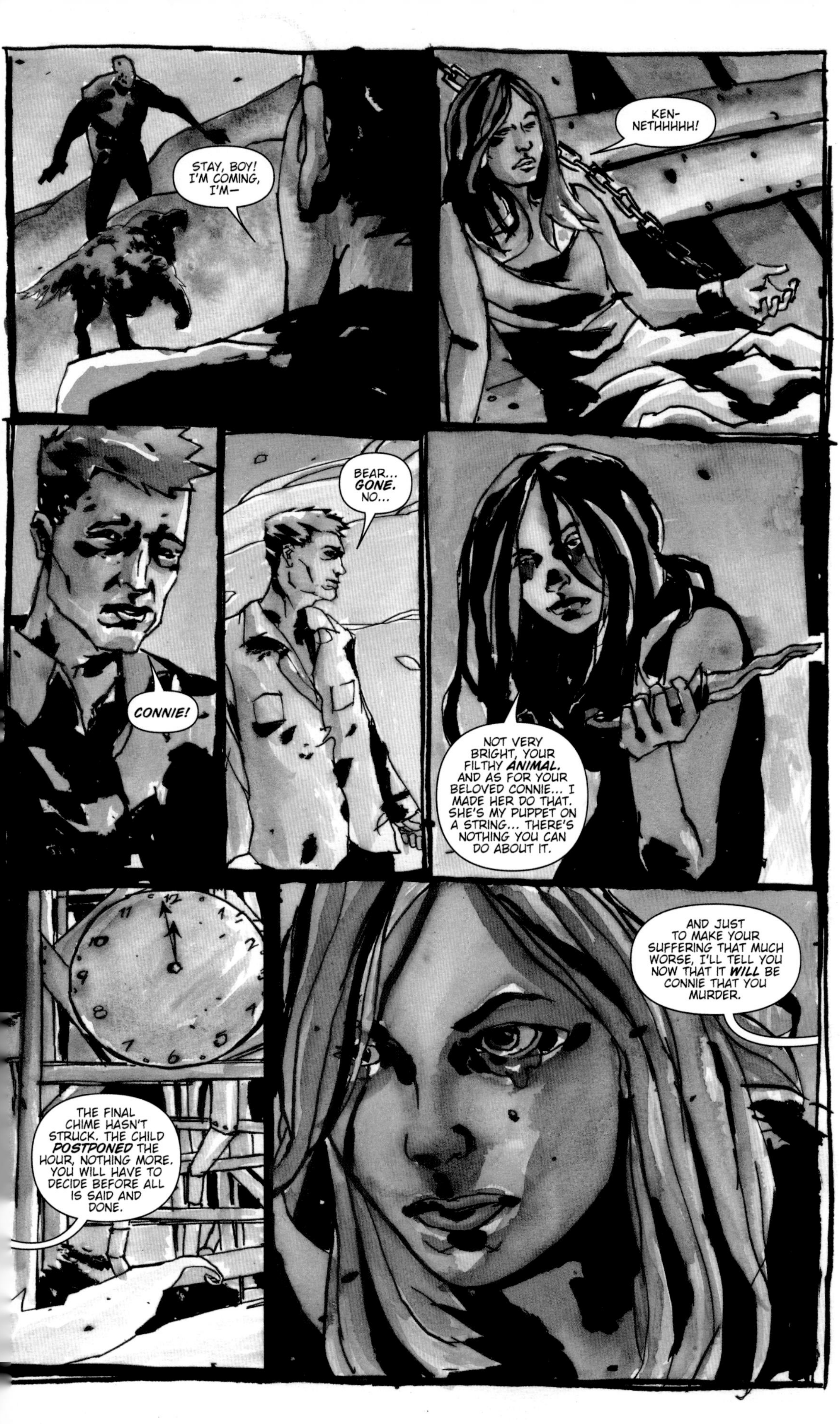
STAY, BOY! I'M COMING, I'M—
KEN-NETHHHHH!
CONNIE!
BEAR... GONE. NO...
NOT VERY BRIGHT, YOUR FILTHY ANIMAL. AND AS FOR YOUR BELOVED CONNIE... I MADE HER DO THAT. SHE'S MY PUPPET ON A STRING... THERE'S NOTHING YOU CAN DO ABOUT IT.
THE FINAL CHIME HASN'T STRUCK. THE CHILD POSTPONED THE HOUR, NOTHING MORE. YOU WILL HAVE TO DECIDE BEFORE ALL IS SAID AND DONE.
AND JUST TO MAKE YOUR SUFFERING THAT MUCH WORSE, I'LL TELL YOU NOW THAT IT WILL BE CONNIE THAT YOU MURDER.

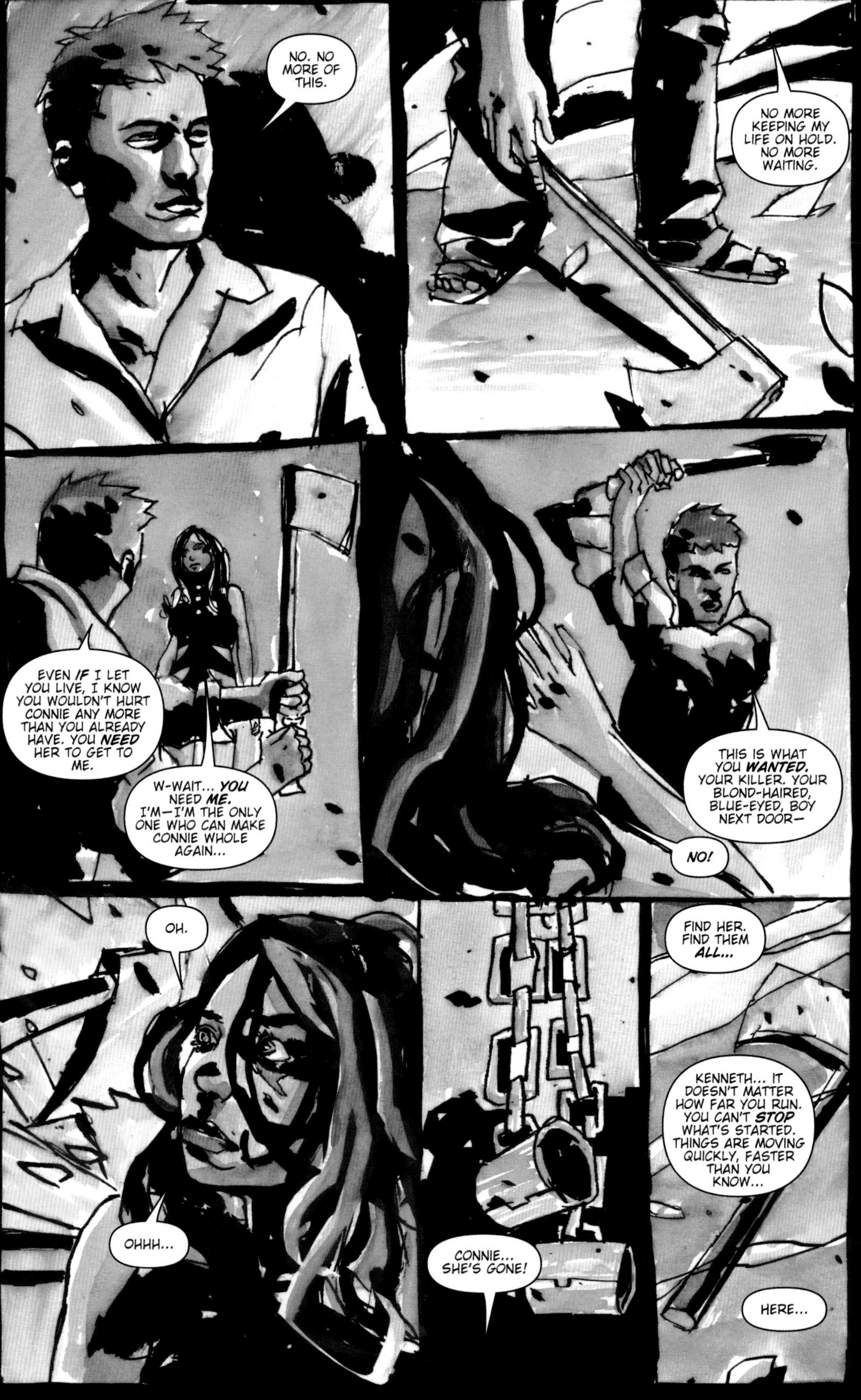
NO. NO MORE OF THIS.
NO MORE KEEPING MY LIFE ON HOLD. NO MORE WAITING.
EVEN *IF* I LET YOU LIVE, I KNOW YOU WOULDN'T HURT CONNIE ANY MORE THAN YOU ALREADY HAVE. YOU *NEED* HER TO GET TO ME.
W-WAIT... *YOU* NEED *ME.* I'M—I'M THE ONLY ONE WHO CAN MAKE CONNIE WHOLE AGAIN...
THIS IS WHAT YOU *WANTED.* YOUR KILLER. YOUR BLOND-HAIRED, BLUE-EYED, BOY NEXT DOOR—
NO!
OH.
OHHH...
CONNIE... SHE'S GONE!
FIND HER. FIND THEM *ALL...*
KENNETH... IT DOESN'T MATTER HOW FAR YOU RUN. YOU CAN'T *STOP* WHAT'S STARTED. THINGS ARE MOVING QUICKLY, FASTER THAN YOU KNOW...
HERE...

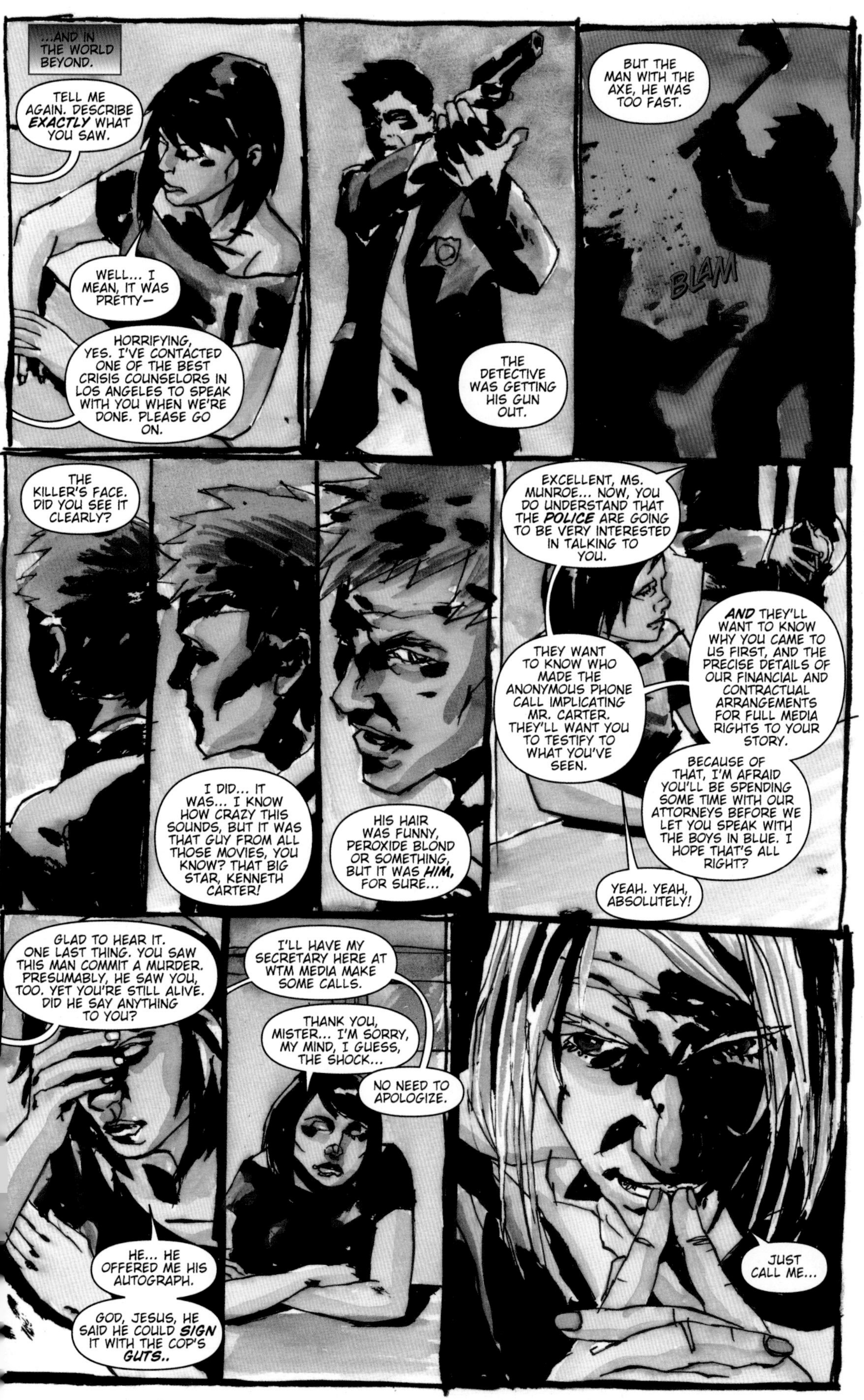

...AND IN THE WORLD BEYOND.
TELL ME AGAIN. DESCRIBE EXACTLY WHAT YOU SAW.
WELL... I MEAN, IT WAS PRETTY—
HORRIFYING, YES. I'VE CONTACTED ONE OF THE BEST CRISIS COUNSELORS IN LOS ANGELES TO SPEAK WITH YOU WHEN WE'RE DONE. PLEASE GO ON.
THE DETECTIVE WAS GETTING HIS GUN OUT.
BUT THE MAN WITH THE AXE, HE WAS TOO FAST.
BLAM
THE KILLER'S FACE. DID YOU SEE IT CLEARLY?
I DID... IT WAS... I KNOW HOW CRAZY THIS SOUNDS, BUT IT WAS THAT GUY FROM ALL THOSE MOVIES, YOU KNOW? THAT BIG STAR, KENNETH CARTER!
HIS HAIR WAS FUNNY, PEROXIDE BLOND OR SOMETHING, BUT IT WAS HIM, FOR SURE...
EXCELLENT, MS. MUNROE... NOW, YOU DO UNDERSTAND THAT THE POLICE ARE GOING TO BE VERY INTERESTED IN TALKING TO YOU.
THEY WANT TO KNOW WHO MADE THE ANONYMOUS PHONE CALL IMPLICATING MR. CARTER. THEY'LL WANT YOU TO TESTIFY TO WHAT YOU'VE SEEN.
AND THEY'LL WANT TO KNOW WHY YOU CAME TO US FIRST, AND THE PRECISE DETAILS OF OUR FINANCIAL AND CONTRACTUAL ARRANGEMENTS FOR FULL MEDIA RIGHTS TO YOUR STORY.
BECAUSE OF THAT, I'M AFRAID YOU'LL BE SPENDING SOME TIME WITH OUR ATTORNEYS BEFORE WE LET YOU SPEAK WITH THE BOYS IN BLUE. I HOPE THAT'S ALL RIGHT?
YEAH. YEAH, ABSOLUTELY!
GLAD TO HEAR IT. ONE LAST THING. YOU SAW THIS MAN COMMIT A MURDER. PRESUMABLY, HE SAW YOU, TOO. YET YOU'RE STILL ALIVE. DID HE SAY ANYTHING TO YOU?
HE... HE OFFERED ME HIS AUTOGRAPH.
GOD, JESUS, HE SAID HE COULD SIGN IT WITH THE COP'S GUTS..
I'LL HAVE MY SECRETARY HERE AT WTM MEDIA MAKE SOME CALLS.
THANK YOU, MISTER... I'M SORRY, MY MIND, I GUESS, THE SHOCK...
NO NEED TO APOLOGIZE.
JUST CALL ME...

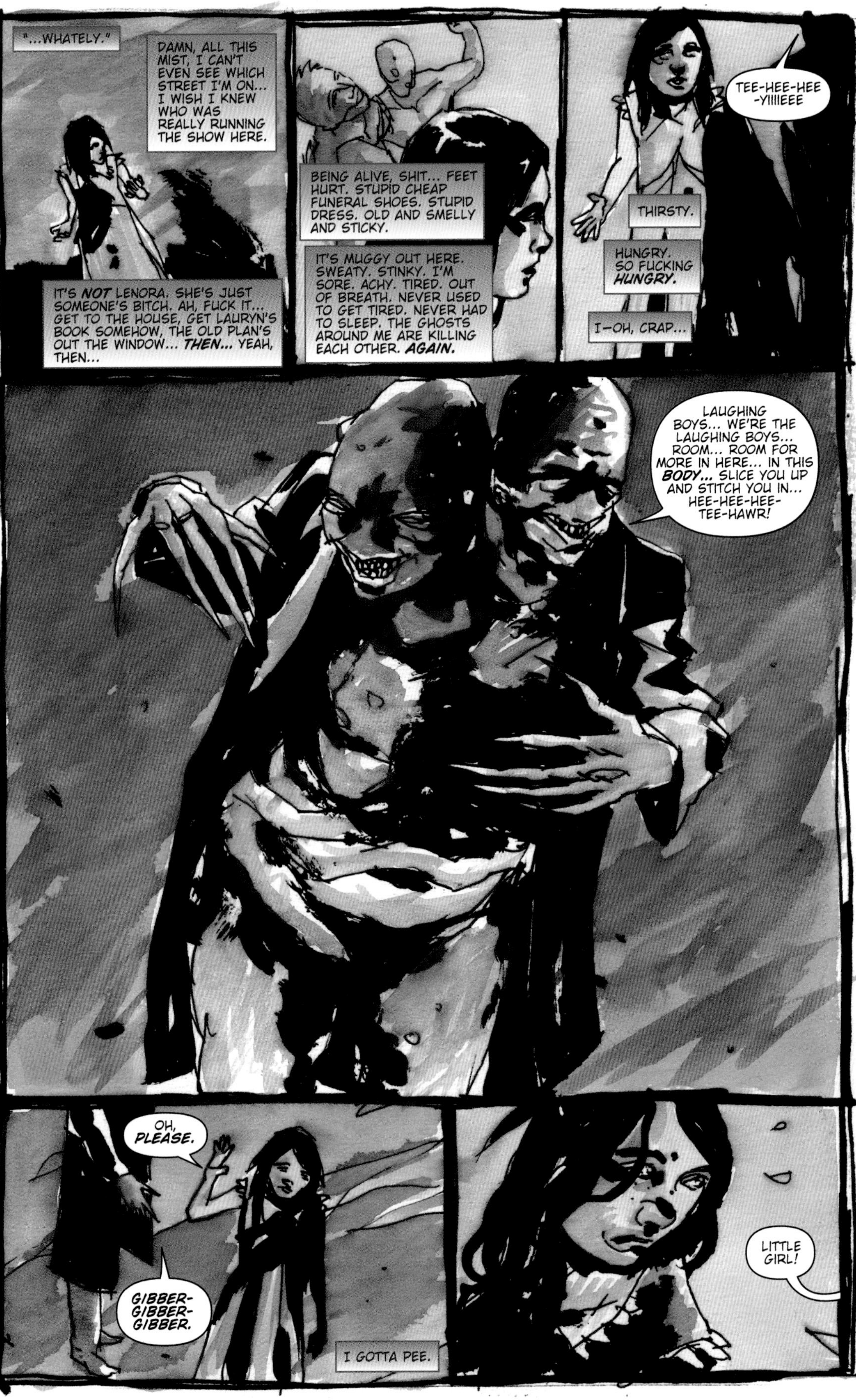
"...WHATELY."
DAMN, ALL THIS MIST, I CAN'T EVEN SEE WHICH STREET I'M ON... I WISH I KNEW WHO WAS REALLY RUNNING THE SHOW HERE.
IT'S NOT LENORA. SHE'S JUST SOMEONE'S BITCH. AH, FUCK IT... GET TO THE HOUSE, GET LAURYN'S BOOK SOMEHOW, THE OLD PLAN'S OUT THE WINDOW... THEN... YEAH, THEN...
BEING ALIVE, SHIT... FEET HURT. STUPID CHEAP FUNERAL SHOES. STUPID DRESS. OLD AND SMELLY AND STICKY.
IT'S MUGGY OUT HERE. SWEATY. STINKY. I'M SORE. ACHY. TIRED. OUT OF BREATH. NEVER USED TO GET TIRED. NEVER HAD TO SLEEP. THE GHOSTS AROUND ME ARE KILLING EACH OTHER. AGAIN.
TEE-HEE-HEE -YIIIIEEE
THIRSTY.
HUNGRY. SO FUCKING HUNGRY.
I—OH, CRAP...
LAUGHING BOYS... WE'RE THE LAUGHING BOYS... ROOM... ROOM FOR MORE IN HERE... IN THIS BODY... SLICE YOU UP AND STITCH YOU IN... HEE-HEE-HEE-TEE-HAWR!
OH, PLEASE.
GIBBER-GIBBER-GIBBER.
I GOTTA PEE.
LITTLE GIRL!

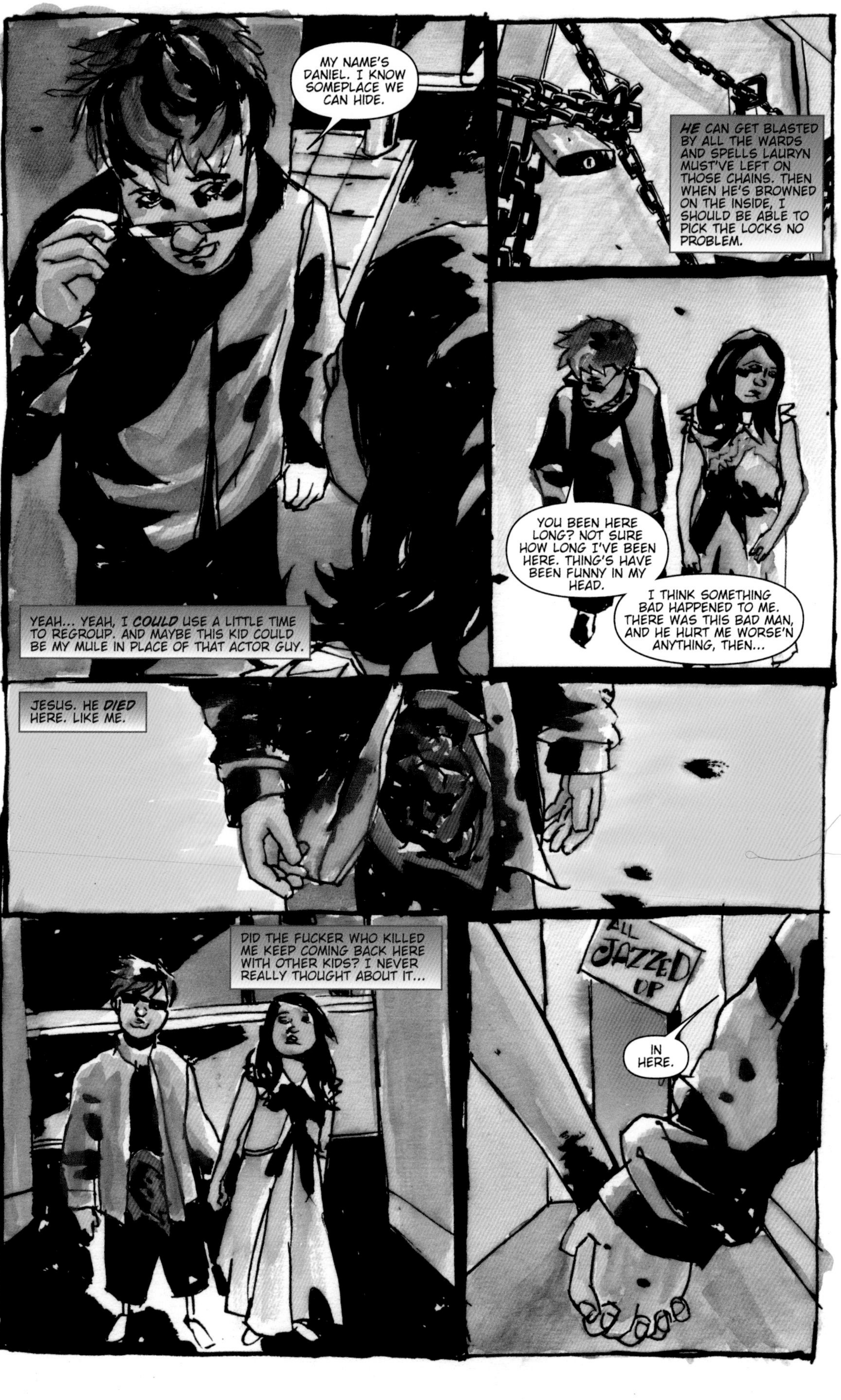

MY NAME'S DANIEL. I KNOW SOMEPLACE WE CAN HIDE.
YEAH... YEAH, I COULD USE A LITTLE TIME TO REGROUP. AND MAYBE THIS KID COULD BE MY MULE IN PLACE OF THAT ACTOR GUY.
HE CAN GET BLASTED BY ALL THE WARDS AND SPELLS LAURYN MUST'VE LEFT ON THOSE CHAINS. THEN WHEN HE'S BROWNED ON THE INSIDE, I SHOULD BE ABLE TO PICK THE LOCKS NO PROBLEM.
YOU BEEN HERE LONG? NOT SURE HOW LONG I'VE BEEN HERE. THING'S HAVE BEEN FUNNY IN MY HEAD.
I THINK SOMETHING BAD HAPPENED TO ME. THERE WAS THIS BAD MAN, AND HE HURT ME WORSE'N ANYTHING, THEN...
JESUS. HE DIED HERE. LIKE ME.
DID THE FUCKER WHO KILLED ME KEEP COMING BACK HERE WITH OTHER KIDS? I NEVER REALLY THOUGHT ABOUT IT...
ALL JAZZED UP
IN HERE.

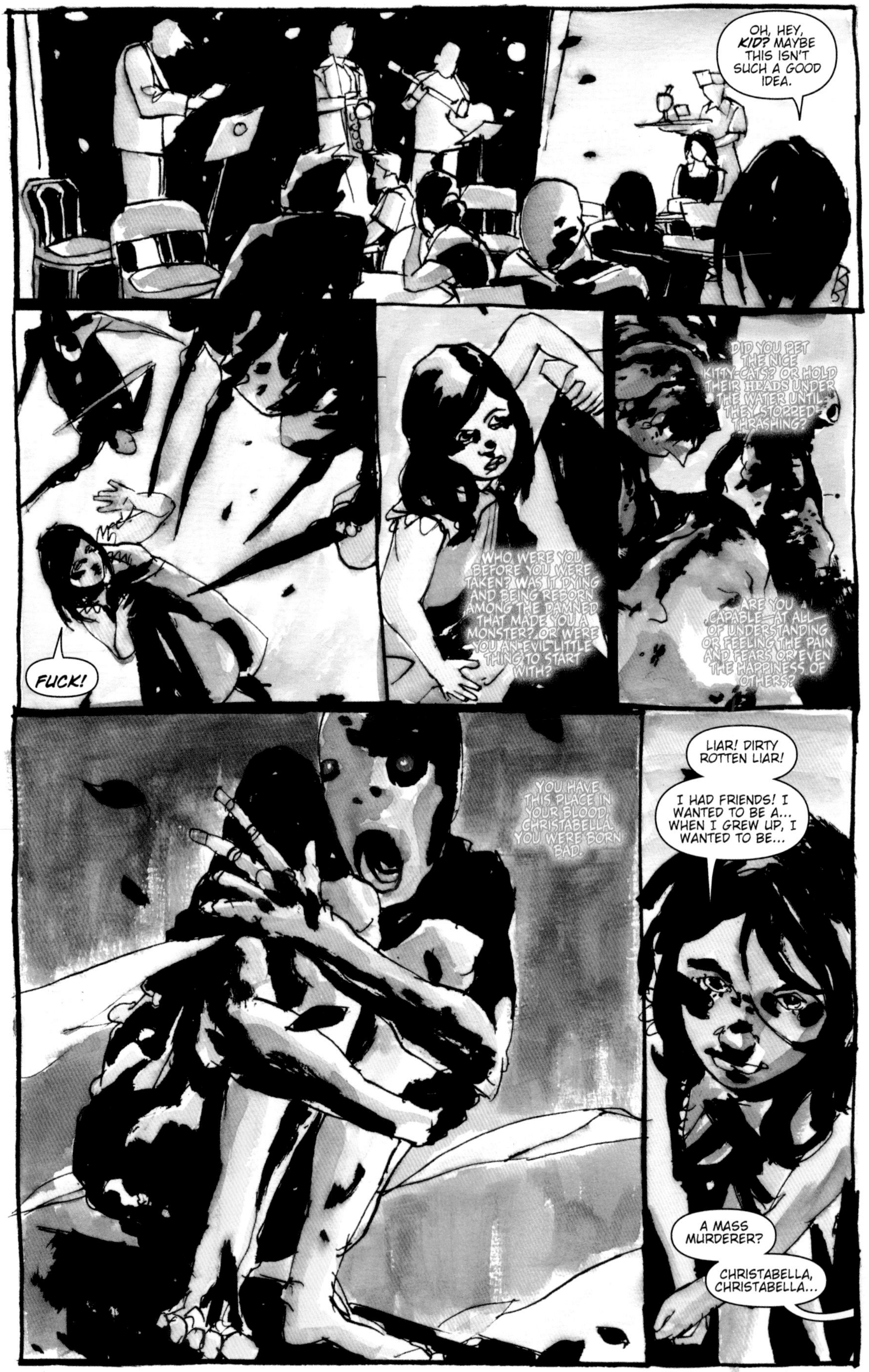

OH, HEY, *KID?* MAYBE THIS ISN'T SUCH A GOOD IDEA.
FUCK!
WHO WERE YOU BEFORE YOU WERE TAKEN? WAS IT DYING AND BEING REBORN AMONG THE DAMNED THAT MADE YOU A MONSTER? OR WERE YOU AN EVIL LITTLE THING TO START WITH?
DID YOU PET THE NICE KITTY-CATS? OR HOLD THEIR HEADS UNDER THE WATER UNTIL THEY STOPPED THRASHING?
ARE YOU CAPABLE—AT ALL—OF UNDERSTANDING OR FEELING THE PAIN AND FEARS OR EVEN THE HAPPINESS OF OTHERS?
YOU HAVE THIS PLACE IN YOUR BLOOD, CHRISTABELLA. YOU WERE BORN BAD.
LIAR! DIRTY ROTTEN LIAR!
I HAD FRIENDS! I WANTED TO BE A... WHEN I GREW UP, I WANTED TO BE...
A MASS MURDERER?
CHRISTABELLA, CHRISTABELLA...

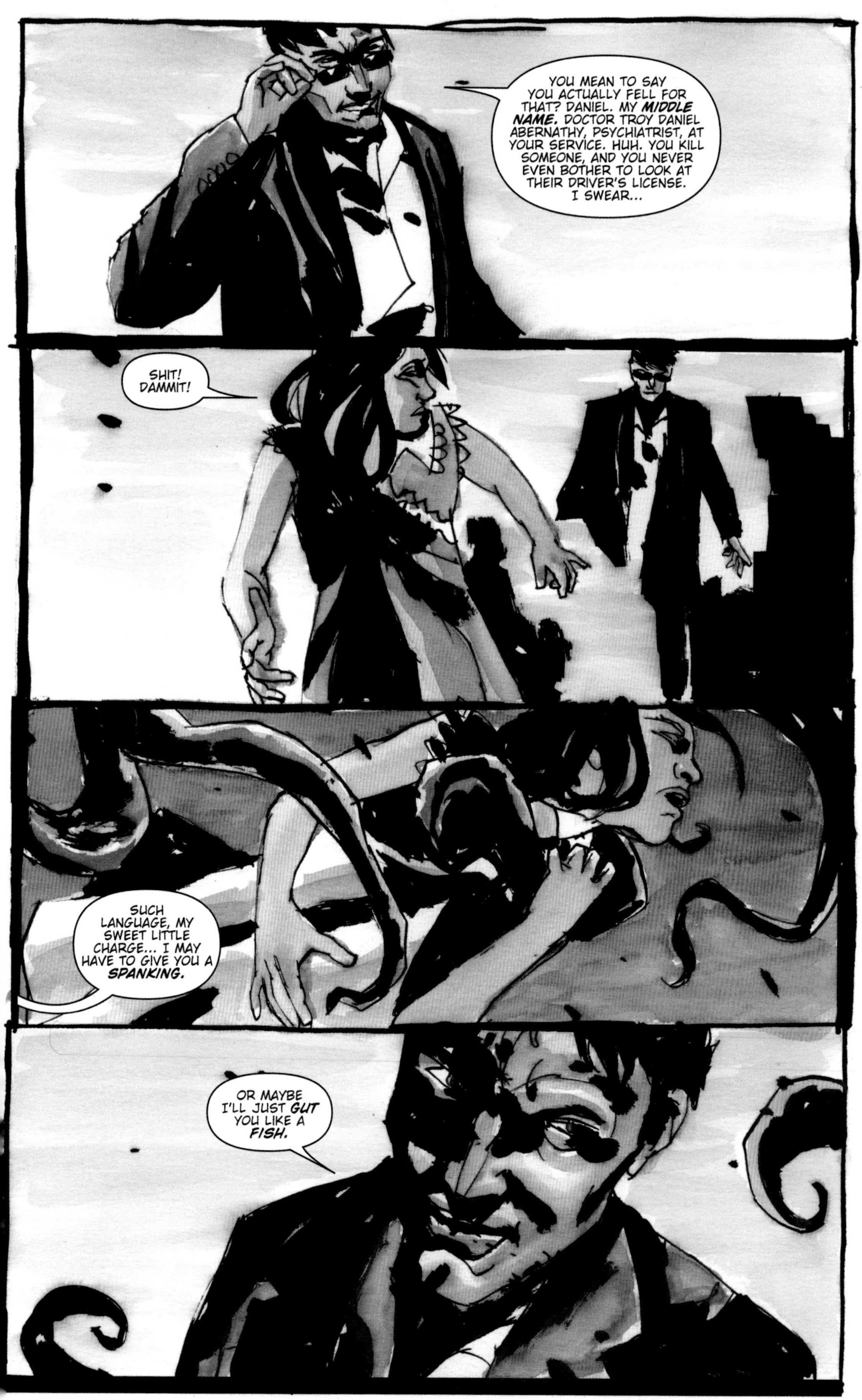
YOU MEAN TO SAY YOU ACTUALLY FELL FOR THAT? DANIEL. MY **MIDDLE NAME.** DOCTOR TROY DANIEL ABERNATHY, PSYCHIATRIST, AT YOUR SERVICE. HUH. YOU KILL SOMEONE, AND YOU NEVER EVEN BOTHER TO LOOK AT THEIR DRIVER'S LICENSE. I SWEAR...
SHIT! DAMMIT!
SUCH LANGUAGE, MY SWEET LITTLE CHARGE... I MAY HAVE TO GIVE YOU A **SPANKING.**
OR MAYBE I'LL JUST **GUT** YOU LIKE A **FISH.**

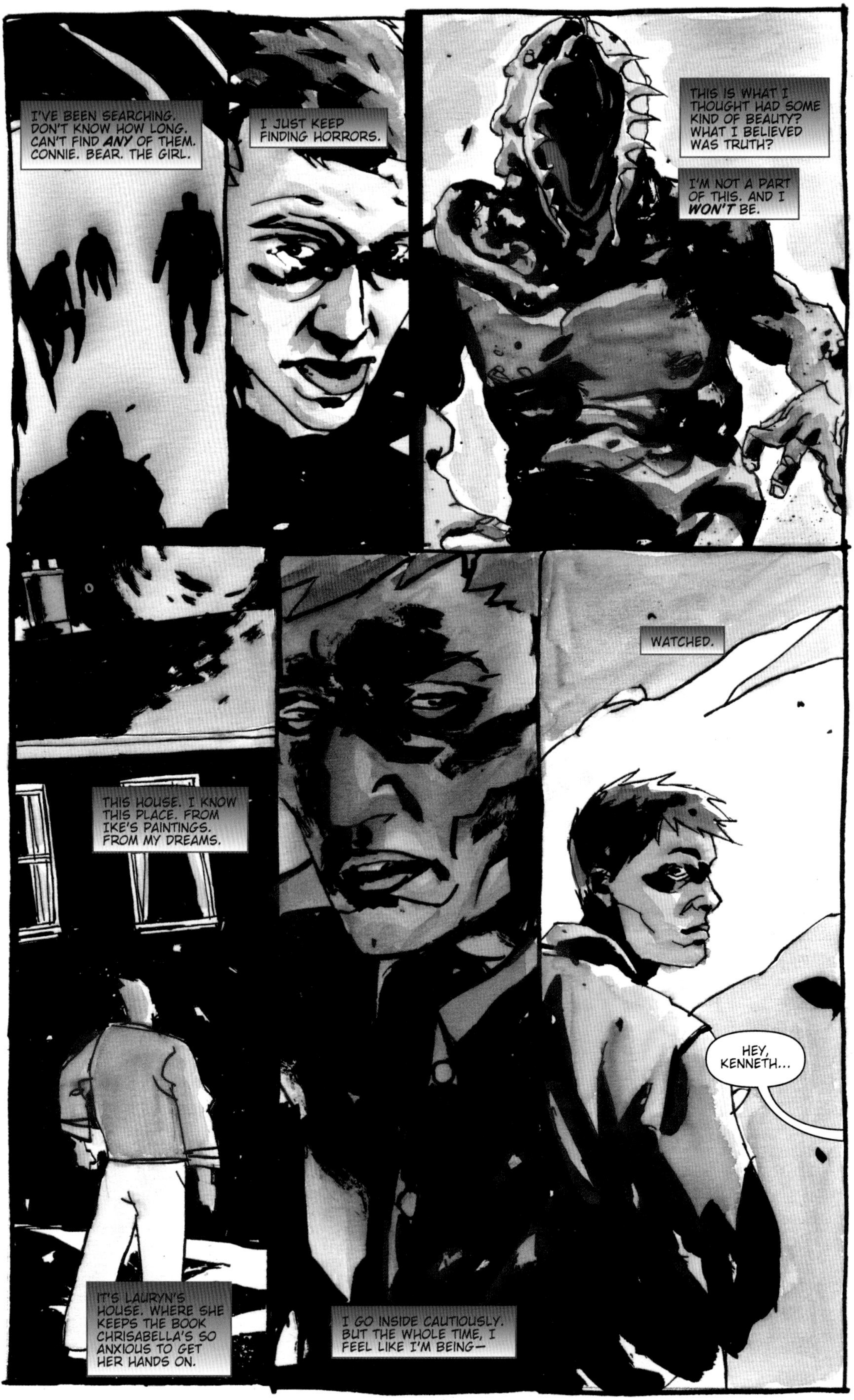
I'VE BEEN SEARCHING. DON'T KNOW HOW LONG. CAN'T FIND *ANY* OF THEM. CONNIE. BEAR. THE GIRL.
I JUST KEEP FINDING HORRORS.
THIS IS WHAT I THOUGHT HAD SOME KIND OF BEAUTY? WHAT I BELIEVED WAS TRUTH?
I'M NOT A PART OF THIS. AND I *WON'T* BE.
THIS HOUSE. I KNOW THIS PLACE. FROM IKE'S PAINTINGS. FROM MY DREAMS.
IT'S LAURYN'S HOUSE. WHERE SHE KEEPS THE BOOK CHRISABELLA'S SO ANXIOUS TO GET HER HANDS ON.
I GO INSIDE CAUTIOUSLY. BUT THE WHOLE TIME, I FEEL LIKE I'M BEING—
WATCHED.
HEY, KENNETH...

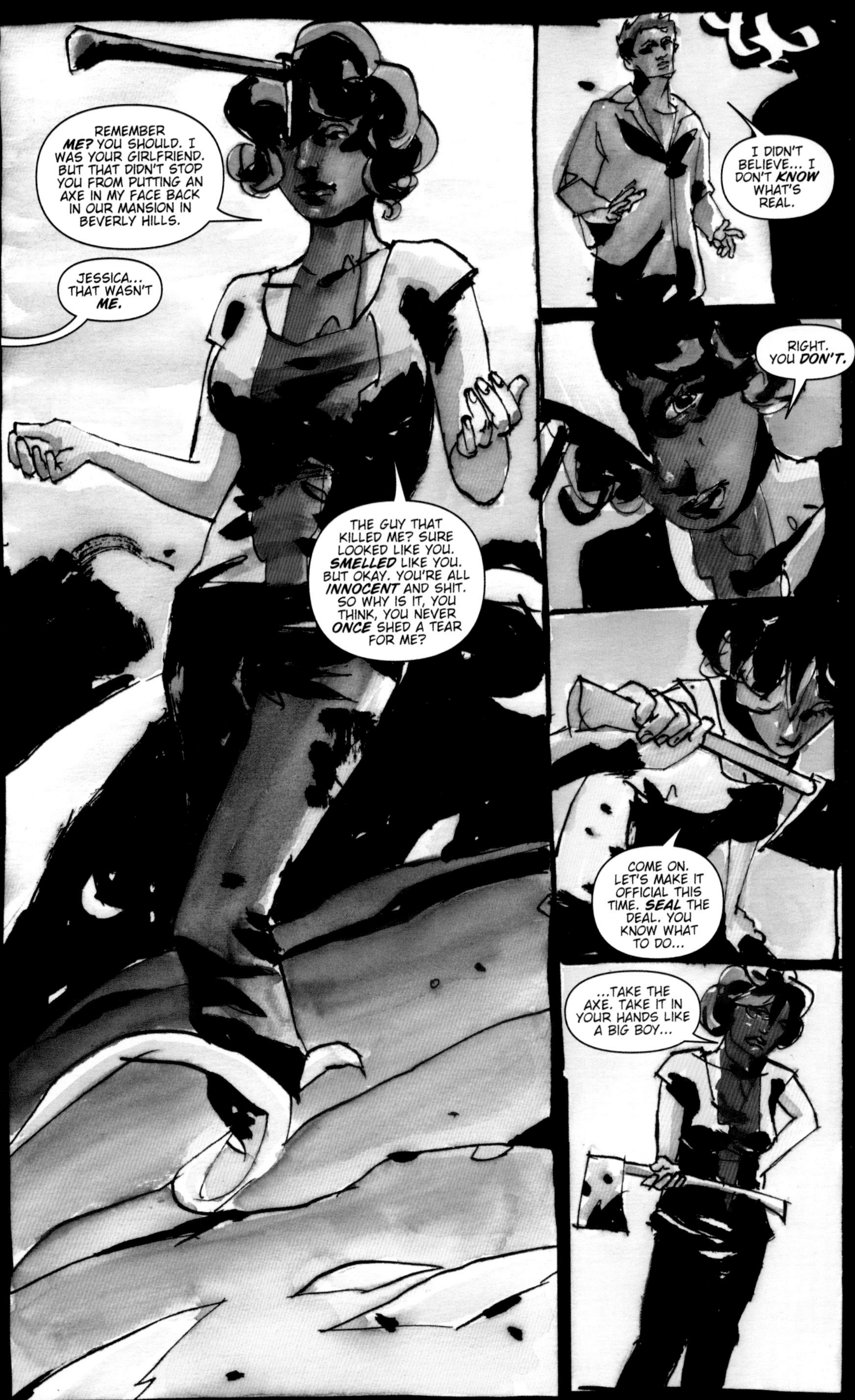
REMEMBER ME? YOU SHOULD. I WAS YOUR GIRLFRIEND. BUT THAT DIDN'T STOP YOU FROM PUTTING AN AXE IN MY FACE BACK IN OUR MANSION IN BEVERLY HILLS.
JESSICA... THAT WASN'T ME.
THE GUY THAT KILLED ME? SURE LOOKED LIKE YOU. SMELLED LIKE YOU. BUT OKAY. YOU'RE ALL INNOCENT AND SHIT. SO WHY IS IT, YOU THINK, YOU NEVER ONCE SHED A TEAR FOR ME?
I DIDN'T BELIEVE... I DON'T KNOW WHAT'S REAL.
RIGHT. YOU DON'T.
COME ON. LET'S MAKE IT OFFICIAL THIS TIME. SEAL THE DEAL. YOU KNOW WHAT TO DO...
...TAKE THE AXE. TAKE IT IN YOUR HANDS LIKE A BIG BOY...

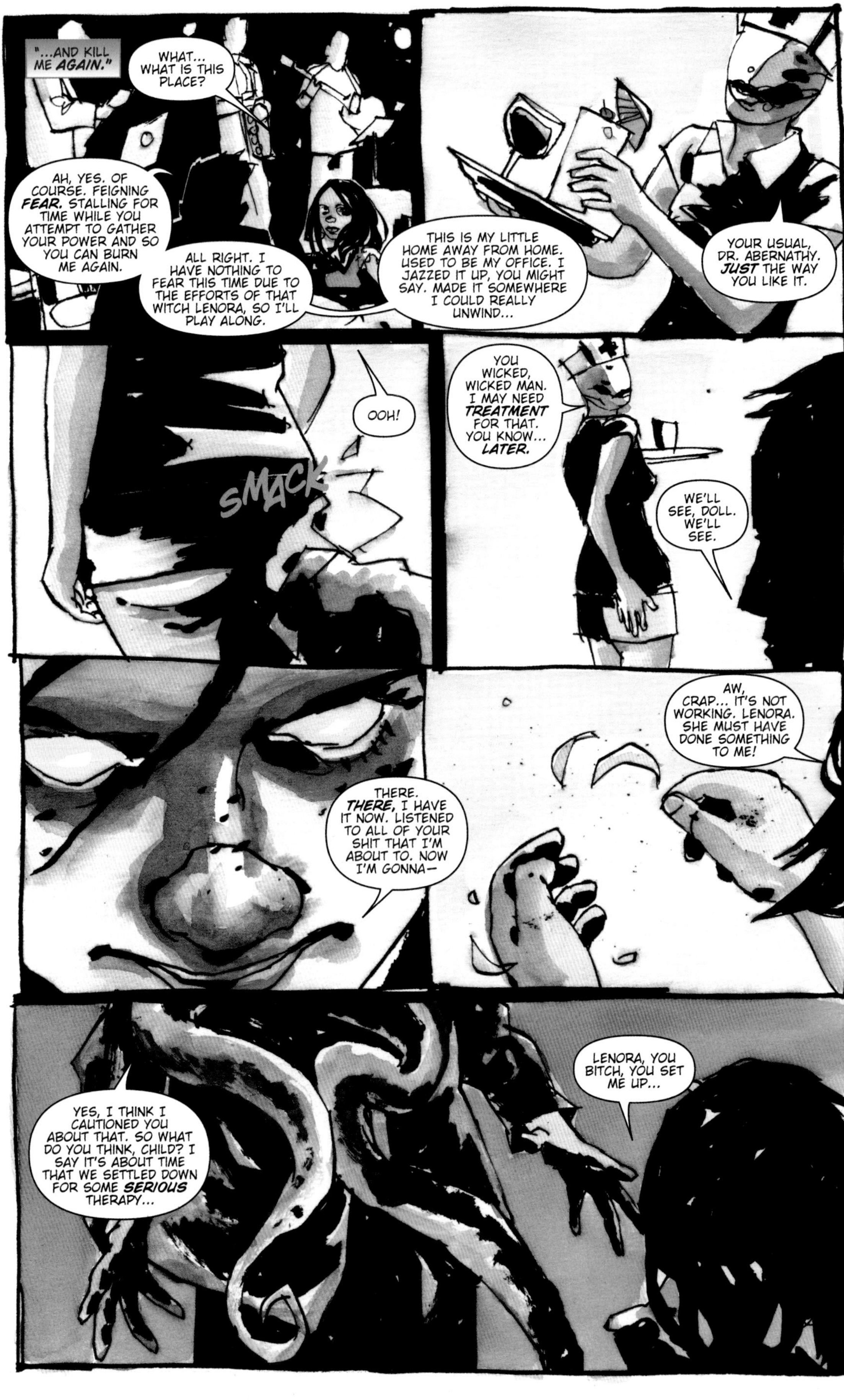
"...AND KILL ME AGAIN."
WHAT... WHAT IS THIS PLACE?
AH, YES. OF COURSE. FEIGNING FEAR. STALLING FOR TIME WHILE YOU ATTEMPT TO GATHER YOUR POWER AND SO YOU CAN BURN ME AGAIN.
ALL RIGHT. I HAVE NOTHING TO FEAR THIS TIME DUE TO THE EFFORTS OF THAT WITCH LENORA, SO I'LL PLAY ALONG.
THIS IS MY LITTLE HOME AWAY FROM HOME. USED TO BE MY OFFICE. I JAZZED IT UP, YOU MIGHT SAY. MADE IT SOMEWHERE I COULD REALLY UNWIND...
YOUR USUAL, DR. ABERNATHY. JUST THE WAY YOU LIKE IT.
OOH!
SMACK
YOU WICKED, WICKED MAN. I MAY NEED TREATMENT FOR THAT. YOU KNOW... LATER.
WE'LL SEE, DOLL. WE'LL SEE.
THERE. THERE, I HAVE IT NOW. LISTENED TO ALL OF YOUR SHIT THAT I'M ABOUT TO. NOW I'M GONNA—
AW, CRAP... IT'S NOT WORKING. LENORA. SHE MUST HAVE DONE SOMETHING TO ME!
YES, I THINK I CAUTIONED YOU ABOUT THAT. SO WHAT DO YOU THINK, CHILD? I SAY IT'S ABOUT TIME THAT WE SETTLED DOWN FOR SOME SERIOUS THERAPY...
LENORA, YOU BITCH, YOU SET ME UP...

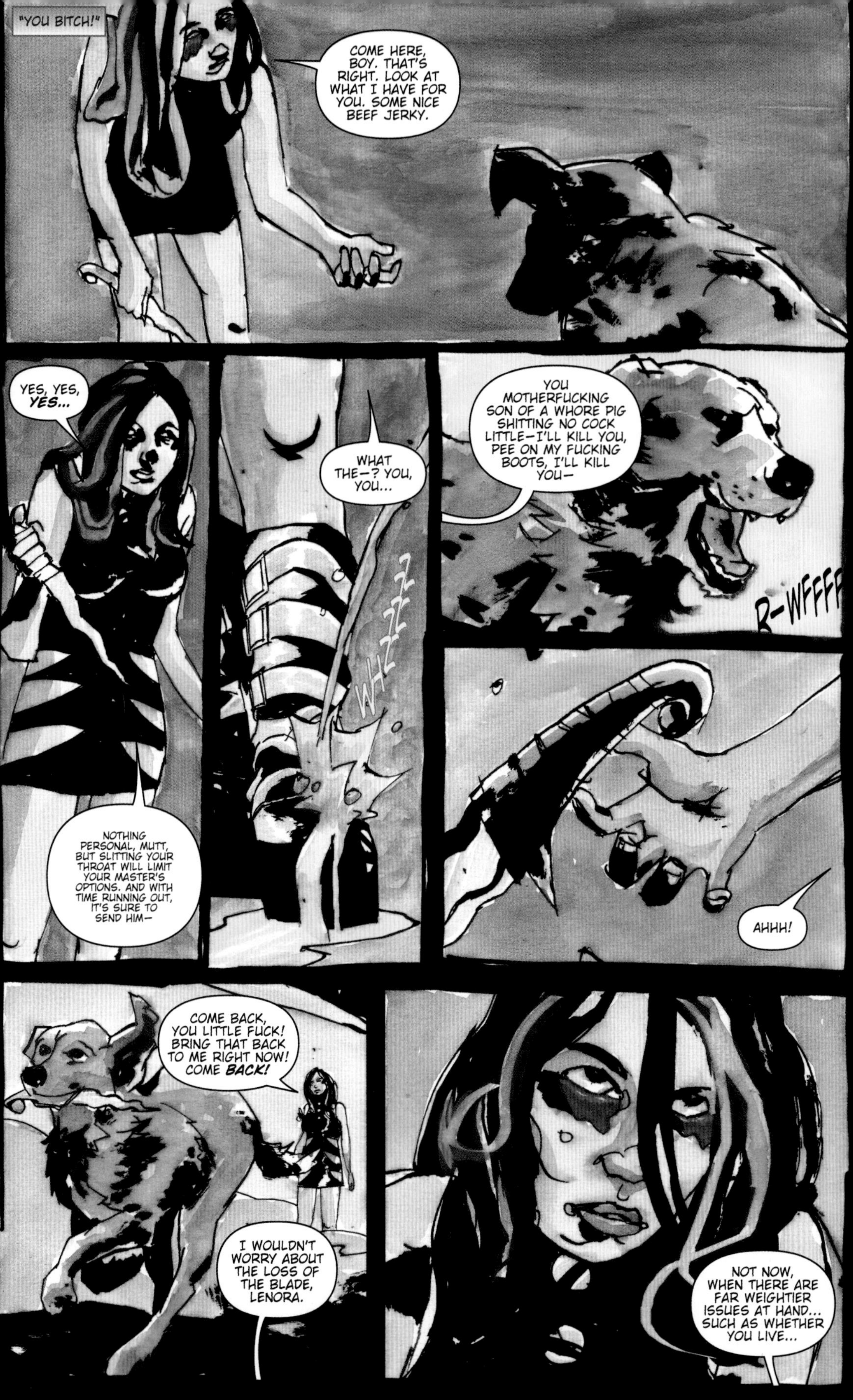
"YOU BITCH!"
COME HERE, BOY. THAT'S RIGHT. LOOK AT WHAT I HAVE FOR YOU. SOME NICE BEEF JERKY.
YES, YES, *YES...*
NOTHING PERSONAL, MUTT, BUT SLITTING YOUR THROAT WILL LIMIT YOUR MASTER'S OPTIONS. AND WITH TIME RUNNING OUT, IT'S SURE TO SEND HIM—
WHZZZZZ
WHAT THE—? YOU, YOU...
YOU MOTHERFUCKING SON OF A WHORE PIG SHITTING NO COCK LITTLE—I'LL KILL YOU, PEE ON MY FUCKING BOOTS, I'LL KILL YOU—
R-WFFFF
AHHH!
COME BACK, YOU LITTLE FUCK! BRING THAT BACK TO ME RIGHT NOW! COME *BACK!*
I WOULDN'T WORRY ABOUT THE LOSS OF THE BLADE, LENORA.
NOT NOW, WHEN THERE ARE FAR WEIGHTIER ISSUES AT HAND... SUCH AS WHETHER YOU LIVE...

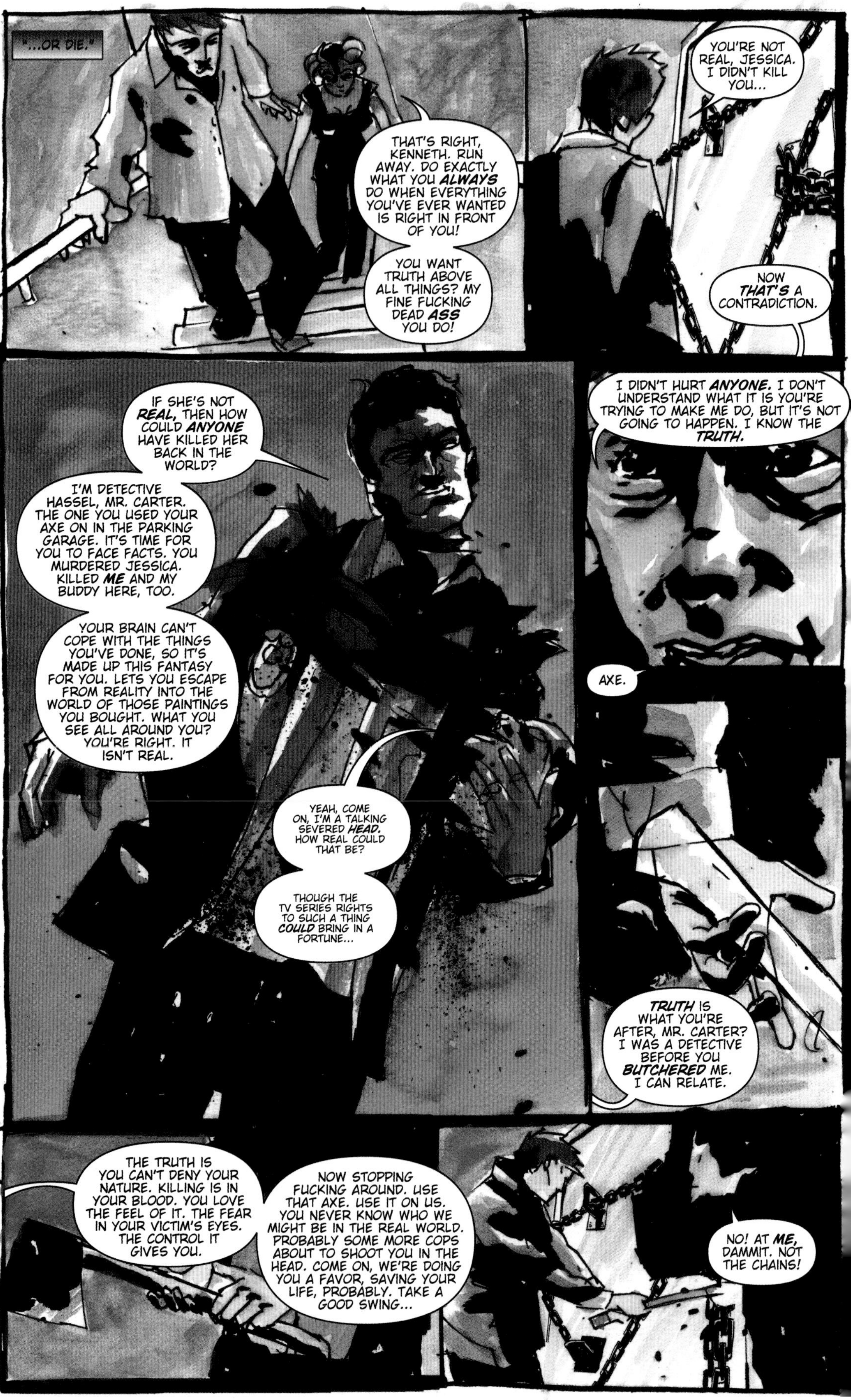
"...OR DIE."
THAT'S RIGHT, KENNETH. RUN AWAY. DO EXACTLY WHAT YOU ALWAYS DO WHEN EVERYTHING YOU'VE EVER WANTED IS RIGHT IN FRONT OF YOU!
YOU WANT TRUTH ABOVE ALL THINGS? MY FINE FUCKING DEAD ASS YOU DO!
YOU'RE NOT REAL, JESSICA. I DIDN'T KILL YOU...
NOW THAT'S A CONTRADICTION.
IF SHE'S NOT REAL, THEN HOW COULD ANYONE HAVE KILLED HER BACK IN THE WORLD?
I'M DETECTIVE HASSEL, MR. CARTER. THE ONE YOU USED YOUR AXE ON IN THE PARKING GARAGE. IT'S TIME FOR YOU TO FACE FACTS. YOU MURDERED JESSICA. KILLED ME AND MY BUDDY HERE, TOO.
YOUR BRAIN CAN'T COPE WITH THE THINGS YOU'VE DONE, SO IT'S MADE UP THIS FANTASY FOR YOU. LETS YOU ESCAPE FROM REALITY INTO THE WORLD OF THOSE PAINTINGS YOU BOUGHT. WHAT YOU SEE ALL AROUND YOU? YOU'RE RIGHT. IT ISN'T REAL.
YEAH, COME ON, I'M A TALKING SEVERED HEAD. HOW REAL COULD THAT BE?
THOUGH THE TV SERIES RIGHTS TO SUCH A THING COULD BRING IN A FORTUNE...
I DIDN'T HURT ANYONE. I DON'T UNDERSTAND WHAT IT IS YOU'RE TRYING TO MAKE ME DO, BUT IT'S NOT GOING TO HAPPEN. I KNOW THE TRUTH.
AXE.
TRUTH IS WHAT YOU'RE AFTER, MR. CARTER? I WAS A DETECTIVE BEFORE YOU BUTCHERED ME. I CAN RELATE.
THE TRUTH IS YOU CAN'T DENY YOUR NATURE. KILLING IS IN YOUR BLOOD. YOU LOVE THE FEEL OF IT. THE FEAR IN YOUR VICTIM'S EYES. THE CONTROL IT GIVES YOU.
NOW STOPPING FUCKING AROUND. USE THAT AXE. USE IT ON US. YOU NEVER KNOW WHO WE MIGHT BE IN THE REAL WORLD. PROBABLY SOME MORE COPS ABOUT TO SHOOT YOU IN THE HEAD. COME ON, WE'RE DOING YOU A FAVOR, SAVING YOUR LIFE, PROBABLY. TAKE A GOOD SWING...
NO! AT ME, DAMMIT. NOT THE CHAINS!

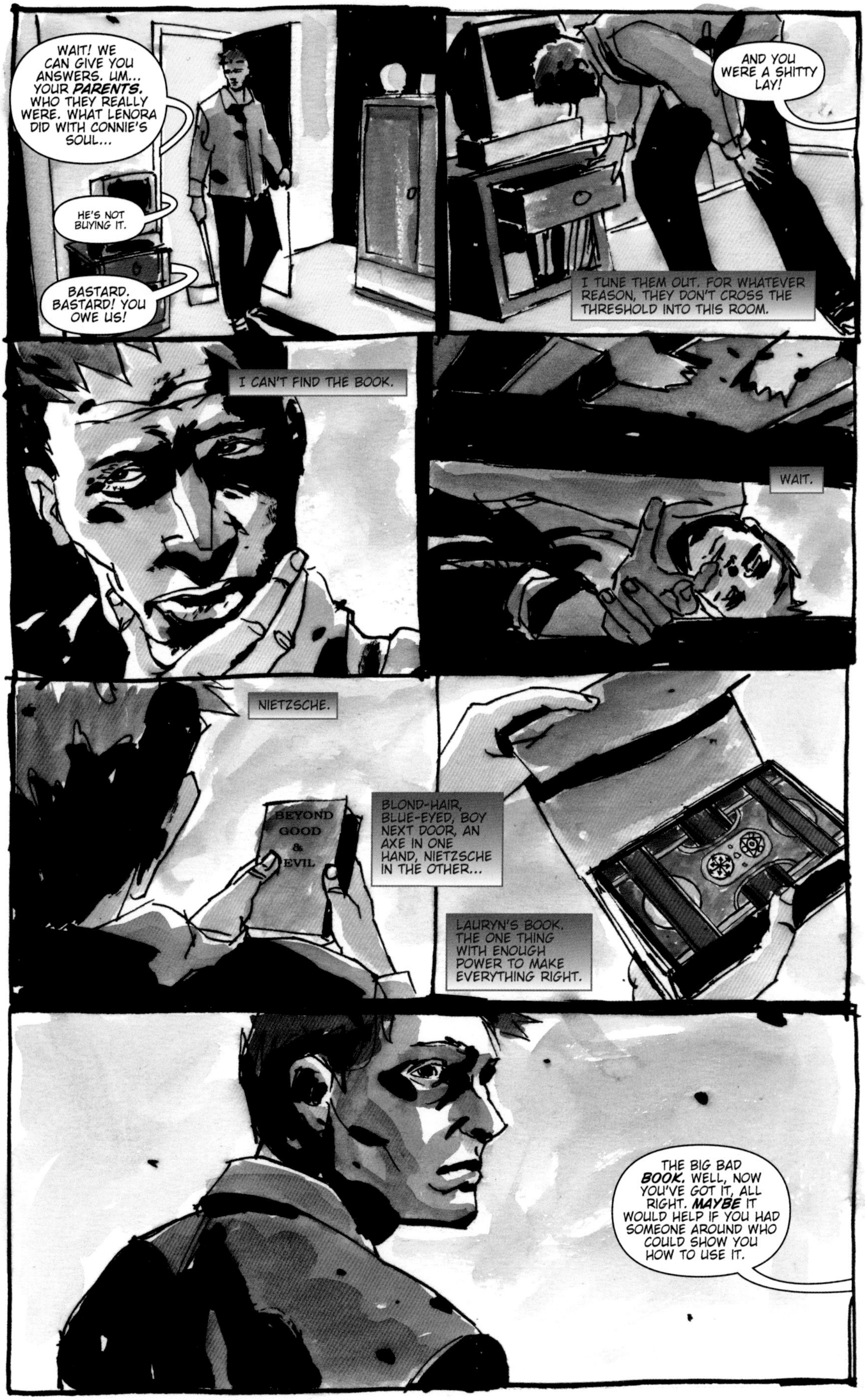
WAIT! WE CAN GIVE YOU ANSWERS. UM... YOUR PARENTS. WHO THEY REALLY WERE. WHAT LENORA DID WITH CONNIE'S SOUL...
HE'S NOT BUYING IT.
BASTARD. BASTARD! YOU OWE US!
AND YOU WERE A SHITTY LAY!
I TUNE THEM OUT. FOR WHATEVER REASON, THEY DON'T CROSS THE THRESHOLD INTO THIS ROOM.
I CAN'T FIND THE BOOK.
WAIT.
NIETZSCHE.
BEYOND GOOD & EVIL
BLOND-HAIR, BLUE-EYED, BOY NEXT DOOR, AN AXE IN ONE HAND, NIETZSCHE IN THE OTHER...
LAURYN'S BOOK. THE ONE THING WITH ENOUGH POWER TO MAKE EVERYTHING RIGHT.
THE BIG BAD BOOK. WELL, NOW YOU'VE GOT IT, ALL RIGHT. MAYBE IT WOULD HELP IF YOU HAD SOMEONE AROUND WHO COULD SHOW YOU HOW TO USE IT.

WHAT, YOU DON'T HAVE ANYTHING TO SAY TO ME, BOY? HOW ABOUT WE START WITH...
HI, DAD! NICE TO SEE YOU AFTER ALL THIS TIME.
JUST WAIT TILL I TELL YOUR MOM ABOUT THIS...

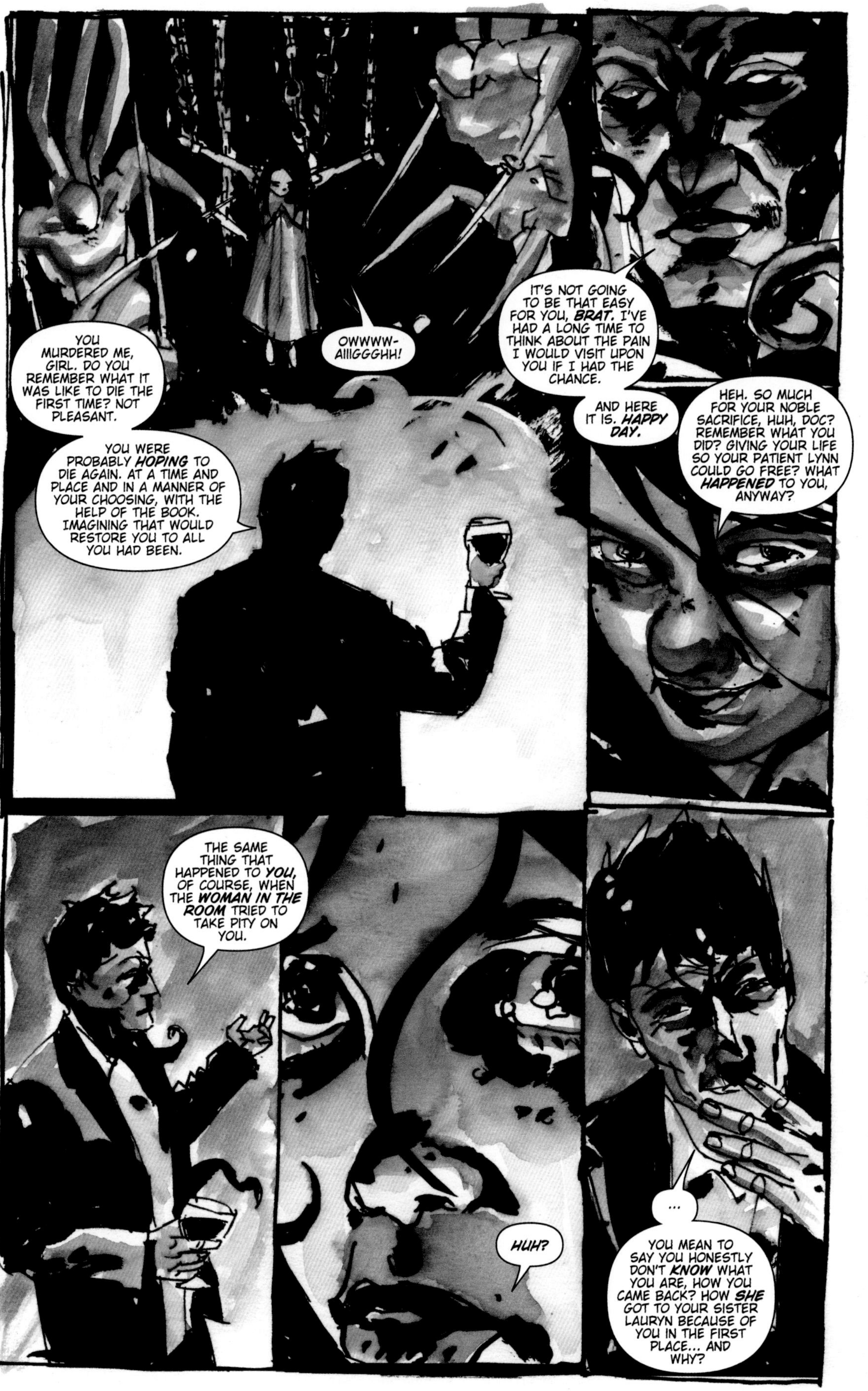
YOU MURDERED ME, GIRL. DO YOU REMEMBER WHAT IT WAS LIKE TO DIE THE FIRST TIME? NOT PLEASANT.
YOU WERE PROBABLY HOPING TO DIE AGAIN. AT A TIME AND PLACE AND IN A MANNER OF YOUR CHOOSING, WITH THE HELP OF THE BOOK. IMAGINING THAT WOULD RESTORE YOU TO ALL YOU HAD BEEN.
OWWWW-AIIIGGGHH!
IT'S NOT GOING TO BE THAT EASY FOR YOU, BRAT. I'VE HAD A LONG TIME TO THINK ABOUT THE PAIN I WOULD VISIT UPON YOU IF I HAD THE CHANCE.
AND HERE IT IS. HAPPY DAY.
HEH. SO MUCH FOR YOUR NOBLE SACRIFICE, HUH, DOC? REMEMBER WHAT YOU DID? GIVING YOUR LIFE SO YOUR PATIENT LYNN COULD GO FREE? WHAT HAPPENED TO YOU, ANYWAY?
THE SAME THING THAT HAPPENED TO YOU, OF COURSE, WHEN THE WOMAN IN THE ROOM TRIED TO TAKE PITY ON YOU.
HUH?
...
YOU MEAN TO SAY YOU HONESTLY DON'T KNOW WHAT YOU ARE, HOW YOU CAME BACK? HOW SHE GOT TO YOUR SISTER LAURYN BECAUSE OF YOU IN THE FIRST PLACE... AND WHY?

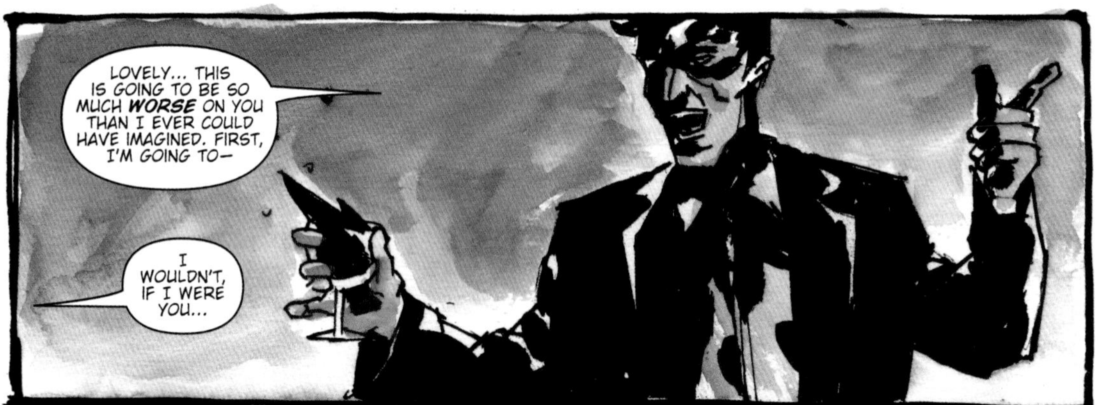
LOVELY... THIS IS GOING TO BE SO MUCH WORSE ON YOU THAN I EVER COULD HAVE IMAGINED. FIRST, I'M GOING TO—
I WOULDN'T, IF I WERE YOU...

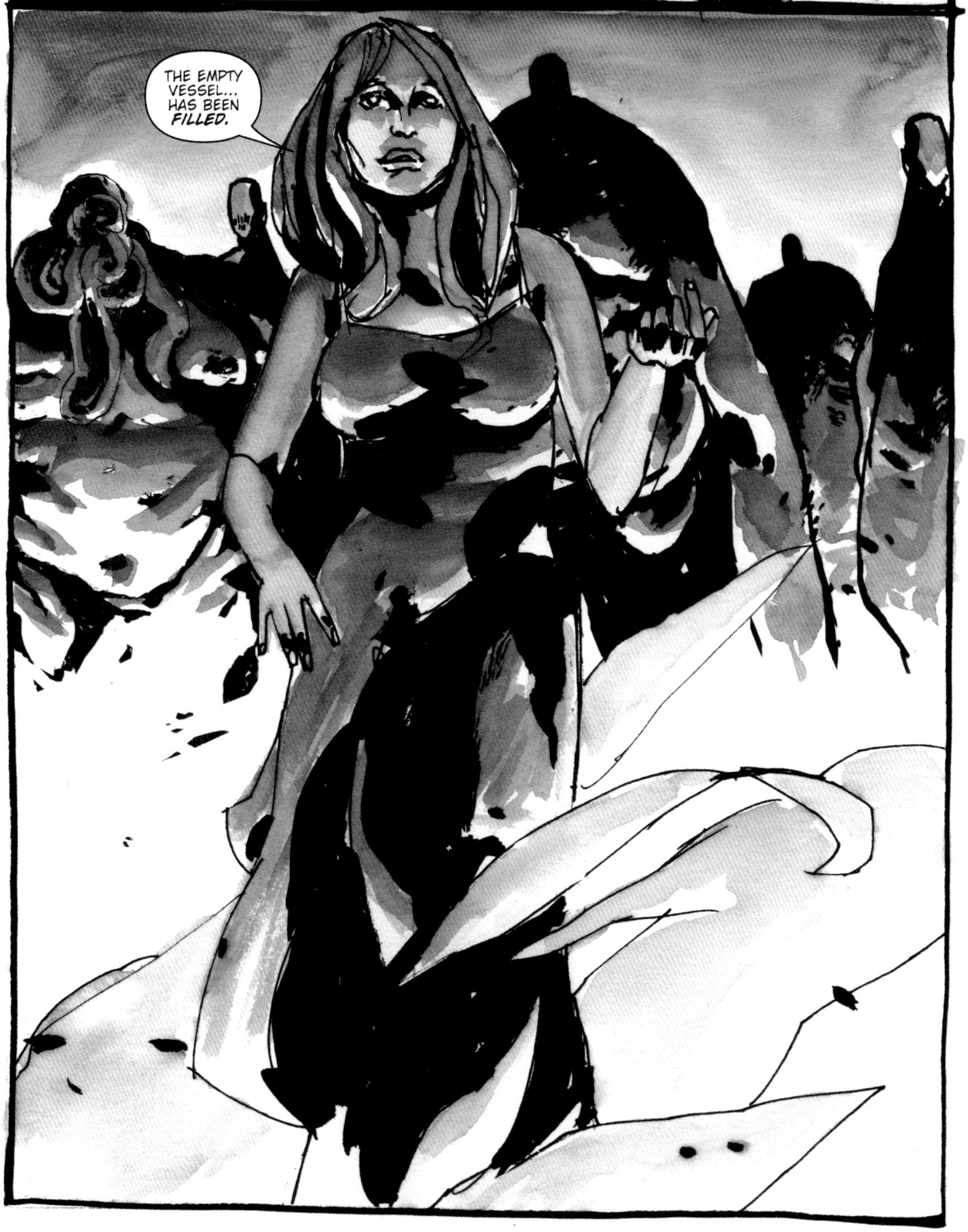
THE EMPTY VESSEL... HAS BEEN FILLED.

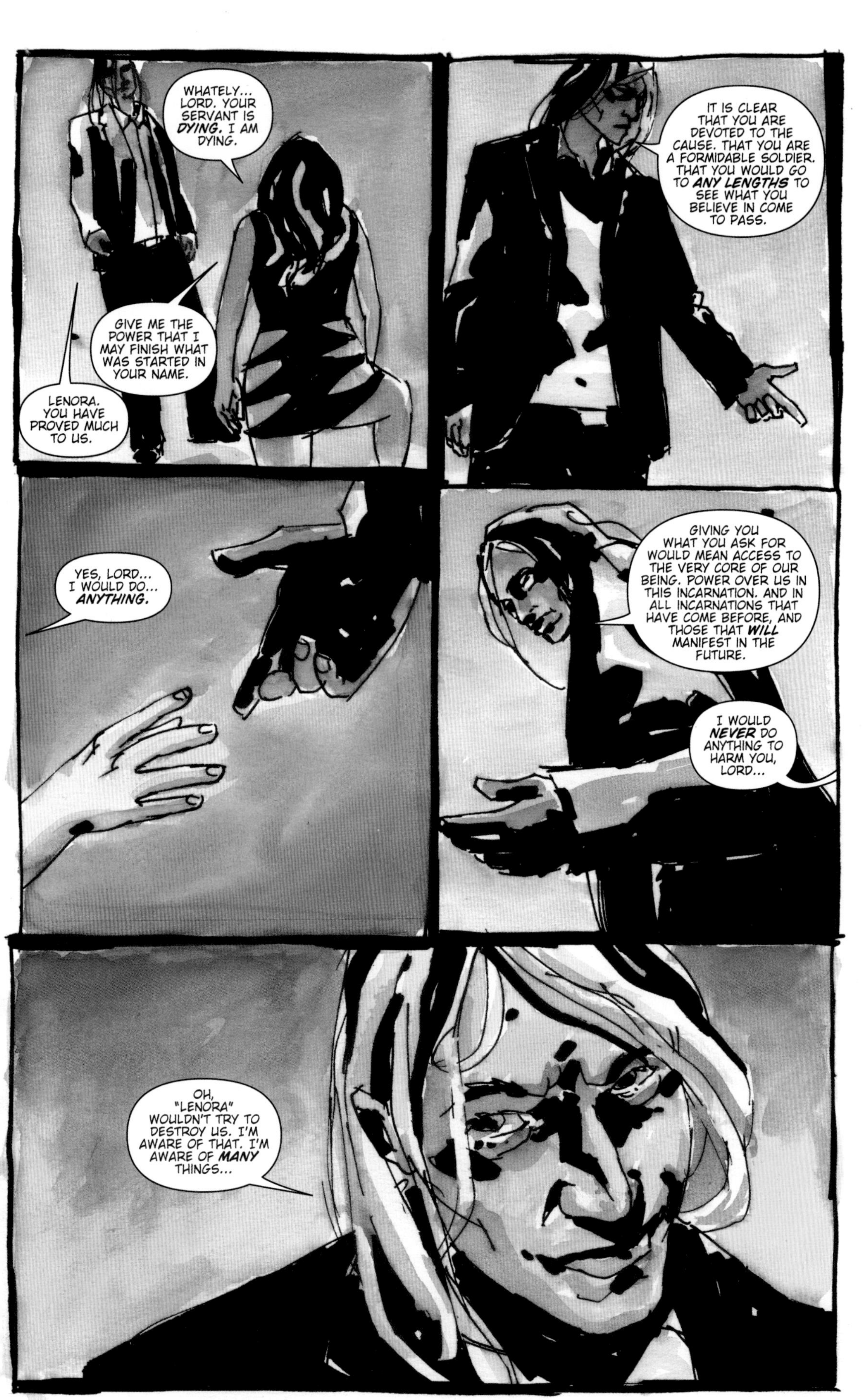
WHATELY... LORD. YOUR SERVANT IS DYING. I AM DYING.
GIVE ME THE POWER THAT I MAY FINISH WHAT WAS STARTED IN YOUR NAME.
LENORA. YOU HAVE PROVED MUCH TO US.
IT IS CLEAR THAT YOU ARE DEVOTED TO THE CAUSE. THAT YOU ARE A FORMIDABLE SOLDIER. THAT YOU WOULD GO TO ANY LENGTHS TO SEE WHAT YOU BELIEVE IN COME TO PASS.
YES, LORD... I WOULD DO... ANYTHING.
GIVING YOU WHAT YOU ASK FOR WOULD MEAN ACCESS TO THE VERY CORE OF OUR BEING. POWER OVER US IN THIS INCARNATION. AND IN ALL INCARNATIONS THAT HAVE COME BEFORE, AND THOSE THAT WILL MANIFEST IN THE FUTURE.
I WOULD NEVER DO ANYTHING TO HARM YOU, LORD...
OH, "LENORA" WOULDN'T TRY TO DESTROY US. I'M AWARE OF THAT. I'M AWARE OF MANY THINGS...

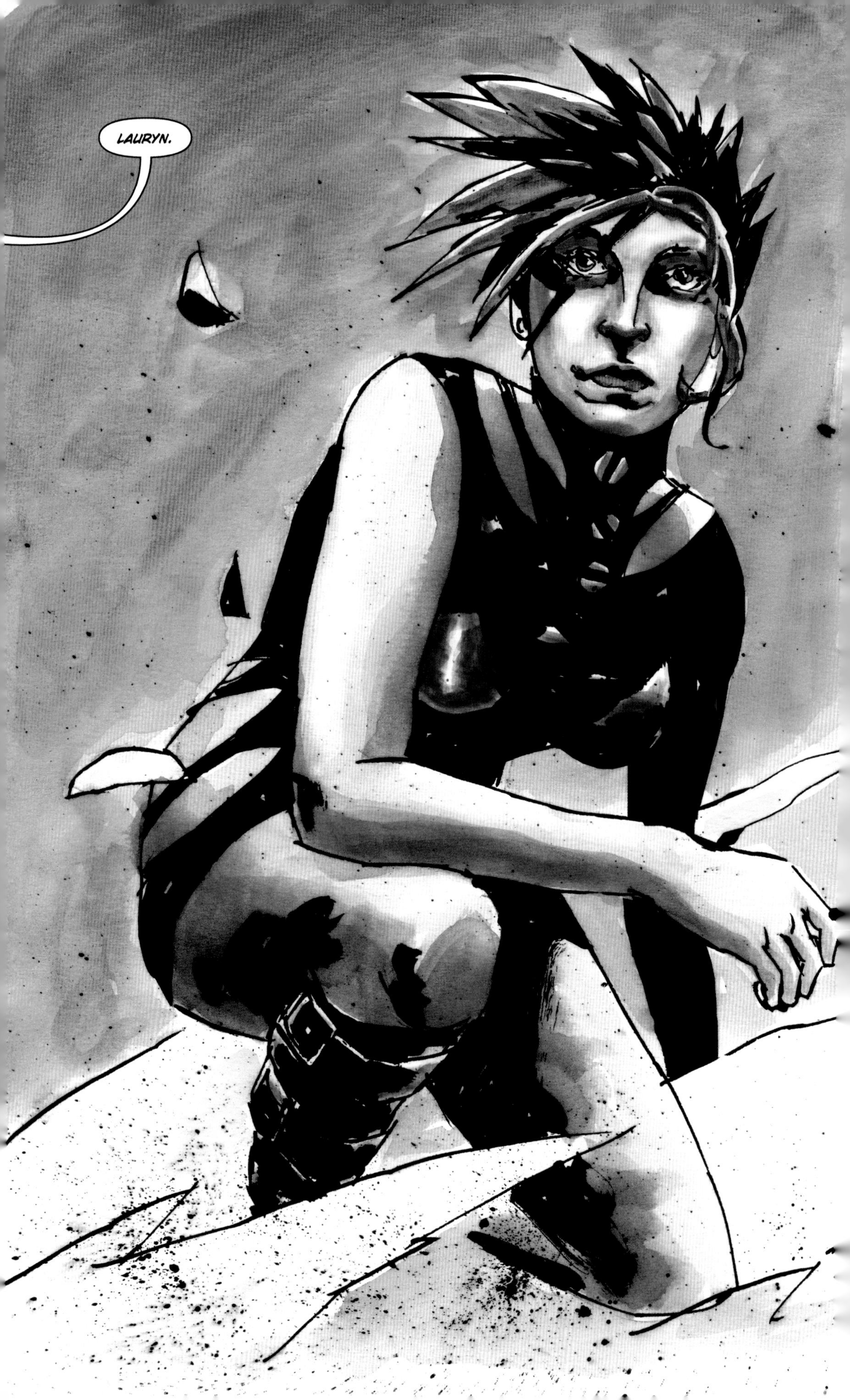
LAURYN.

CHAPTER
5

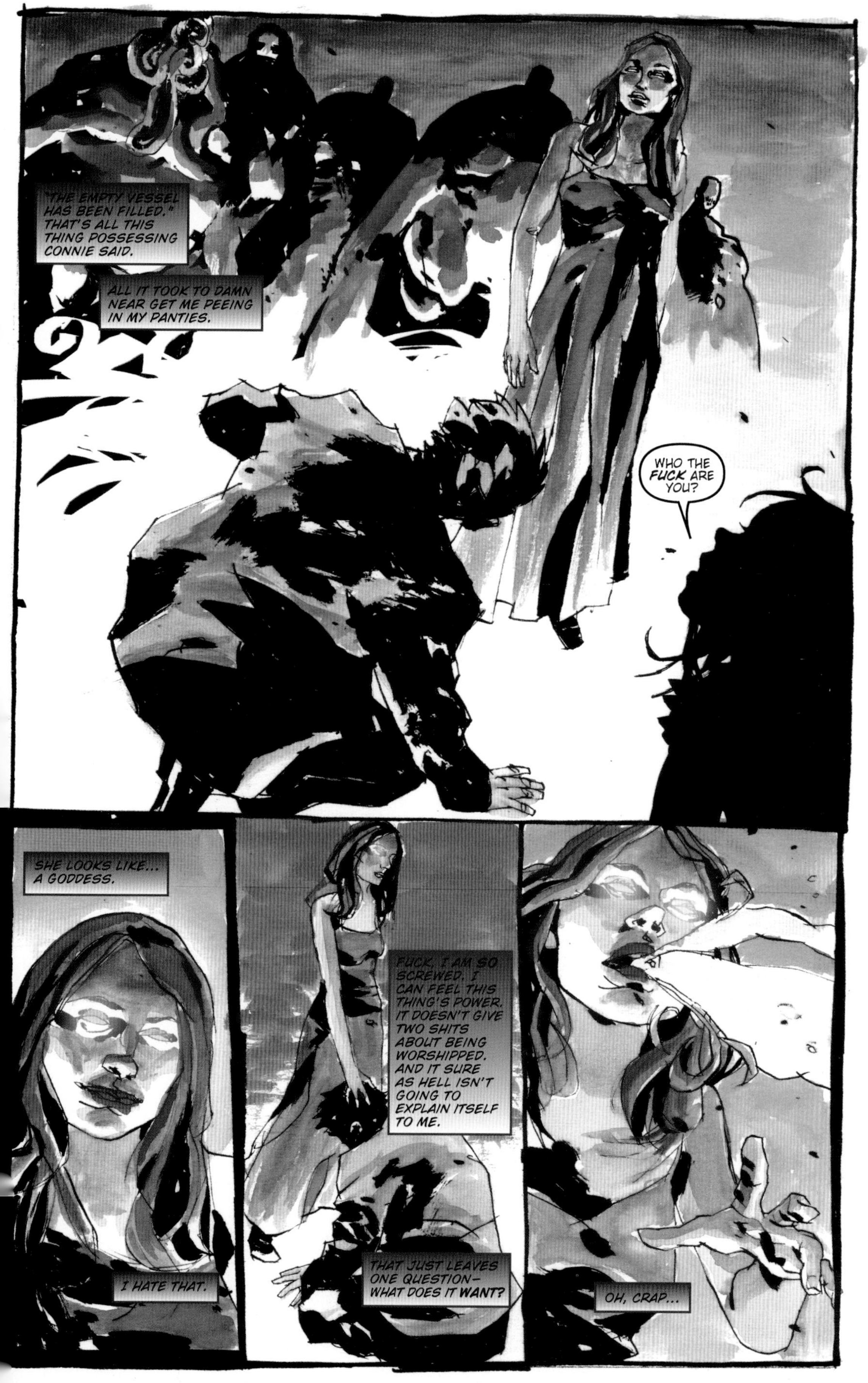

"THE EMPTY VESSEL HAS BEEN FILLED." THAT'S ALL THIS THING POSSESSING CONNIE SAID.
ALL IT TOOK TO DAMN NEAR GET ME PEEING IN MY PANTIES.
WHO THE FUCK ARE YOU?
SHE LOOKS LIKE... A GODDESS.
I HATE THAT.
FUCK, I AM SO SCREWED. I CAN FEEL THIS THING'S POWER. IT DOESN'T GIVE TWO SHITS ABOUT BEING WORSHIPPED. AND IT SURE AS HELL ISN'T GOING TO EXPLAIN ITSELF TO ME.
THAT JUST LEAVES ONE QUESTION– WHAT DOES IT WANT?
OH, CRAP...

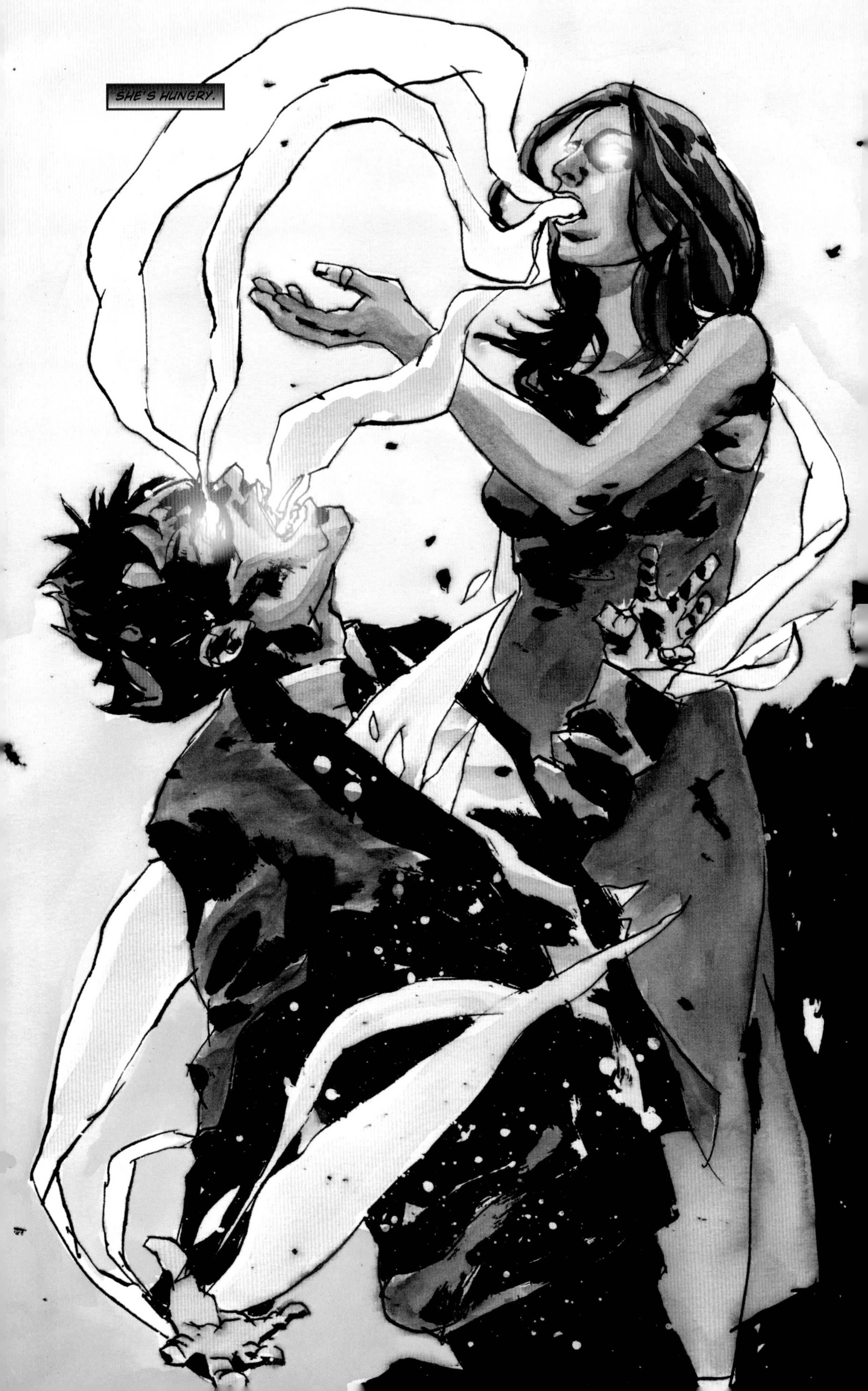
SHE'S HUNGRY.

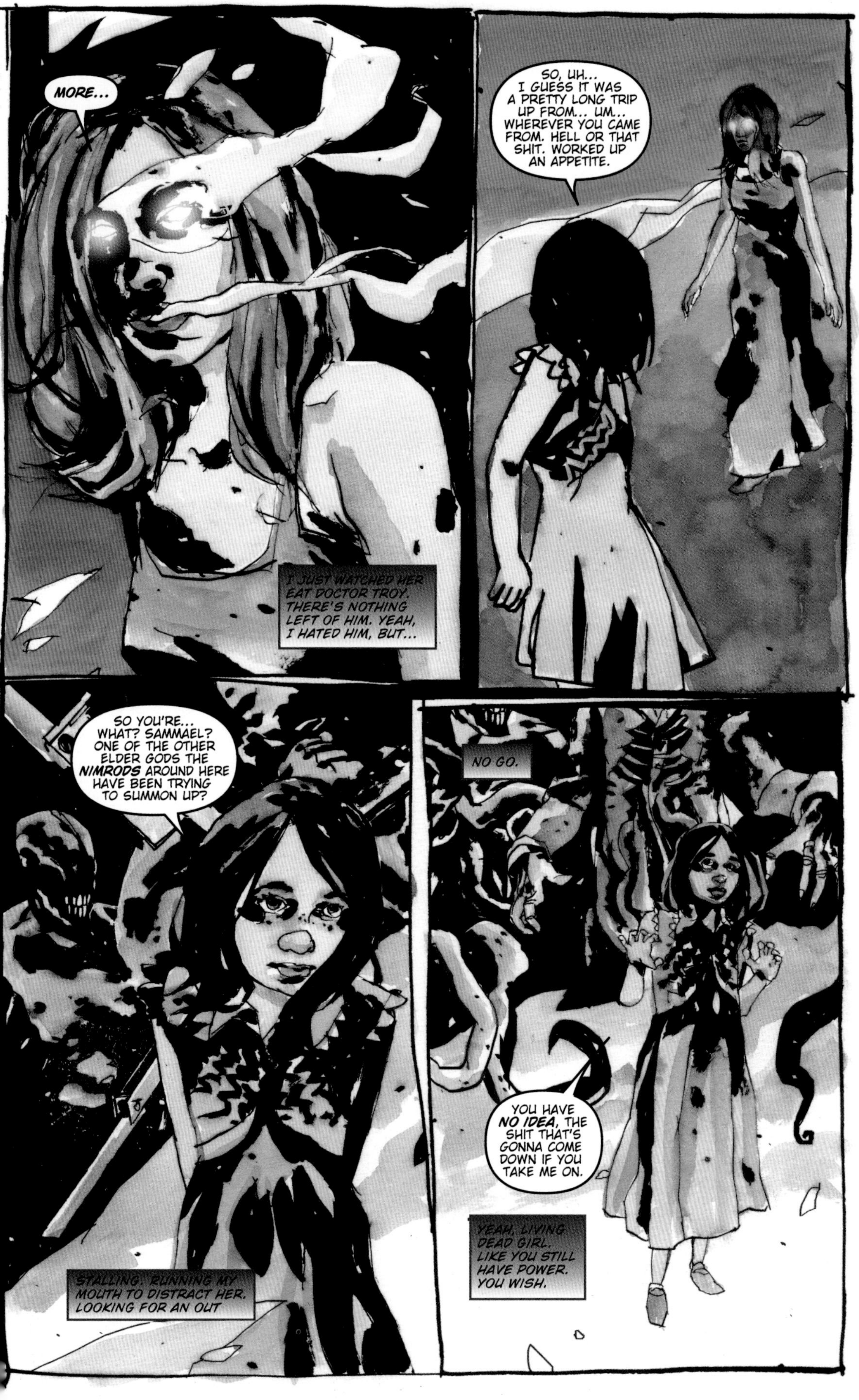
MORE...
I JUST WATCHED HER EAT DOCTOR TROY. THERE'S NOTHING LEFT OF HIM. YEAH, I HATED HIM, BUT...
SO, UH... I GUESS IT WAS A PRETTY LONG TRIP UP FROM... UM... WHEREVER YOU CAME FROM. HELL OR THAT SHIT. WORKED UP AN APPETITE.
SO YOU'RE... WHAT? SAMMAEL? ONE OF THE OTHER ELDER GODS THE NIMRODS AROUND HERE HAVE BEEN TRYING TO SUMMON UP?
STALLING. RUNNING MY MOUTH TO DISTRACT HER. LOOKING FOR AN OUT
NO GO.
YOU HAVE NO IDEA, THE SHIT THAT'S GONNA COME DOWN IF YOU TAKE ME ON.
YEAH, LIVING DEAD GIRL. LIKE YOU STILL HAVE POWER. YOU WISH.

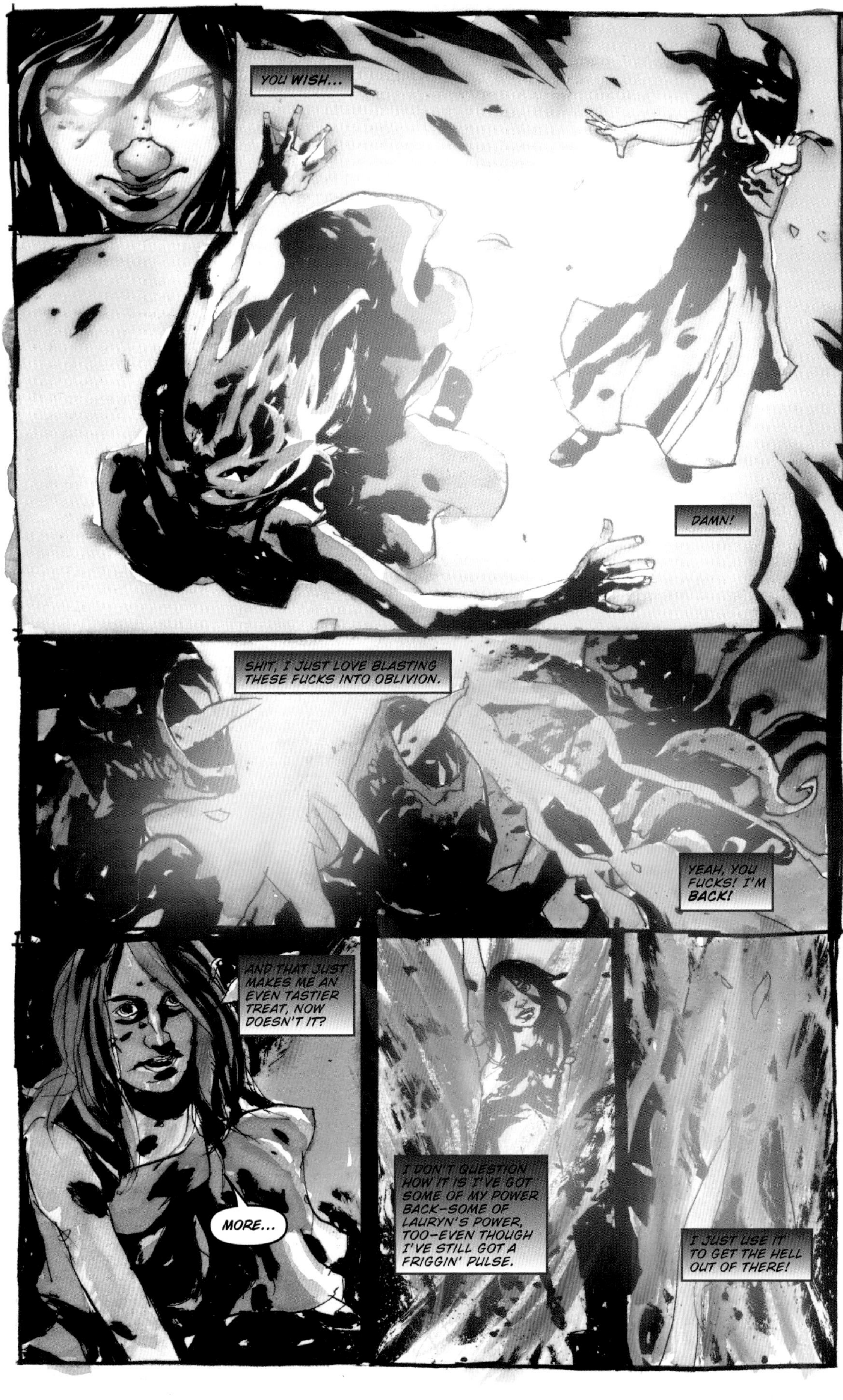
YOU WISH...
DAMN!
SHIT, I JUST LOVE BLASTING THESE FUCKS INTO OBLIVION.
YEAH, YOU FUCKS! I'M BACK!
AND THAT JUST MAKES ME AN EVEN TASTIER TREAT, NOW DOESN'T IT?
MORE...
I DON'T QUESTION HOW IT IS I'VE GOT SOME OF MY POWER BACK—SOME OF LAURYN'S POWER, TOO—EVEN THOUGH I'VE STILL GOT A FRIGGIN' PULSE.
I JUST USE IT TO GET THE HELL OUT OF THERE!

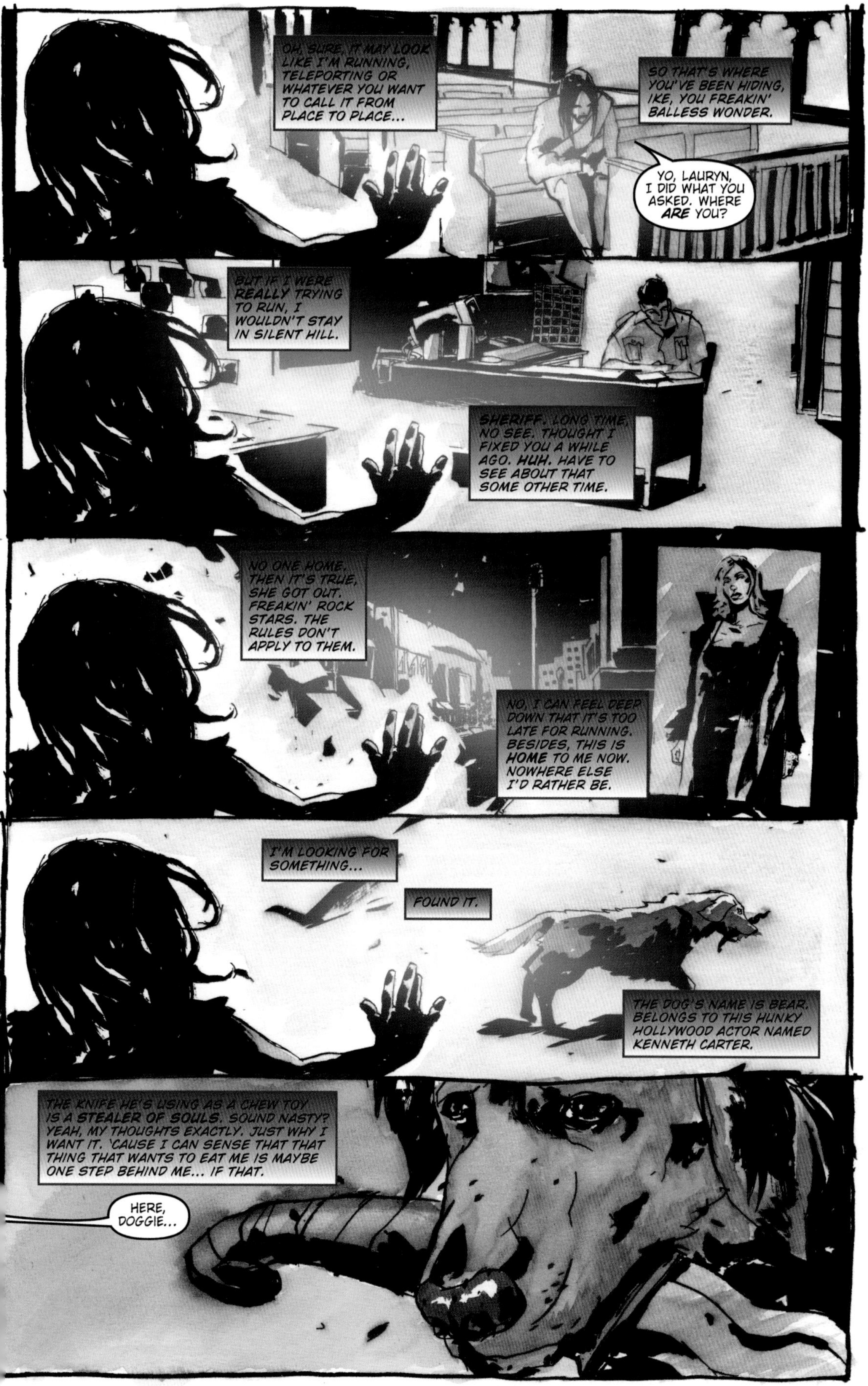
OH, SURE, IT MAY LOOK LIKE I'M RUNNING, TELEPORTING OR WHATEVER YOU WANT TO CALL IT FROM PLACE TO PLACE...
SO THAT'S WHERE YOU'VE BEEN HIDING, IKE, YOU FREAKIN' BALLESS WONDER.
YO, LAURYN, I DID WHAT YOU ASKED. WHERE ARE YOU?
BUT IF I WERE REALLY TRYING TO RUN, I WOULDN'T STAY IN SILENT HILL.
SHERIFF. LONG TIME, NO SEE. THOUGHT I FIXED YOU A WHILE AGO. HUH. HAVE TO SEE ABOUT THAT SOME OTHER TIME.
NO ONE HOME. THEN IT'S TRUE, SHE GOT OUT. FREAKIN' ROCK STARS. THE RULES DON'T APPLY TO THEM.
NO, I CAN FEEL DEEP DOWN THAT IT'S TOO LATE FOR RUNNING. BESIDES, THIS IS HOME TO ME NOW. NOWHERE ELSE I'D RATHER BE.
I'M LOOKING FOR SOMETHING...
FOUND IT.
THE DOG'S NAME IS BEAR. BELONGS TO THIS HUNKY HOLLYWOOD ACTOR NAMED KENNETH CARTER.
THE KNIFE HE'S USING AS A CHEW TOY IS A STEALER OF SOULS. SOUND NASTY? YEAH, MY THOUGHTS EXACTLY. JUST WHY I WANT IT. 'CAUSE I CAN SENSE THAT THAT THING THAT WANTS TO EAT ME IS MAYBE ONE STEP BEHIND ME... IF THAT.
HERE, DOGGIE...

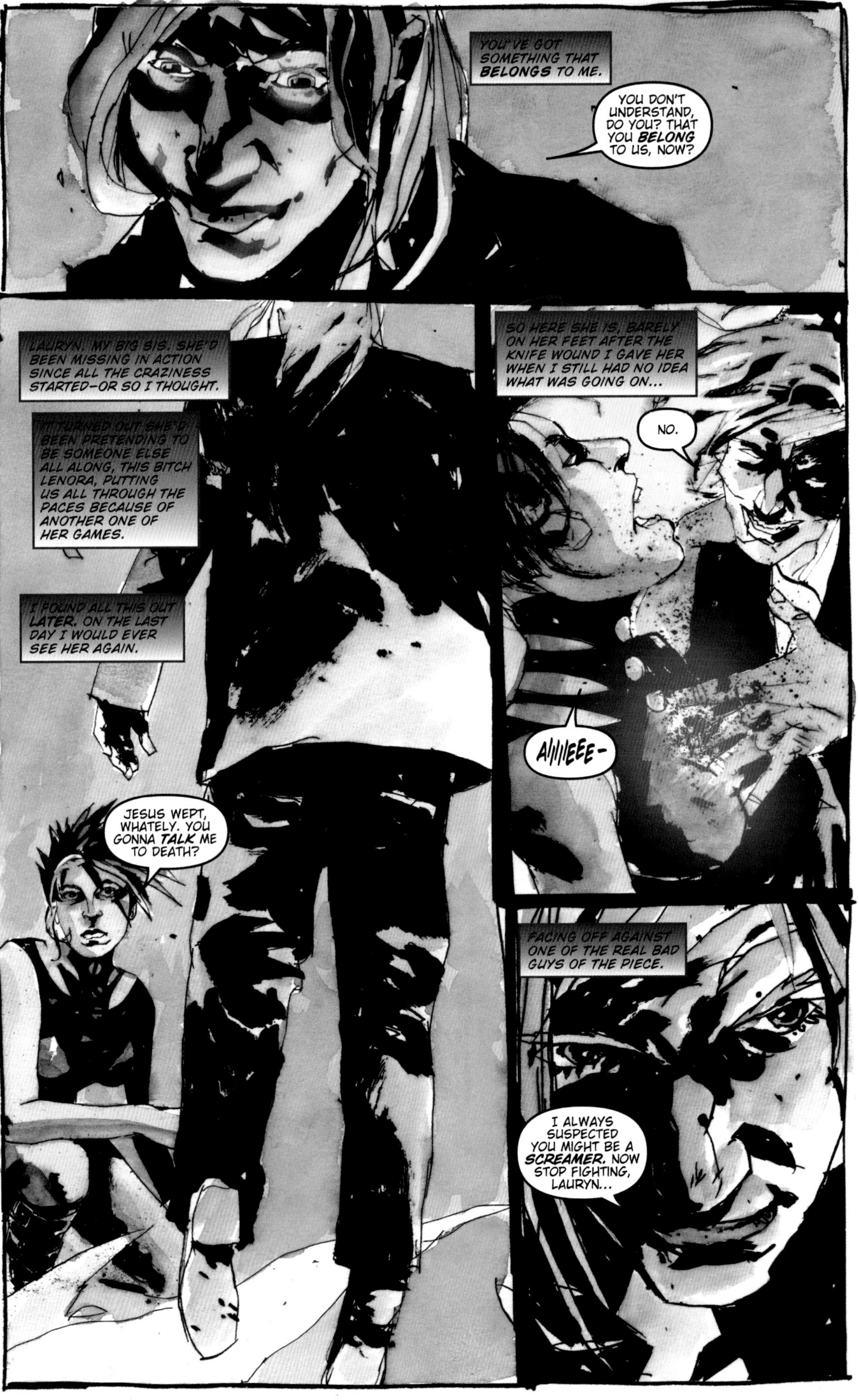
YOU'VE GOT SOMETHING THAT BELONGS TO ME.
YOU DON'T UNDERSTAND, DO YOU? THAT YOU BELONG TO US, NOW?
LAURYN. MY BIG SIS. SHE'D BEEN MISSING IN ACTION SINCE ALL THE CRAZINESS STARTED—OR SO I THOUGHT.
IT TURNED OUT SHE'D BEEN PRETENDING TO BE SOMEONE ELSE ALL ALONG, THIS BITCH LENORA, PUTTING US ALL THROUGH THE PACES BECAUSE OF ANOTHER ONE OF HER GAMES.
I FOUND ALL THIS OUT LATER. ON THE LAST DAY I WOULD EVER SEE HER AGAIN.
JESUS WEPT, WHATELY. YOU GONNA TALK ME TO DEATH?
SO HERE SHE IS, BARELY ON HER FEET AFTER THE KNIFE WOUND I GAVE HER WHEN I STILL HAD NO IDEA WHAT WAS GOING ON...
NO.
AIIIIEEE-
FACING OFF AGAINST ONE OF THE REAL BAD GUYS OF THE PIECE.
I ALWAYS SUSPECTED YOU MIGHT BE A SCREAMER. NOW STOP FIGHTING, LAURYN...

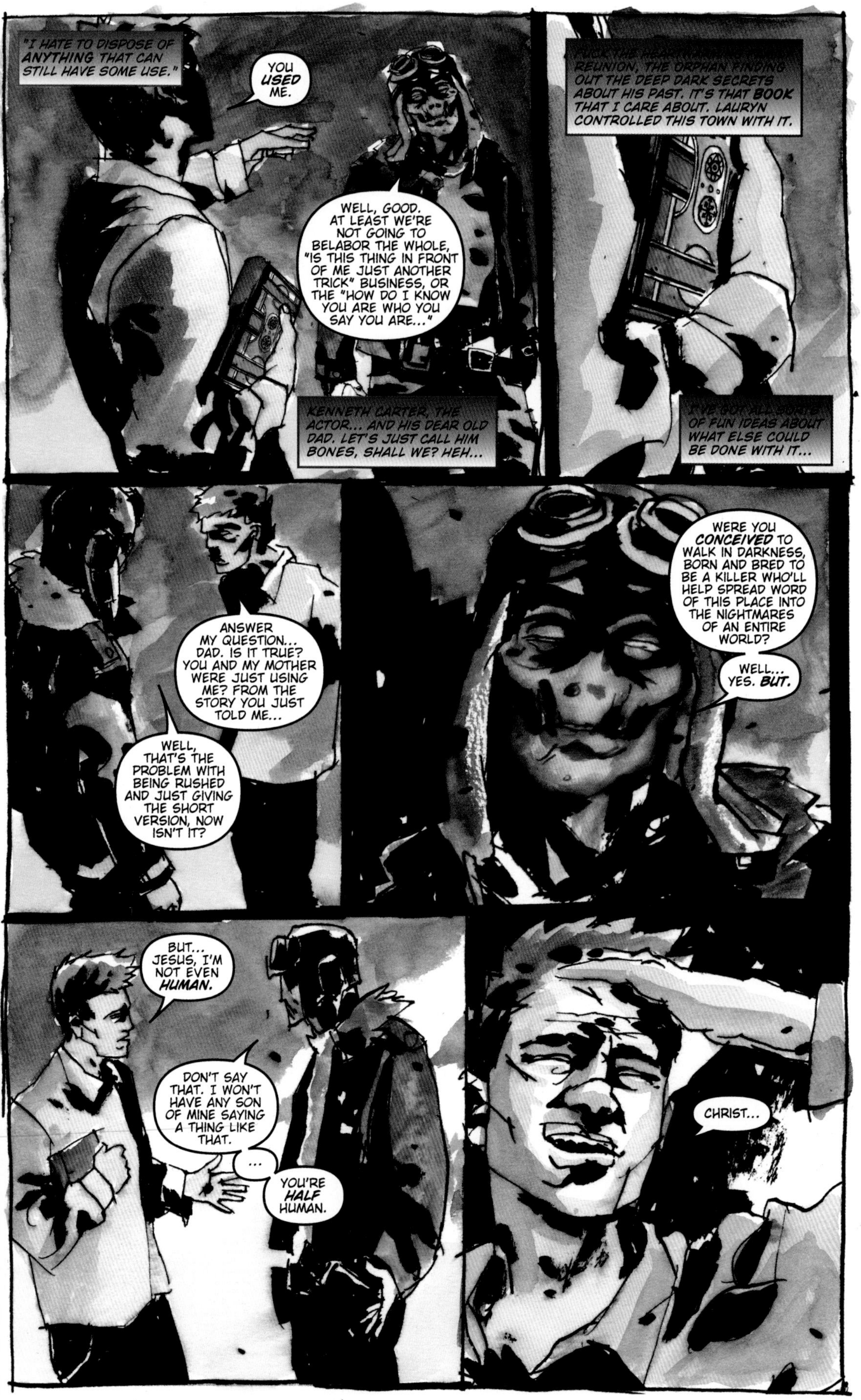
"I HATE TO DISPOSE OF ANYTHING THAT CAN STILL HAVE SOME USE."
YOU USED ME.
WELL, GOOD. AT LEAST WE'RE NOT GOING TO BELABOR THE WHOLE, "IS THIS THING IN FRONT OF ME JUST ANOTHER TRICK" BUSINESS, OR THE "HOW DO I KNOW YOU ARE WHO YOU SAY YOU ARE..."
KENNETH CARTER, THE ACTOR... AND HIS DEAR OLD DAD. LET'S JUST CALL HIM BONES, SHALL WE? HEH...
FUCK THE HEARTWARMING FAMILY REUNION, THE ORPHAN FINDING OUT THE DEEP DARK SECRETS ABOUT HIS PAST. IT'S THAT BOOK THAT I CARE ABOUT. LAURYN CONTROLLED THIS TOWN WITH IT.
I'VE GOT ALL SORTS OF FUN IDEAS ABOUT WHAT ELSE COULD BE DONE WITH IT...
ANSWER MY QUESTION... DAD. IS IT TRUE? YOU AND MY MOTHER WERE JUST USING ME? FROM THE STORY YOU JUST TOLD ME...
WELL, THAT'S THE PROBLEM WITH BEING RUSHED AND JUST GIVING THE SHORT VERSION, NOW ISN'T IT?
WERE YOU CONCEIVED TO WALK IN DARKNESS, BORN AND BRED TO BE A KILLER WHO'LL HELP SPREAD WORD OF THIS PLACE INTO THE NIGHTMARES OF AN ENTIRE WORLD?
WELL... YES. BUT.
BUT... JESUS, I'M NOT EVEN HUMAN.
DON'T SAY THAT. I WON'T HAVE ANY SON OF MINE SAYING A THING LIKE THAT.
...
YOU'RE HALF HUMAN.
CHRIST...

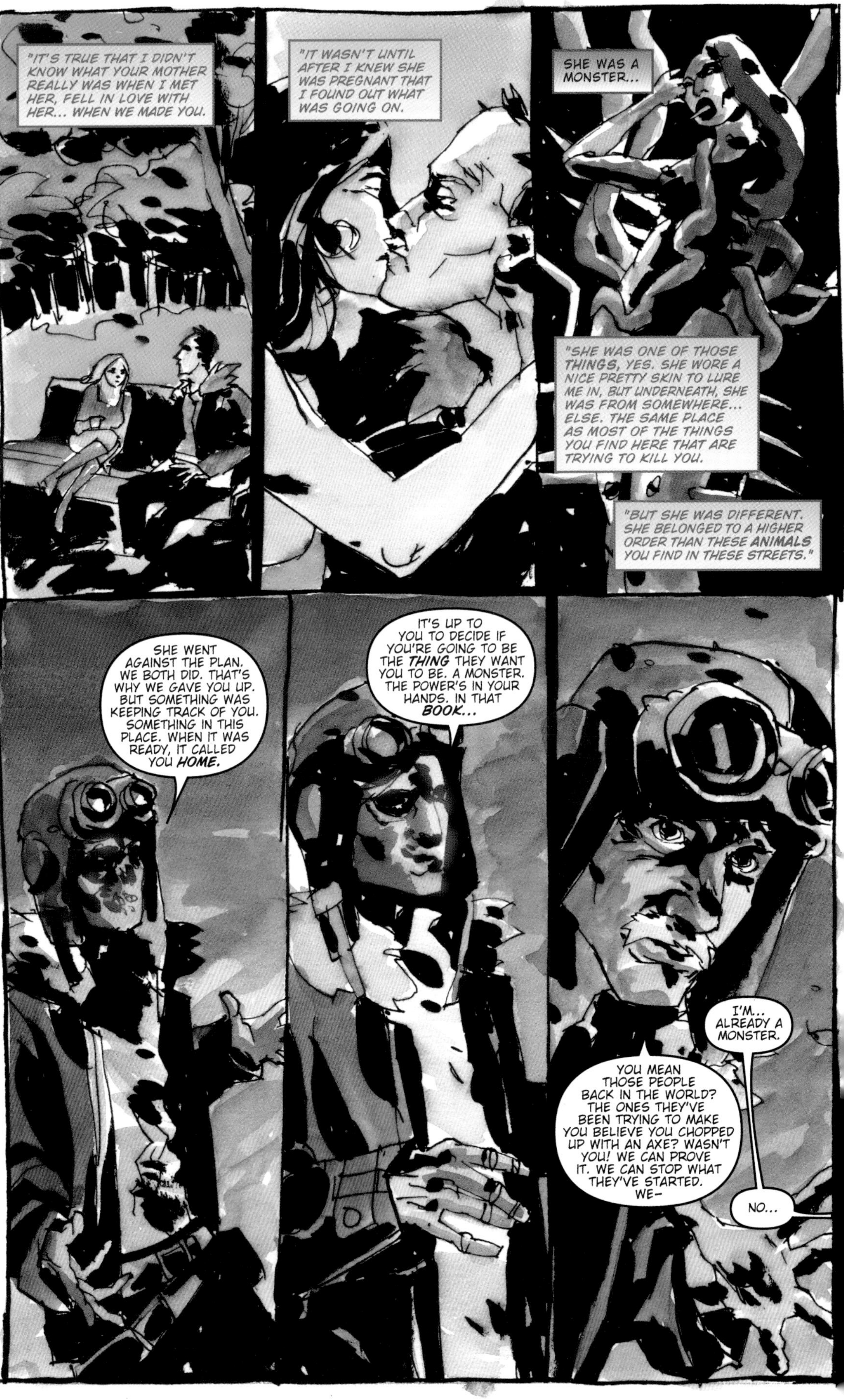

"IT'S TRUE THAT I DIDN'T KNOW WHAT YOUR MOTHER REALLY WAS WHEN I MET HER, FELL IN LOVE WITH HER... WHEN WE MADE YOU.
"IT WASN'T UNTIL AFTER I KNEW SHE WAS PREGNANT THAT I FOUND OUT WHAT WAS GOING ON.
SHE WAS A MONSTER...
"SHE WAS ONE OF THOSE THINGS, YES. SHE WORE A NICE PRETTY SKIN TO LURE ME IN, BUT UNDERNEATH, SHE WAS FROM SOMEWHERE... ELSE. THE SAME PLACE AS MOST OF THE THINGS YOU FIND HERE THAT ARE TRYING TO KILL YOU.
"BUT SHE WAS DIFFERENT. SHE BELONGED TO A HIGHER ORDER THAN THESE ANIMALS YOU FIND IN THESE STREETS."
SHE WENT AGAINST THE PLAN. WE BOTH DID. THAT'S WHY WE GAVE YOU UP. BUT SOMETHING WAS KEEPING TRACK OF YOU. SOMETHING IN THIS PLACE. WHEN IT WAS READY, IT CALLED YOU HOME.
IT'S UP TO YOU TO DECIDE IF YOU'RE GOING TO BE THE THING THEY WANT YOU TO BE. A MONSTER. THE POWER'S IN YOUR HANDS. IN THAT BOOK...
I'M... ALREADY A MONSTER.
YOU MEAN THOSE PEOPLE BACK IN THE WORLD? THE ONES THEY'VE BEEN TRYING TO MAKE YOU BELIEVE YOU CHOPPED UP WITH AN AXE? WASN'T YOU! WE CAN PROVE IT. WE CAN STOP WHAT THEY'VE STARTED. WE–
NO...

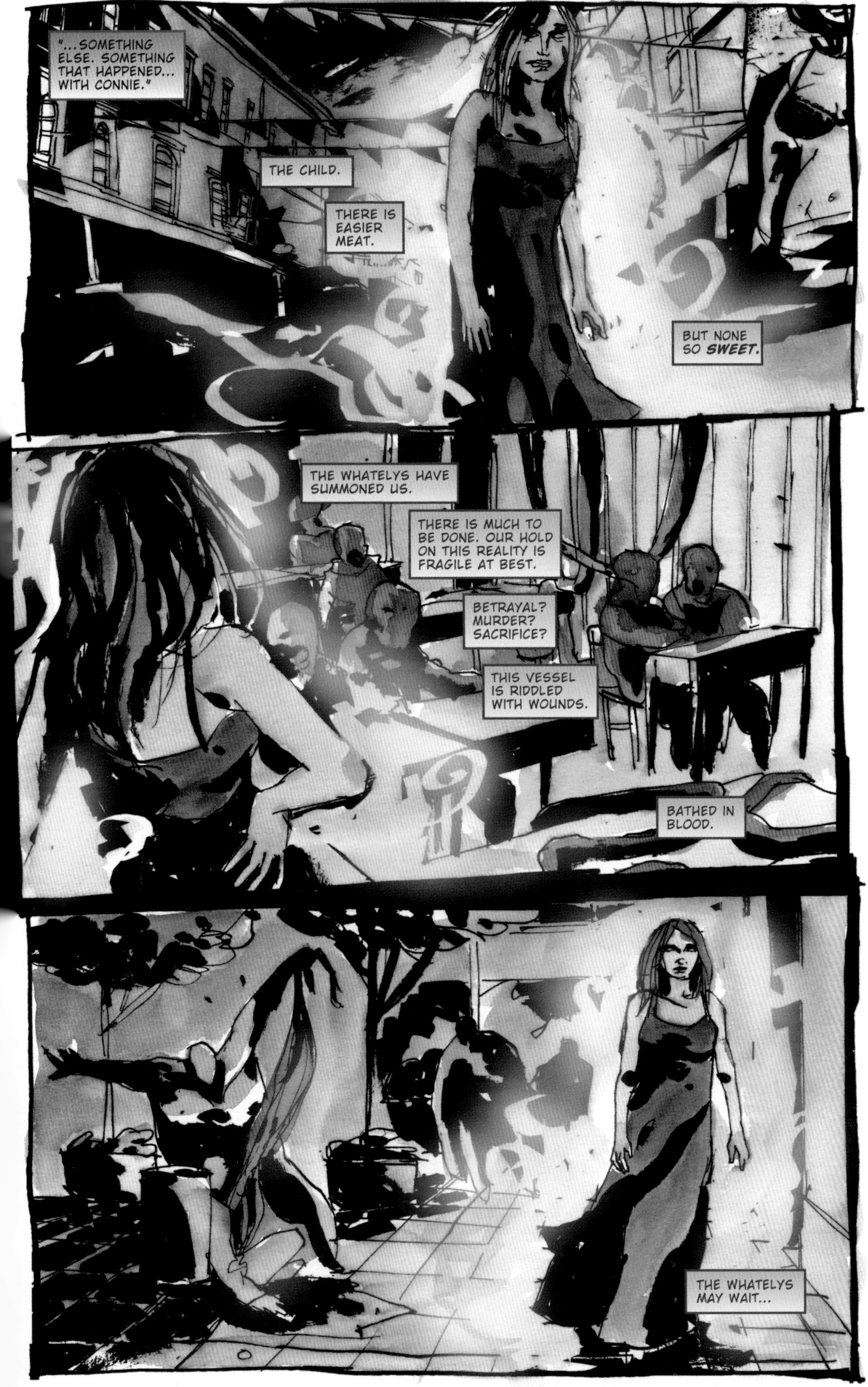
"...SOMETHING ELSE. SOMETHING THAT HAPPENED... WITH CONNIE."
THE CHILD.
THERE IS EASIER MEAT.
BUT NONE SO SWEET.
THE WHATELYS HAVE SUMMONED US.
THERE IS MUCH TO BE DONE. OUR HOLD ON THIS REALITY IS FRAGILE AT BEST.
BETRAYAL? MURDER? SACRIFICE?
THIS VESSEL IS RIDDLED WITH WOUNDS.
BATHED IN BLOOD.
THE WHATELYS MAY WAIT...

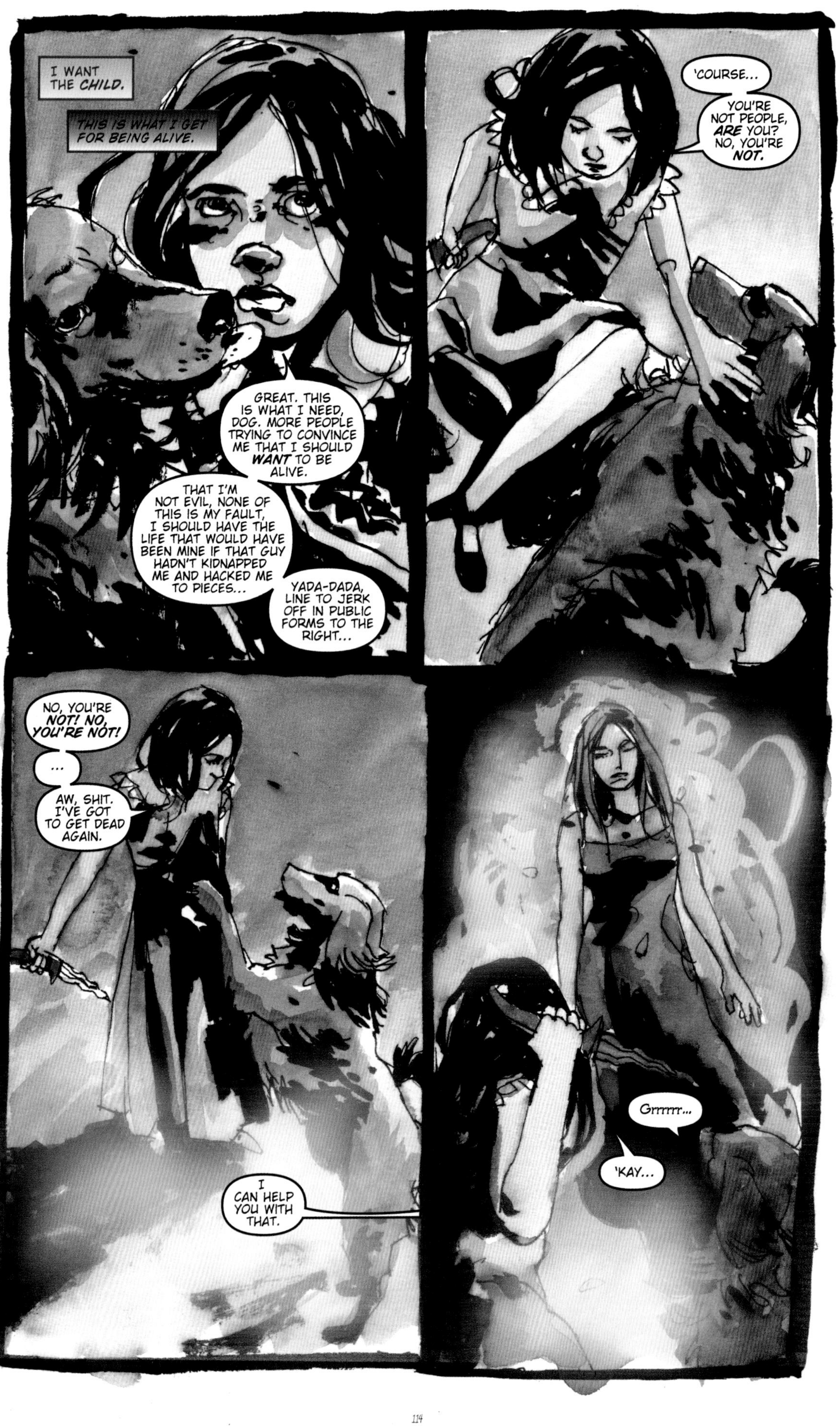
I WANT THE CHILD.
THIS IS WHAT I GET FOR BEING ALIVE.
GREAT. THIS IS WHAT I NEED, DOG. MORE PEOPLE TRYING TO CONVINCE ME THAT I SHOULD WANT TO BE ALIVE.
THAT I'M NOT EVIL, NONE OF THIS IS MY FAULT, I SHOULD HAVE THE LIFE THAT WOULD HAVE BEEN MINE IF THAT GUY HADN'T KIDNAPPED ME AND HACKED ME TO PIECES...
YADA-DADA, LINE TO JERK OFF IN PUBLIC FORMS TO THE RIGHT...
'COURSE...
YOU'RE NOT PEOPLE, ARE YOU? NO, YOU'RE NOT.
NO, YOU'RE NOT! NO, YOU'RE NOT!
...
AW, SHIT. I'VE GOT TO GET DEAD AGAIN.
I CAN HELP YOU WITH THAT.
Grrrrrr...
'KAY...

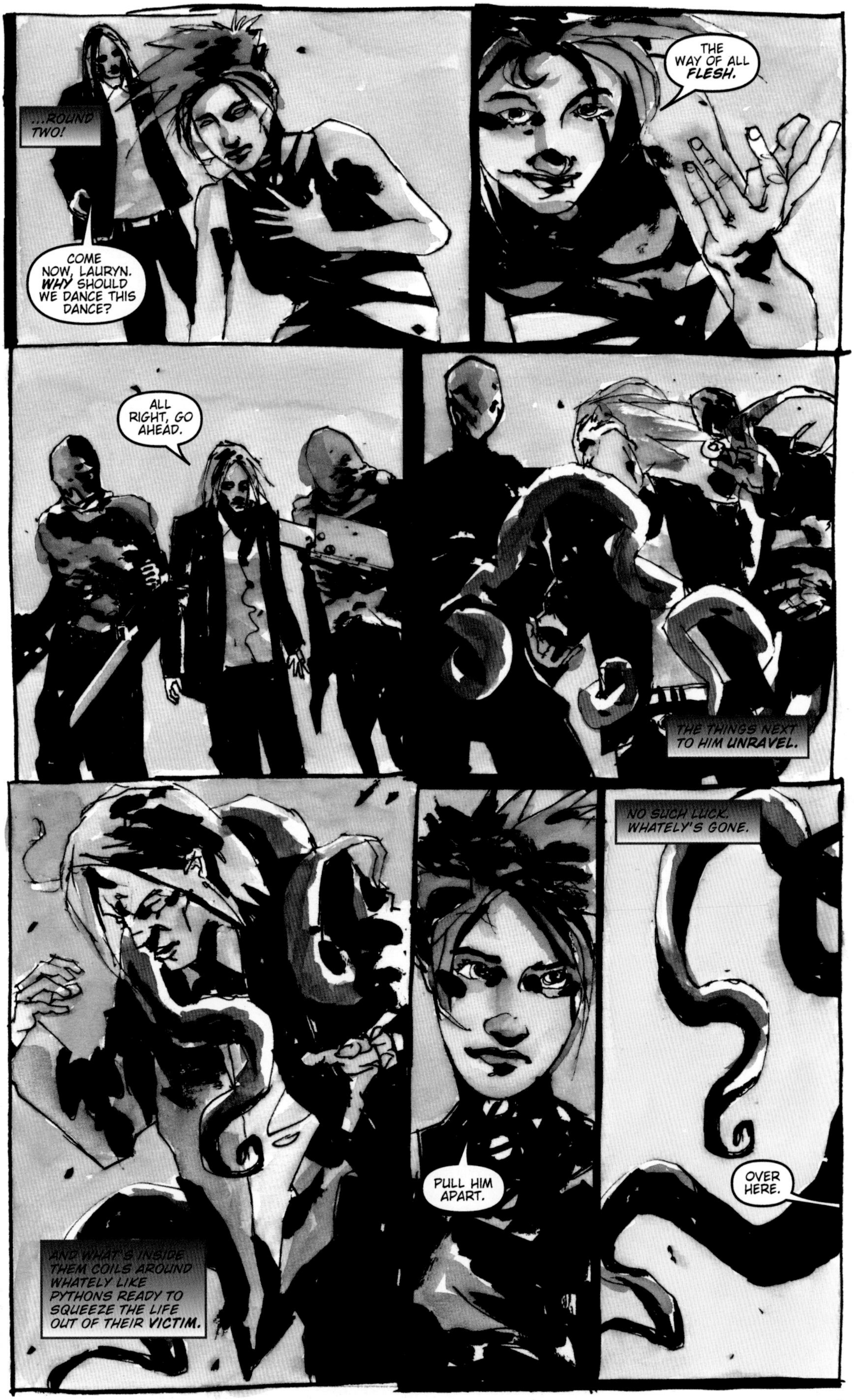

...ROUND TWO!
COME NOW, LAURYN. WHY SHOULD WE DANCE THIS DANCE?
THE WAY OF ALL FLESH.
ALL RIGHT, GO AHEAD.
THE THINGS NEXT TO HIM UNRAVEL.
AND WHAT'S INSIDE THEM COILS AROUND WHATELY LIKE PYTHONS READY TO SQUEEZE THE LIFE OUT OF THEIR VICTIM.
PULL HIM APART.
NO SUCH LUCK. WHATELY'S GONE.
OVER HERE.

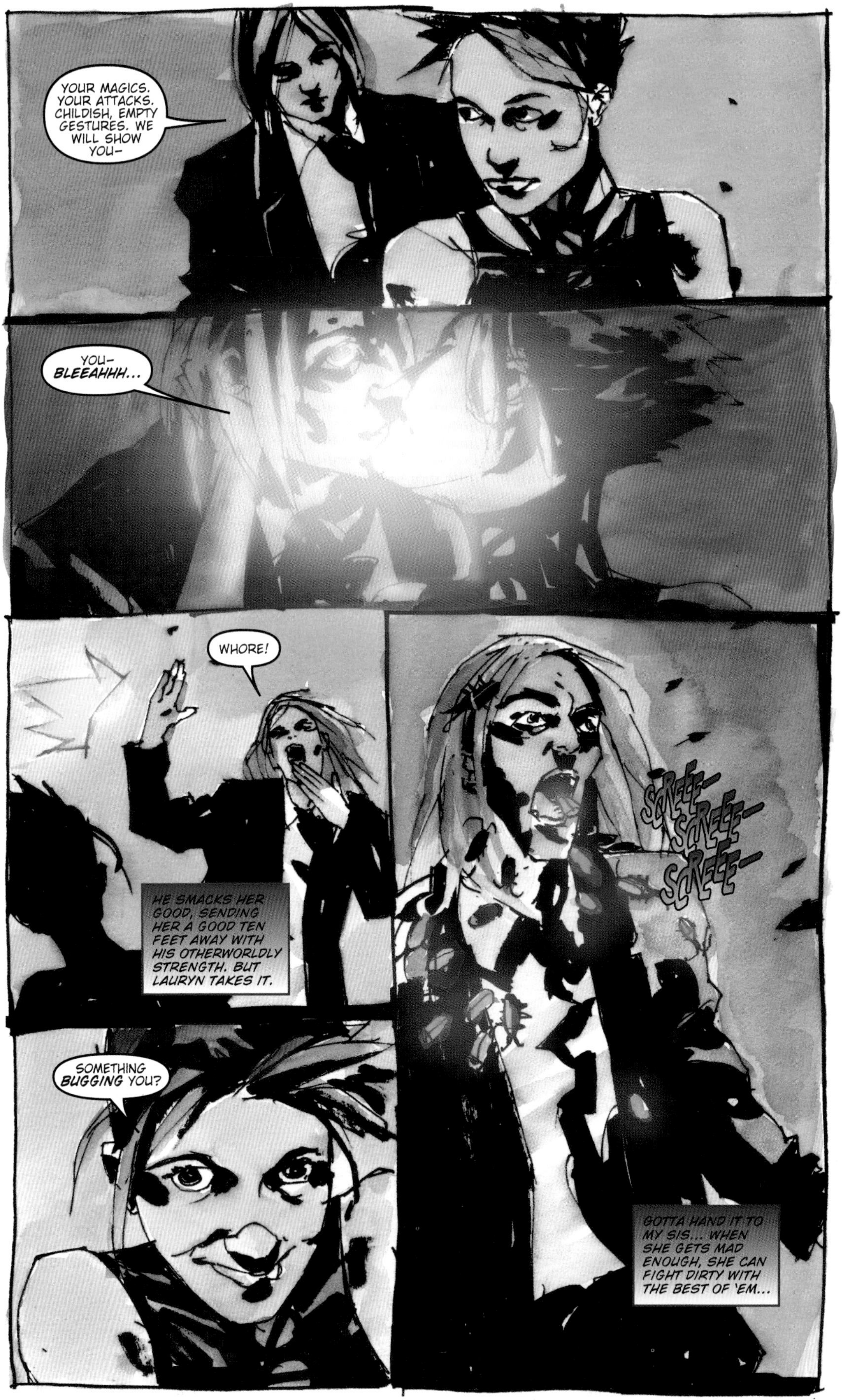
YOUR MAGICS. YOUR ATTACKS. CHILDISH, EMPTY GESTURES. WE WILL SHOW YOU-
YOU- *BLEEAHHH...*
WHORE!
HE SMACKS HER GOOD, SENDING HER A GOOD TEN FEET AWAY WITH HIS OTHERWORLDLY STRENGTH. BUT LAURYN TAKES IT.
SCREEE-
SCREEE-
SCREEE-
SOMETHING *BUGGING* YOU?
GOTTA HAND IT TO MY SIS... WHEN SHE GETS MAD ENOUGH, SHE CAN FIGHT DIRTY WITH THE BEST OF 'EM...

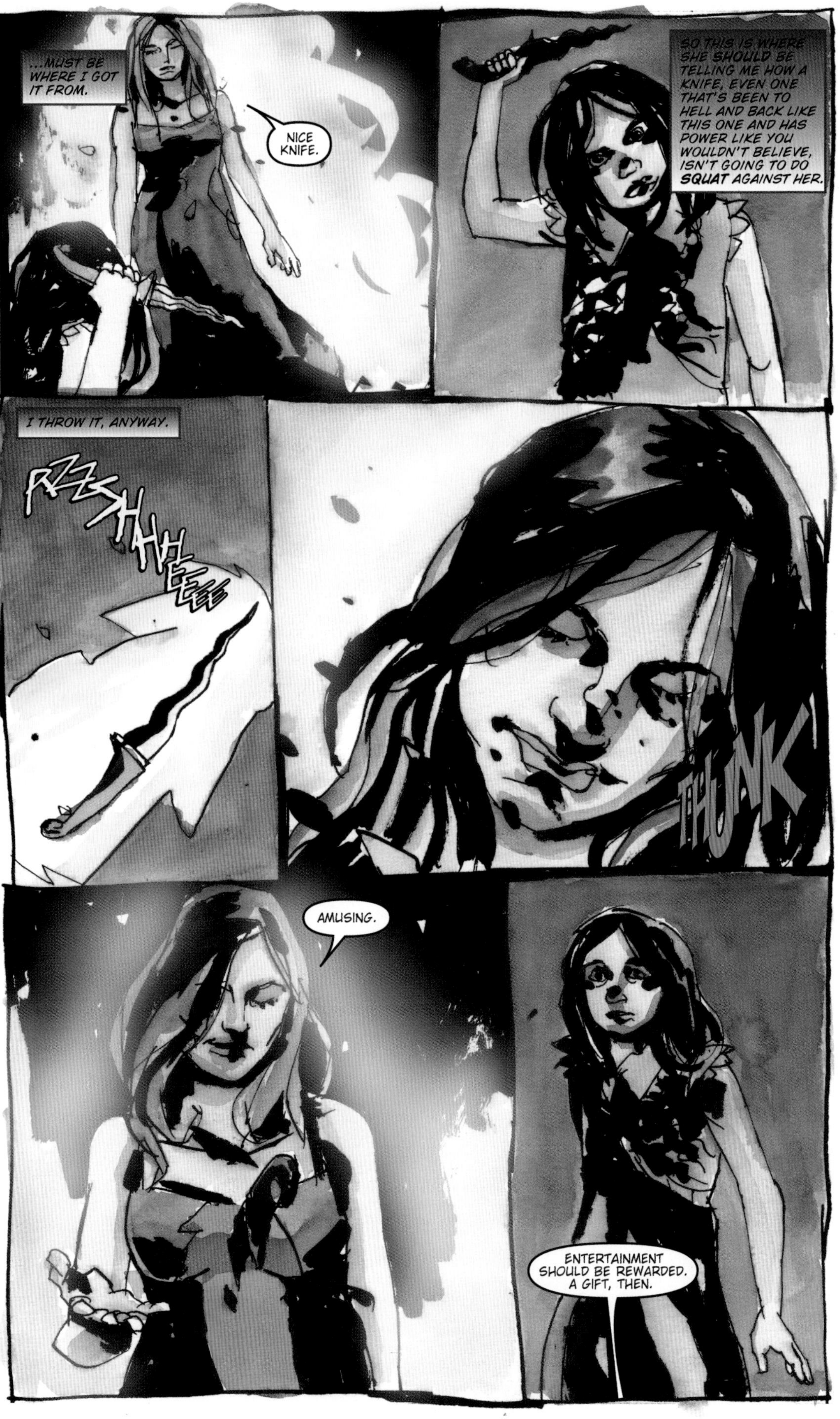

...MUST BE WHERE I GOT IT FROM.
NICE KNIFE.
SO THIS IS WHERE SHE SHOULD BE TELLING ME HOW A KNIFE, EVEN ONE THAT'S BEEN TO HELL AND BACK LIKE THIS ONE AND HAS POWER LIKE YOU WOULDN'T BELIEVE, ISN'T GOING TO DO SQUAT AGAINST HER.
I THROW IT, ANYWAY.
RZZSHHHEEEEE
THUNK
AMUSING.
ENTERTAINMENT SHOULD BE REWARDED. A GIFT, THEN.

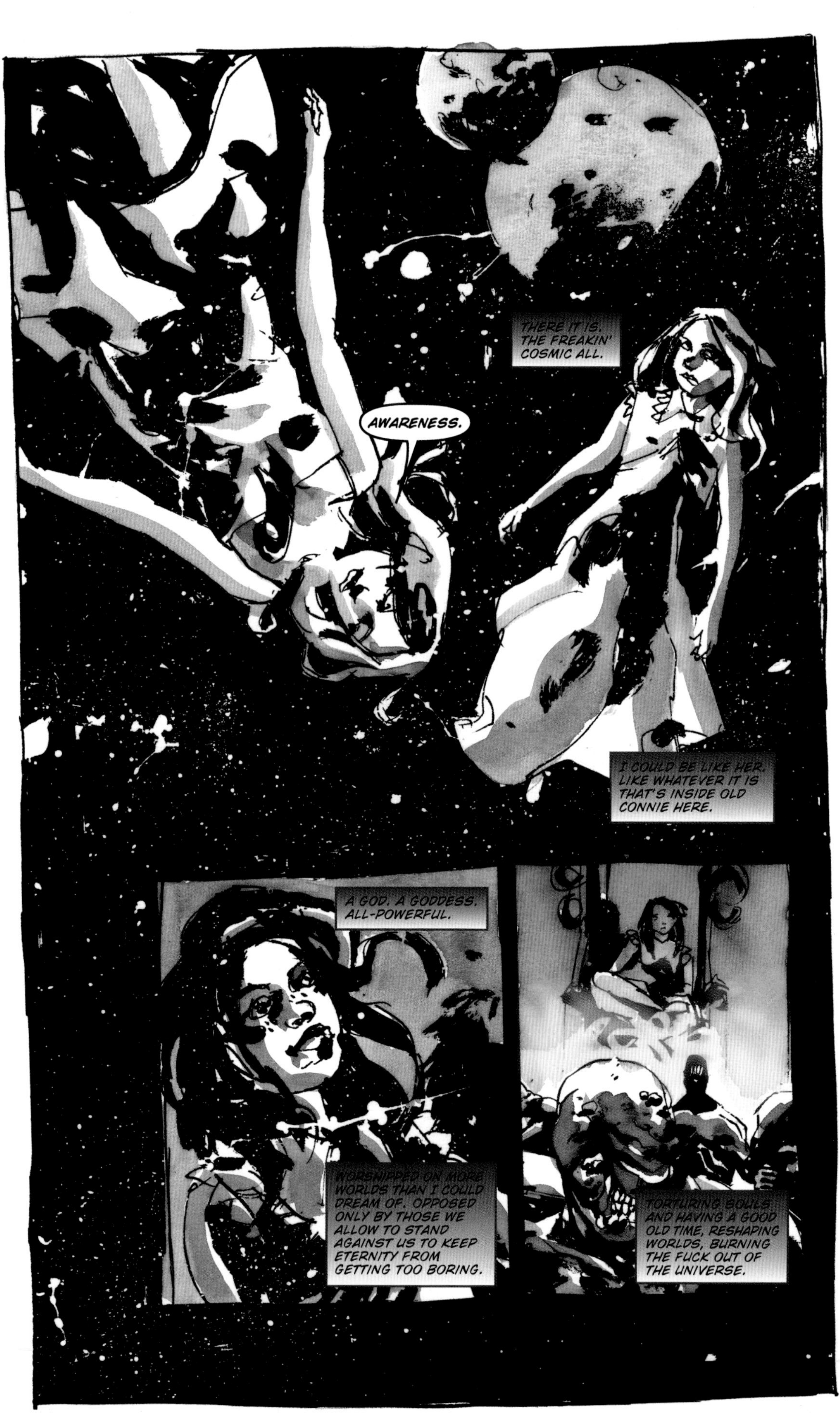
THERE IT IS. THE FREAKIN' COSMIC ALL.
AWARENESS.
I COULD BE LIKE HER. LIKE WHATEVER IT IS THAT'S INSIDE OLD CONNIE HERE.
A GOD. A GODDESS. ALL-POWERFUL.
WORSHIPPED ON MORE WORLDS THAN I COULD DREAM OF. OPPOSED ONLY BY THOSE WE ALLOW TO STAND AGAINST US TO KEEP ETERNITY FROM GETTING TOO BORING.
TORTURING SOULS AND HAVING A GOOD OLD TIME, RESHAPING WORLDS, BURNING THE FUCK OUT OF THE UNIVERSE.

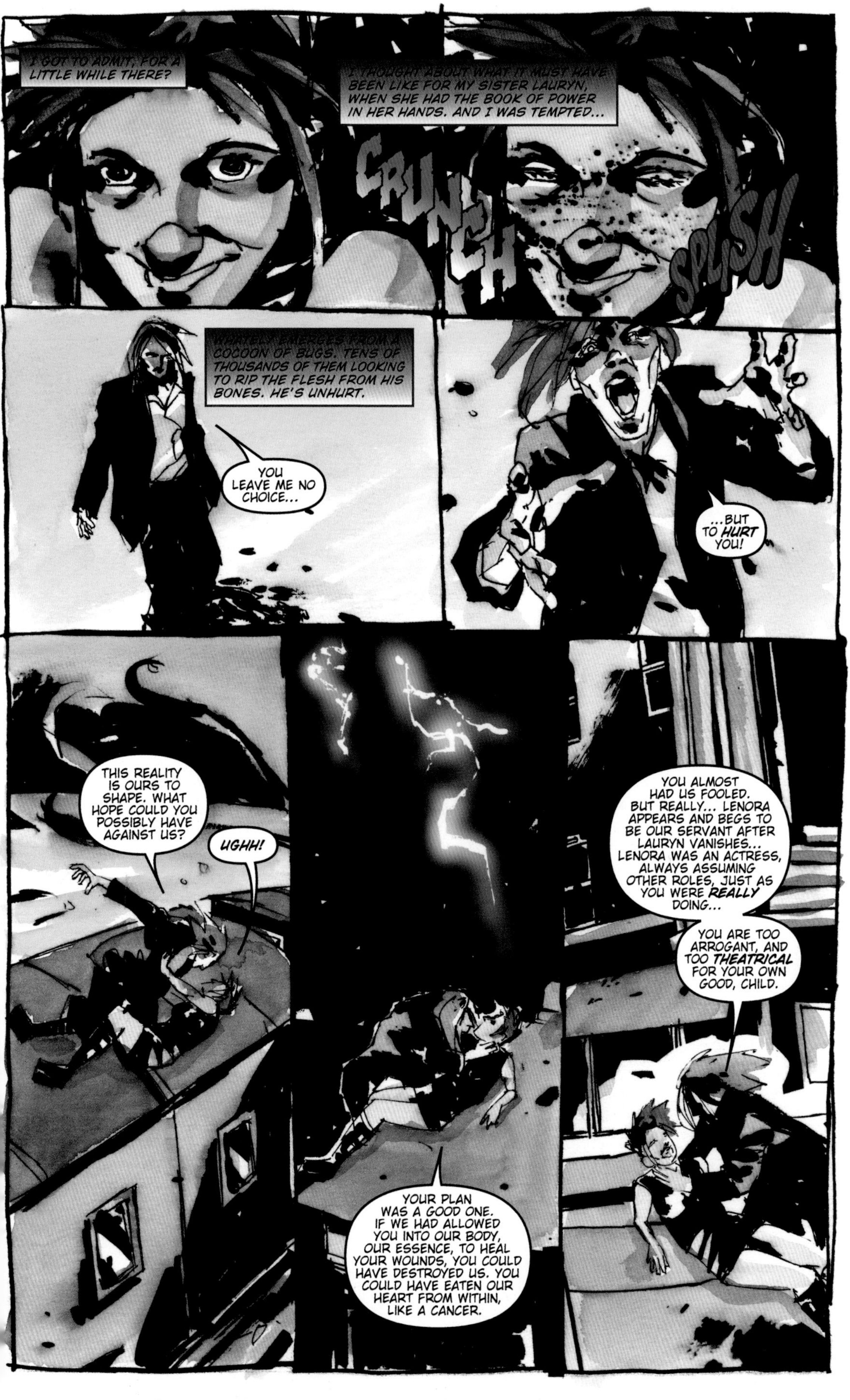
I GOT TO ADMIT, FOR A LITTLE WHILE THERE?
I THOUGHT ABOUT WHAT IT MUST HAVE BEEN LIKE FOR MY SISTER LAURYN, WHEN SHE HAD THE BOOK OF POWER IN HER HANDS. AND I WAS TEMPTED...
CRUNCH
SPLISH
WHATELY EMERGES FROM A COCOON OF BUGS. TENS OF THOUSANDS OF THEM LOOKING TO RIP THE FLESH FROM HIS BONES. HE'S UNHURT.
YOU LEAVE ME NO CHOICE...
...BUT TO HURT YOU!
THIS REALITY IS OURS TO SHAPE. WHAT HOPE COULD YOU POSSIBLY HAVE AGAINST US?
UGHH!
YOUR PLAN WAS A GOOD ONE. IF WE HAD ALLOWED YOU INTO OUR BODY, OUR ESSENCE, TO HEAL YOUR WOUNDS, YOU COULD HAVE DESTROYED US. YOU COULD HAVE EATEN OUR HEART FROM WITHIN, LIKE A CANCER.
YOU ALMOST HAD US FOOLED. BUT REALLY... LENORA APPEARS AND BEGS TO BE OUR SERVANT AFTER LAURYN VANISHES... LENORA WAS AN ACTRESS, ALWAYS ASSUMING OTHER ROLES, JUST AS YOU WERE REALLY DOING...
YOU ARE TOO ARROGANT, AND TOO THEATRICAL FOR YOUR OWN GOOD, CHILD.

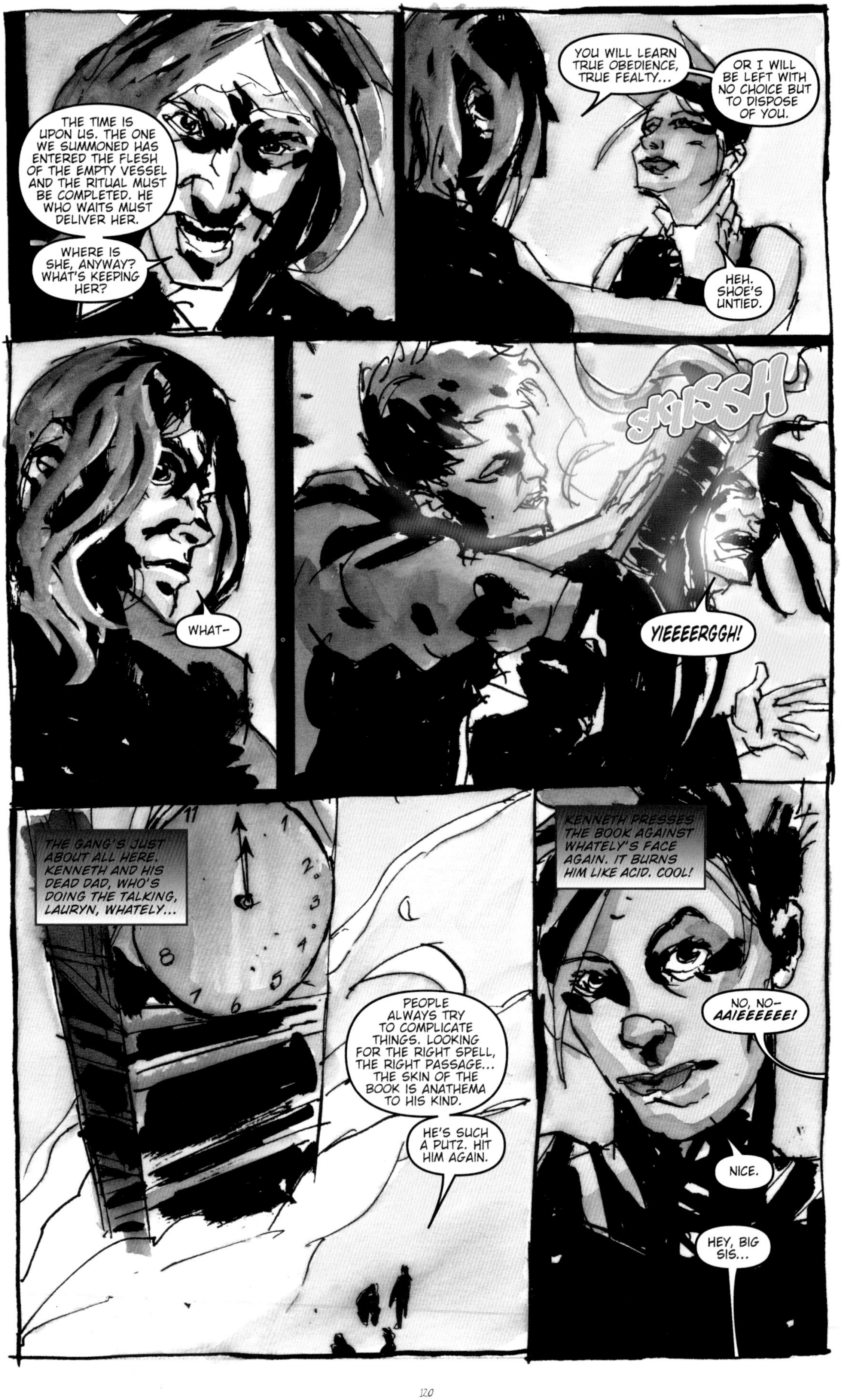
THE TIME IS UPON US. THE ONE WE SUMMONED HAS ENTERED THE FLESH OF THE EMPTY VESSEL AND THE RITUAL MUST BE COMPLETED. HE WHO WAITS MUST DELIVER HER.
WHERE IS SHE, ANYWAY? WHAT'S KEEPING HER?
YOU WILL LEARN TRUE OBEDIENCE, TRUE FEALTY...
OR I WILL BE LEFT WITH NO CHOICE BUT TO DISPOSE OF YOU.
HEH. SHOE'S UNTIED.
WHAT-
SKISSSH
YIEEEERGGH!
THE GANG'S JUST ABOUT ALL HERE. KENNETH AND HIS DEAD DAD, WHO'S DOING THE TALKING, LAURYN, WHATELY...
PEOPLE ALWAYS TRY TO COMPLICATE THINGS. LOOKING FOR THE RIGHT SPELL, THE RIGHT PASSAGE... THE SKIN OF THE BOOK IS ANATHEMA TO HIS KIND.
HE'S SUCH A PUTZ. HIT HIM AGAIN.
KENNETH PRESSES THE BOOK AGAINST WHATELY'S FACE AGAIN. IT BURNS HIM LIKE ACID. COOL!
NO, NO- AAIEEEEEE!
NICE.
HEY, BIG SIS...

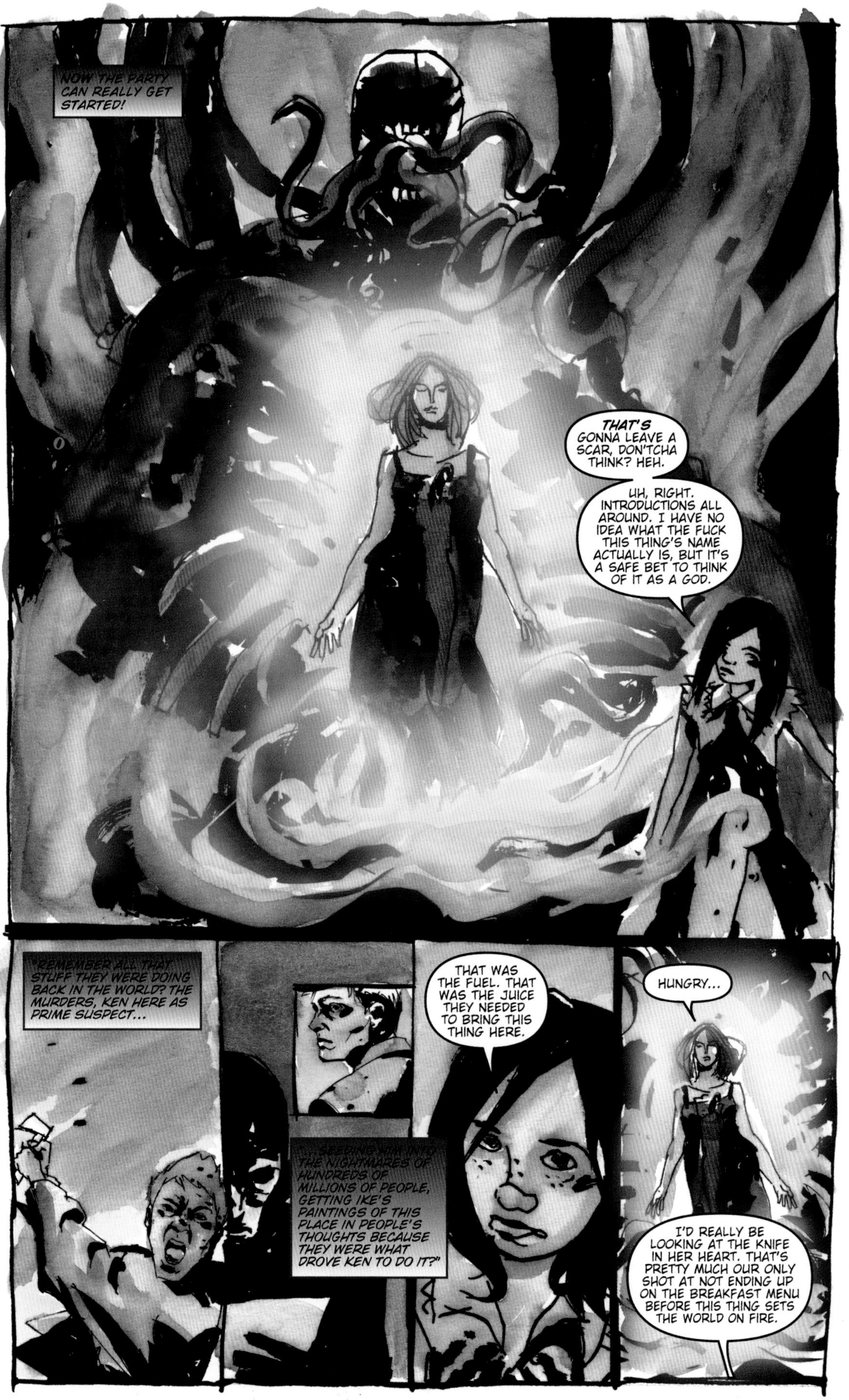
NOW THE PARTY CAN REALLY GET STARTED!
THAT'S GONNA LEAVE A SCAR, DON'TCHA THINK? HEH.
UH, RIGHT. INTRODUCTIONS ALL AROUND. I HAVE NO IDEA WHAT THE FUCK THIS THING'S NAME ACTUALLY IS, BUT IT'S A SAFE BET TO THINK OF IT AS A GOD.
"REMEMBER ALL THAT STUFF THEY WERE DOING BACK IN THE WORLD? THE MURDERS, KEN HERE AS PRIME SUSPECT...
"...SEEDING HIM INTO THE NIGHTMARES OF HUNDREDS OF MILLIONS OF PEOPLE, GETTING IKE'S PAINTINGS OF THIS PLACE IN PEOPLE'S THOUGHTS BECAUSE THEY WERE WHAT DROVE KEN TO DO IT?"
THAT WAS THE FUEL. THAT WAS THE JUICE THEY NEEDED TO BRING THIS THING HERE.
HUNGRY...
I'D REALLY BE LOOKING AT THE KNIFE IN HER HEART. THAT'S PRETTY MUCH OUR ONLY SHOT AT NOT ENDING UP ON THE BREAKFAST MENU BEFORE THIS THING SETS THE WORLD ON FIRE.

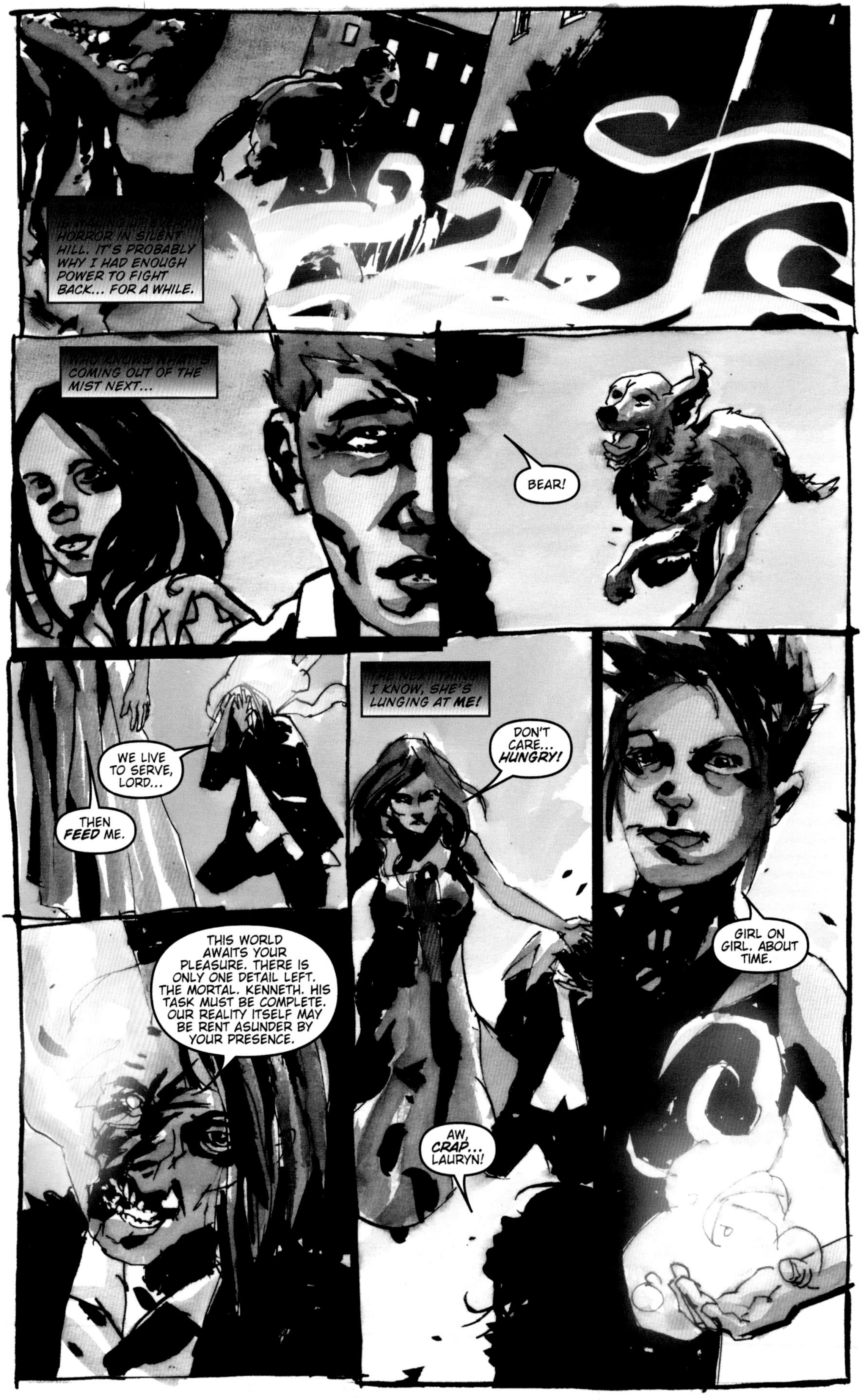
HORROR IN SILENT HILL. IT'S PROBABLY WHY I HAD ENOUGH POWER TO FIGHT BACK... FOR A WHILE.
COMING OUT OF THE MIST NEXT...
BEAR!
WE LIVE TO SERVE, LORD...
THEN FEED ME.
I KNOW, SHE'S LUNGING AT ME!
DON'T CARE... HUNGRY!
GIRL ON GIRL. ABOUT TIME.
THIS WORLD AWAITS YOUR PLEASURE. THERE IS ONLY ONE DETAIL LEFT. THE MORTAL. KENNETH. HIS TASK MUST BE COMPLETE. OUR REALITY ITSELF MAY BE RENT ASUNDER BY YOUR PRESENCE.
AW, CRAP... LAURYN!

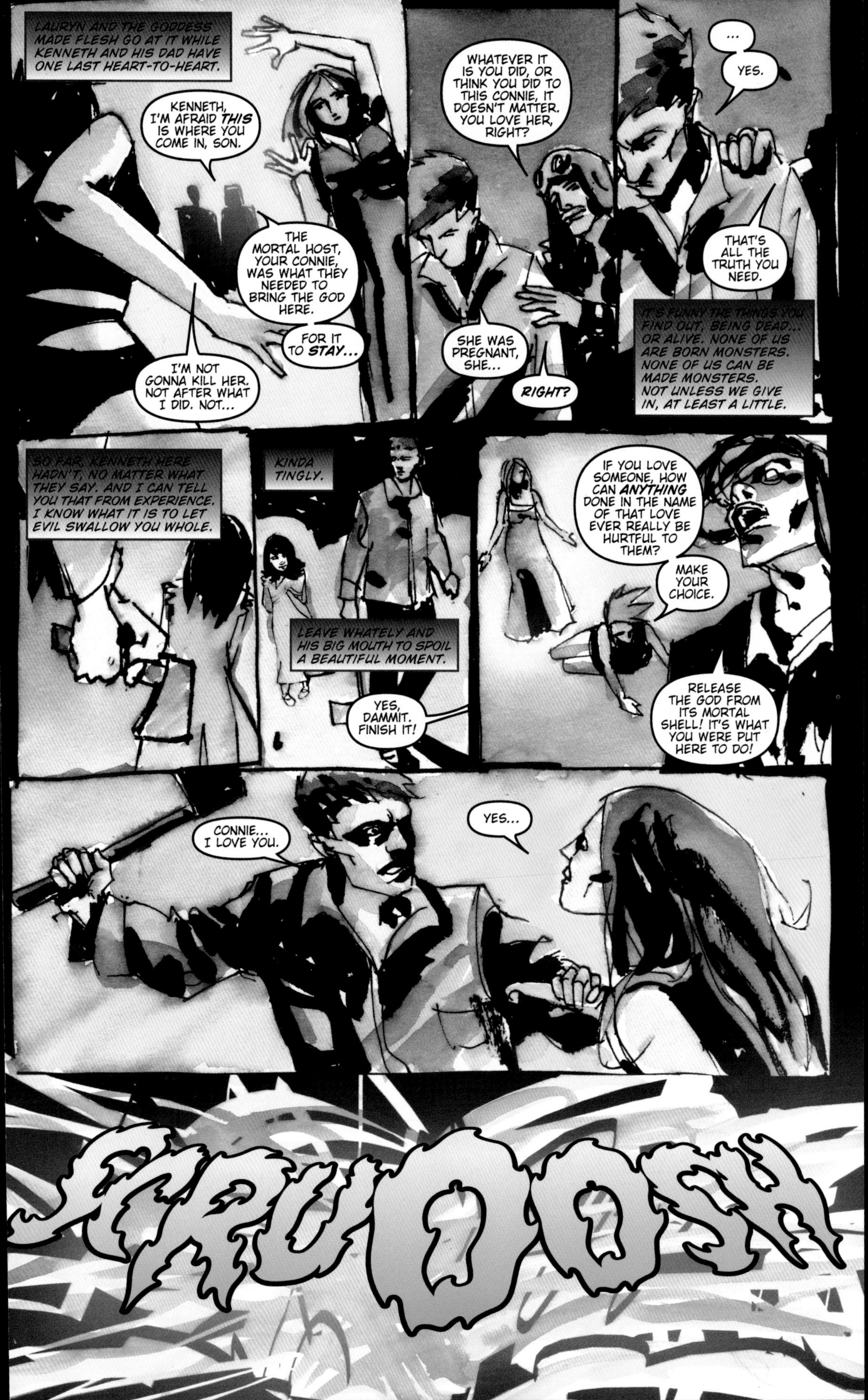
LAURYN AND THE GODDESS MADE FLESH GO AT IT WHILE KENNETH AND HIS DAD HAVE ONE LAST HEART-TO-HEART.
KENNETH, I'M AFRAID *THIS* IS WHERE YOU COME IN, SON.
THE MORTAL HOST, YOUR CONNIE, WAS WHAT THEY NEEDED TO BRING THE GOD HERE.
FOR IT TO *STAY...*
I'M NOT GONNA KILL HER. NOT AFTER WHAT I DID. NOT...
WHATEVER IT IS YOU DID, OR THINK YOU DID TO THIS CONNIE, IT DOESN'T MATTER. YOU LOVE HER, RIGHT?
SHE WAS PREGNANT, SHE...
RIGHT?
...
YES.
THAT'S ALL THE TRUTH YOU NEED.
IT'S FUNNY THE THINGS YOU FIND OUT, BEING DEAD... OR ALIVE. NONE OF US ARE BORN MONSTERS. NONE OF US CAN BE MADE MONSTERS. NOT UNLESS WE GIVE IN, AT LEAST A LITTLE.
SO FAR, KENNETH HERE HADN'T, NO MATTER WHAT THEY SAY. AND I CAN TELL YOU THAT FROM EXPERIENCE. I KNOW WHAT IT IS TO LET EVIL SWALLOW YOU WHOLE.
KINDA TINGLY.
LEAVE WHATELY AND HIS BIG MOUTH TO SPOIL A BEAUTIFUL MOMENT.
YES, DAMMIT. FINISH IT!
IF YOU LOVE SOMEONE, HOW CAN *ANYTHING* DONE IN THE NAME OF THAT LOVE EVER REALLY BE HURTFUL TO THEM?
MAKE YOUR CHOICE.
RELEASE THE GOD FROM ITS MORTAL SHELL! IT'S WHAT YOU WERE PUT HERE TO DO!
CONNIE... I LOVE YOU.
YES...

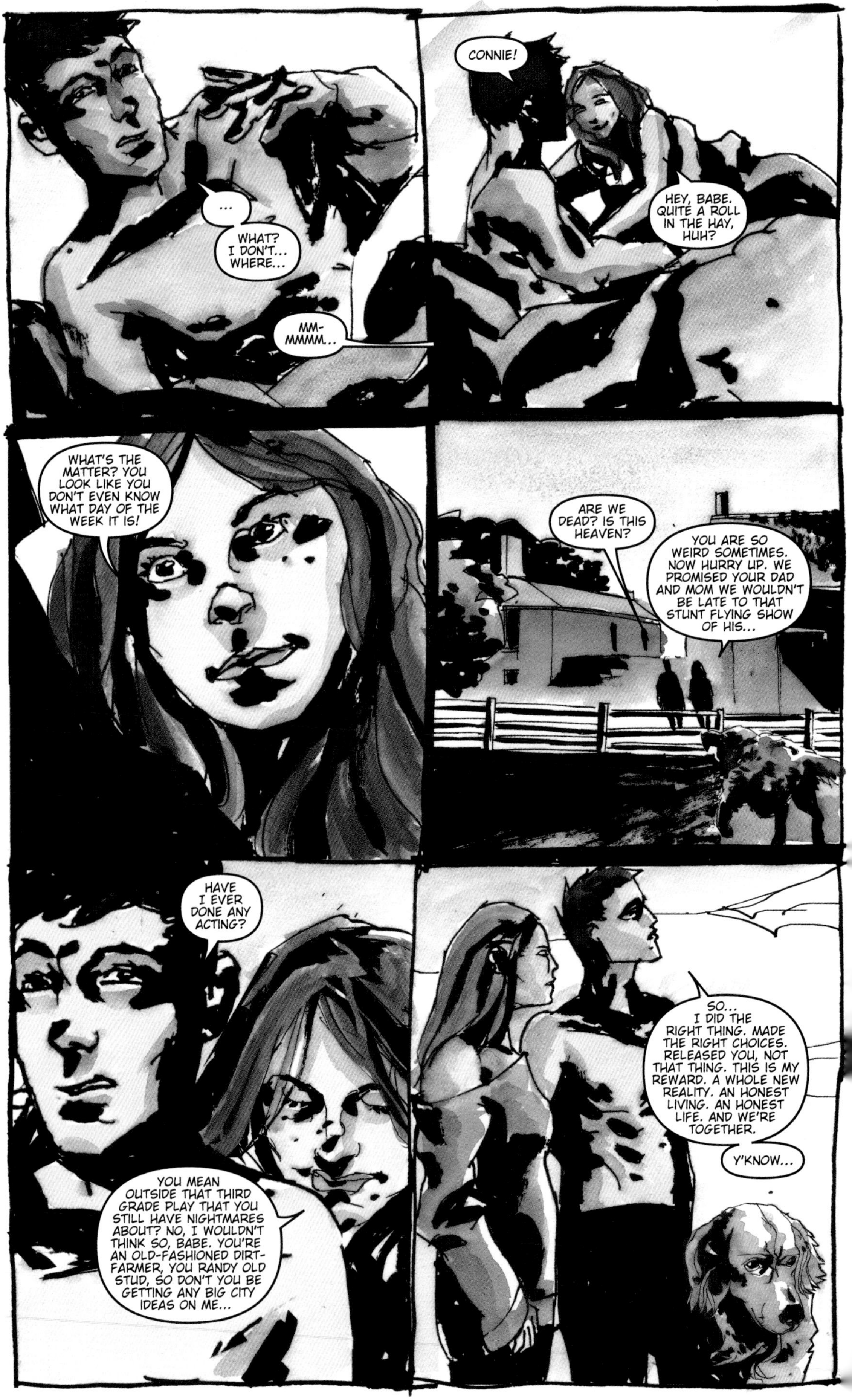
...
WHAT? I DON'T... WHERE...
MM-MMMM...
CONNIE!
HEY, BABE. QUITE A ROLL IN THE HAY, HUH?
WHAT'S THE MATTER? YOU LOOK LIKE YOU DON'T EVEN KNOW WHAT DAY OF THE WEEK IT IS!
ARE WE DEAD? IS THIS HEAVEN?
YOU ARE SO WEIRD SOMETIMES. NOW HURRY UP. WE PROMISED YOUR DAD AND MOM WE WOULDN'T BE LATE TO THAT STUNT FLYING SHOW OF HIS...
HAVE I EVER DONE ANY ACTING?
YOU MEAN OUTSIDE THAT THIRD GRADE PLAY THAT YOU STILL HAVE NIGHTMARES ABOUT? NO, I WOULDN'T THINK SO, BABE. YOU'RE AN OLD-FASHIONED DIRT-FARMER, YOU RANDY OLD STUD, SO DON'T YOU BE GETTING ANY BIG CITY IDEAS ON ME...
SO... I DID THE RIGHT THING. MADE THE RIGHT CHOICES. RELEASED YOU, NOT THAT THING. THIS IS MY REWARD. A WHOLE NEW REALITY. AN HONEST LIVING. AN HONEST LIFE. AND WE'RE TOGETHER.
Y'KNOW...

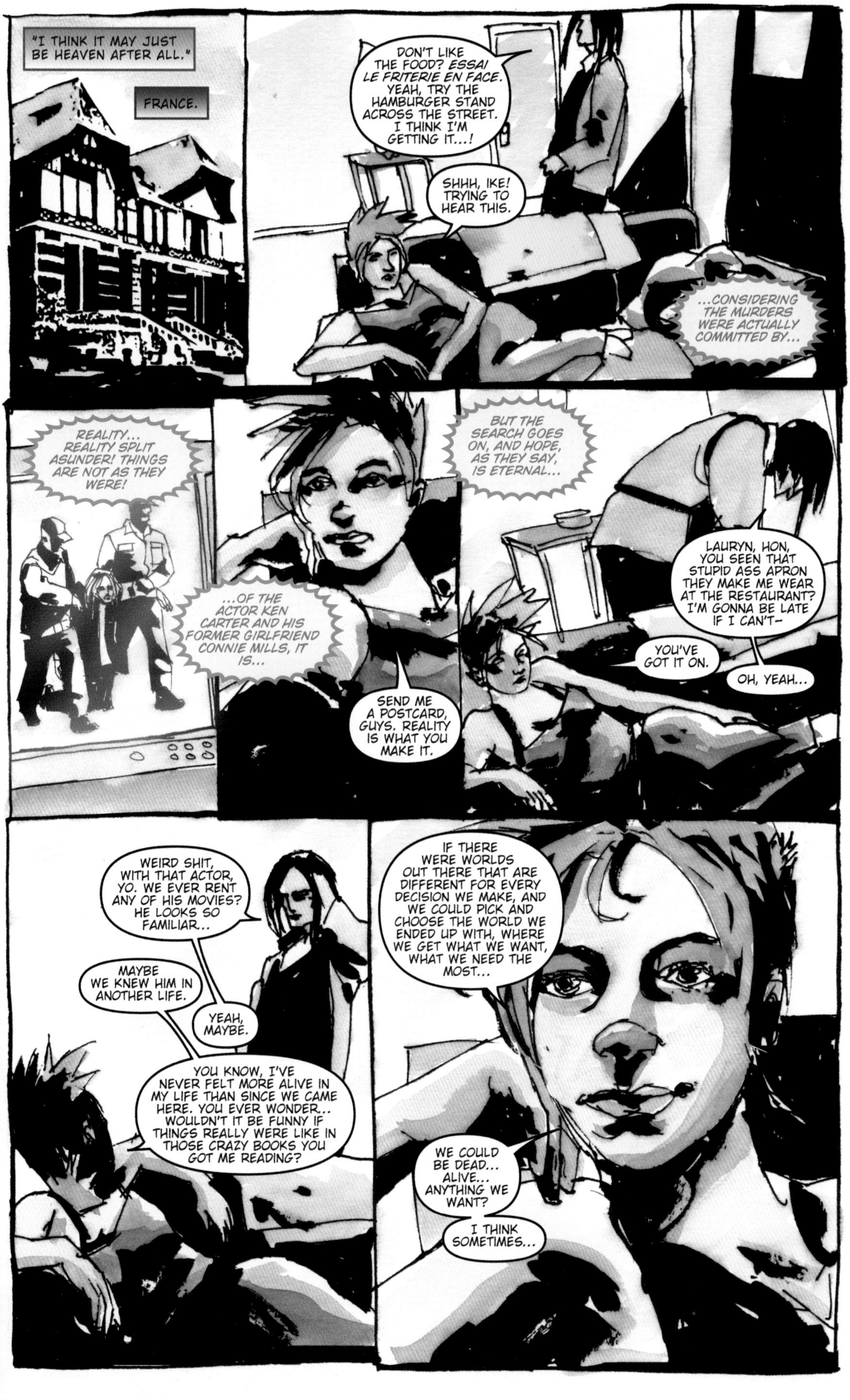
"I THINK IT MAY JUST BE HEAVEN AFTER ALL."
FRANCE.
DON'T LIKE THE FOOD? ESSAI LE FRITERIE EN FACE. YEAH, TRY THE HAMBURGER STAND ACROSS THE STREET. I THINK I'M GETTING IT...!
SHHH, IKE! TRYING TO HEAR THIS.
...CONSIDERING THE MURDERS WERE ACTUALLY COMMITTED BY...
REALITY... REALITY SPLIT ASUNDER! THINGS ARE NOT AS THEY WERE!
...OF THE ACTOR KEN CARTER AND HIS FORMER GIRLFRIEND CONNIE MILLS, IT IS...
SEND ME A POSTCARD, GUYS. REALITY IS WHAT YOU MAKE IT.
BUT THE SEARCH GOES ON, AND HOPE, AS THEY SAY, IS ETERNAL...
LAURYN, HON, YOU SEEN THAT STUPID ASS APRON THEY MAKE ME WEAR AT THE RESTAURANT? I'M GONNA BE LATE IF I CAN'T–
YOU'VE GOT IT ON.
OH, YEAH...
WEIRD SHIT, WITH THAT ACTOR, YO. WE EVER RENT ANY OF HIS MOVIES? HE LOOKS SO FAMILIAR...
MAYBE WE KNEW HIM IN ANOTHER LIFE.
YEAH, MAYBE.
YOU KNOW, I'VE NEVER FELT MORE ALIVE IN MY LIFE THAN SINCE WE CAME HERE. YOU EVER WONDER... WOULDN'T IT BE FUNNY IF THINGS REALLY WERE LIKE IN THOSE CRAZY BOOKS YOU GOT ME READING?
IF THERE WERE WORLDS OUT THERE THAT ARE DIFFERENT FOR EVERY DECISION WE MAKE, AND WE COULD PICK AND CHOOSE THE WORLD WE ENDED UP WITH, WHERE WE GET WHAT WE WANT, WHAT WE NEED THE MOST...
WE COULD BE DEAD... ALIVE... ANYTHING WE WANT?
I THINK SOMETIMES...

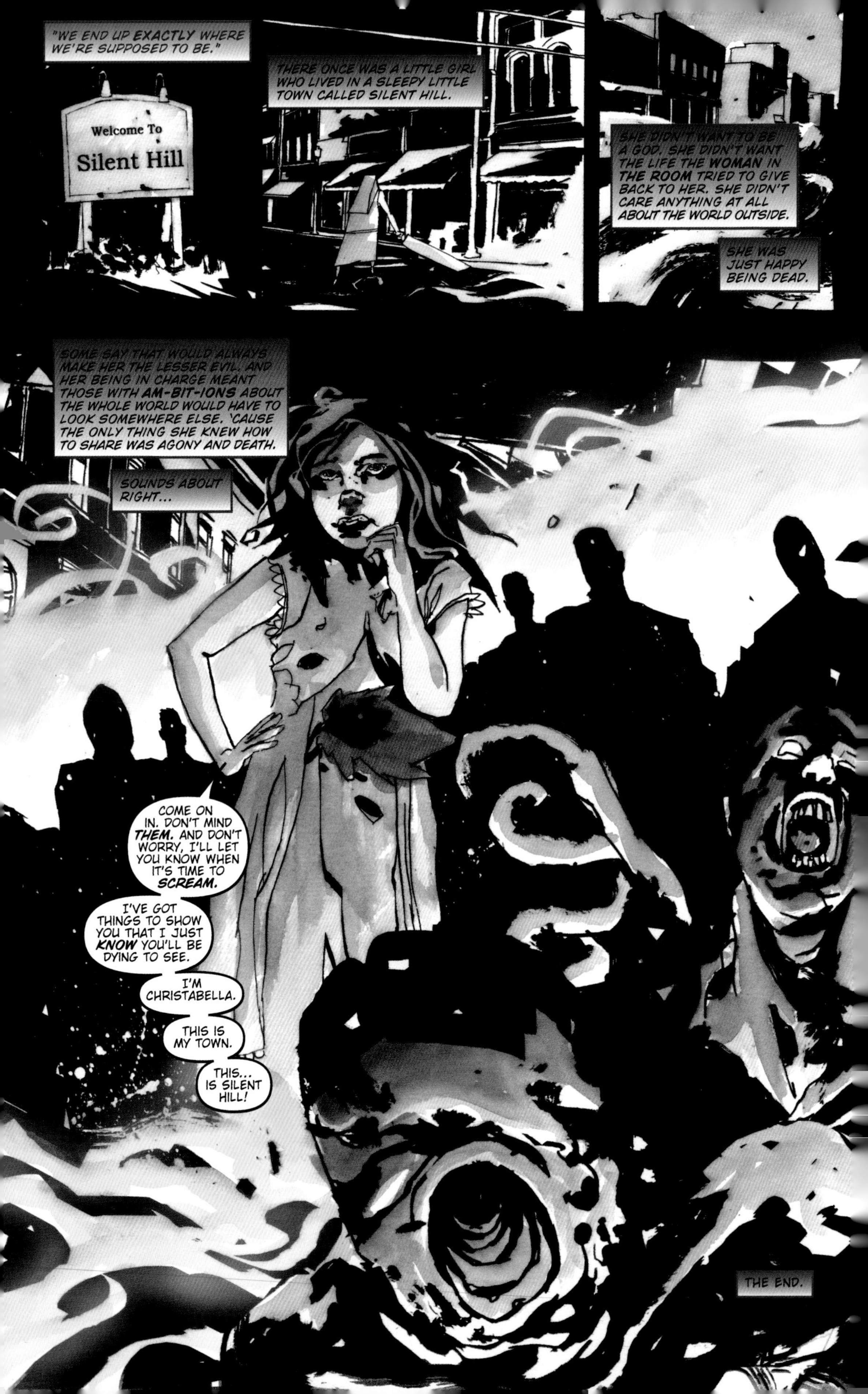
"WE END UP EXACTLY WHERE WE'RE SUPPOSED TO BE."
Welcome To Silent Hill
THERE ONCE WAS A LITTLE GIRL WHO LIVED IN A SLEEPY LITTLE TOWN CALLED SILENT HILL.
SHE DIDN'T WANT TO BE A GOD. SHE DIDN'T WANT THE LIFE THE WOMAN IN THE ROOM TRIED TO GIVE BACK TO HER. SHE DIDN'T CARE ANYTHING AT ALL ABOUT THE WORLD OUTSIDE.
SHE WAS JUST HAPPY BEING DEAD.
SOME SAY THAT WOULD ALWAYS MAKE HER THE LESSER EVIL. AND HER BEING IN CHARGE MEANT THOSE WITH AM-BIT-IONS ABOUT THE WHOLE WORLD WOULD HAVE TO LOOK SOMEWHERE ELSE. 'CAUSE THE ONLY THING SHE KNEW HOW TO SHARE WAS AGONY AND DEATH.
SOUNDS ABOUT RIGHT...
COME ON IN. DON'T MIND THEM. AND DON'T WORRY, I'LL LET YOU KNOW WHEN IT'S TIME TO SCREAM.
I'VE GOT THINGS TO SHOW YOU THAT I JUST KNOW YOU'LL BE DYING TO SEE.
I'M CHRISTABELLA.
THIS IS MY TOWN.
THIS... IS SILENT HILL!
THE END.

SILENT
HILL™
DEAD/ALIVE

COVER GALLERY

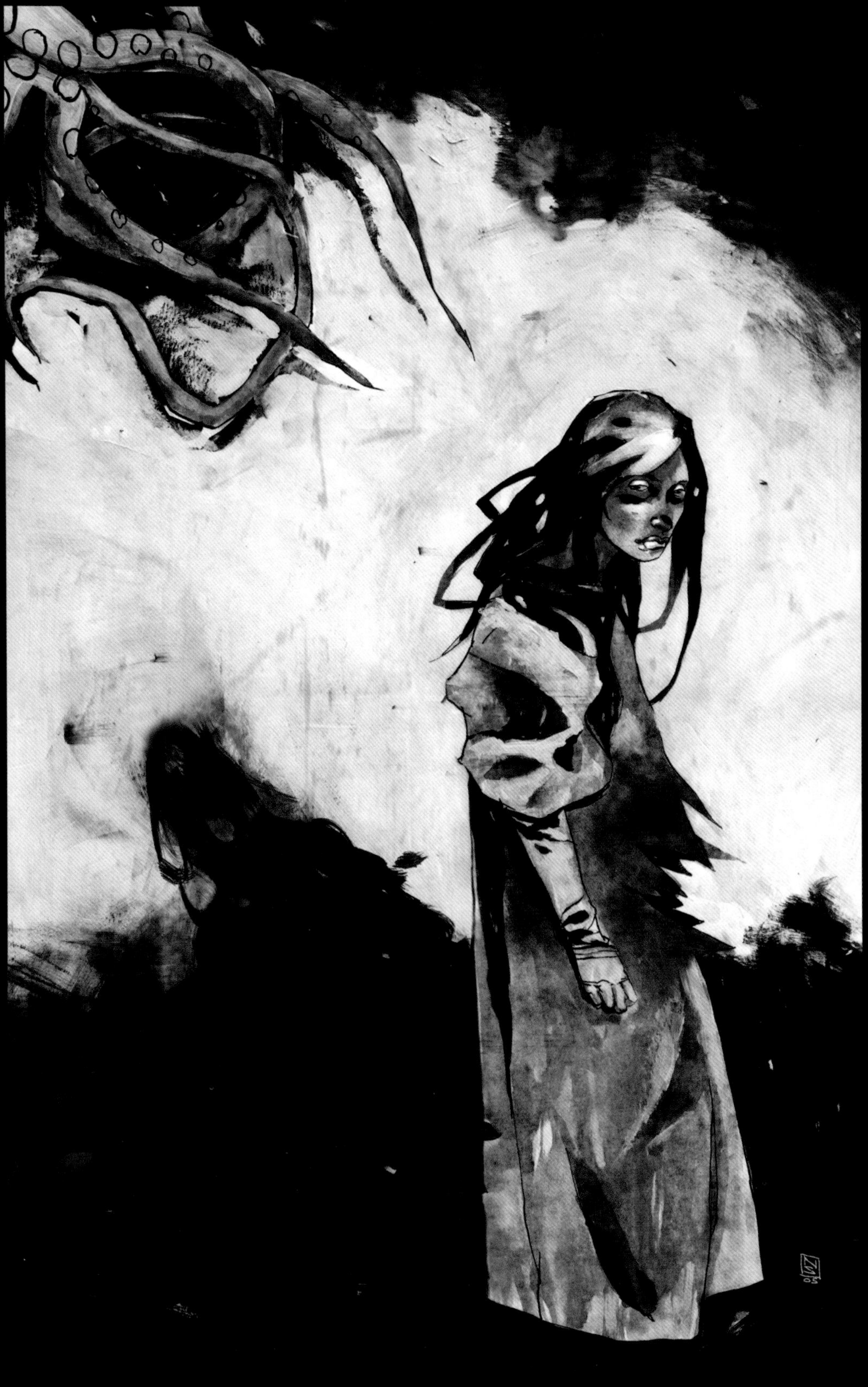

Issue no. 1, Art by Nick Stakal

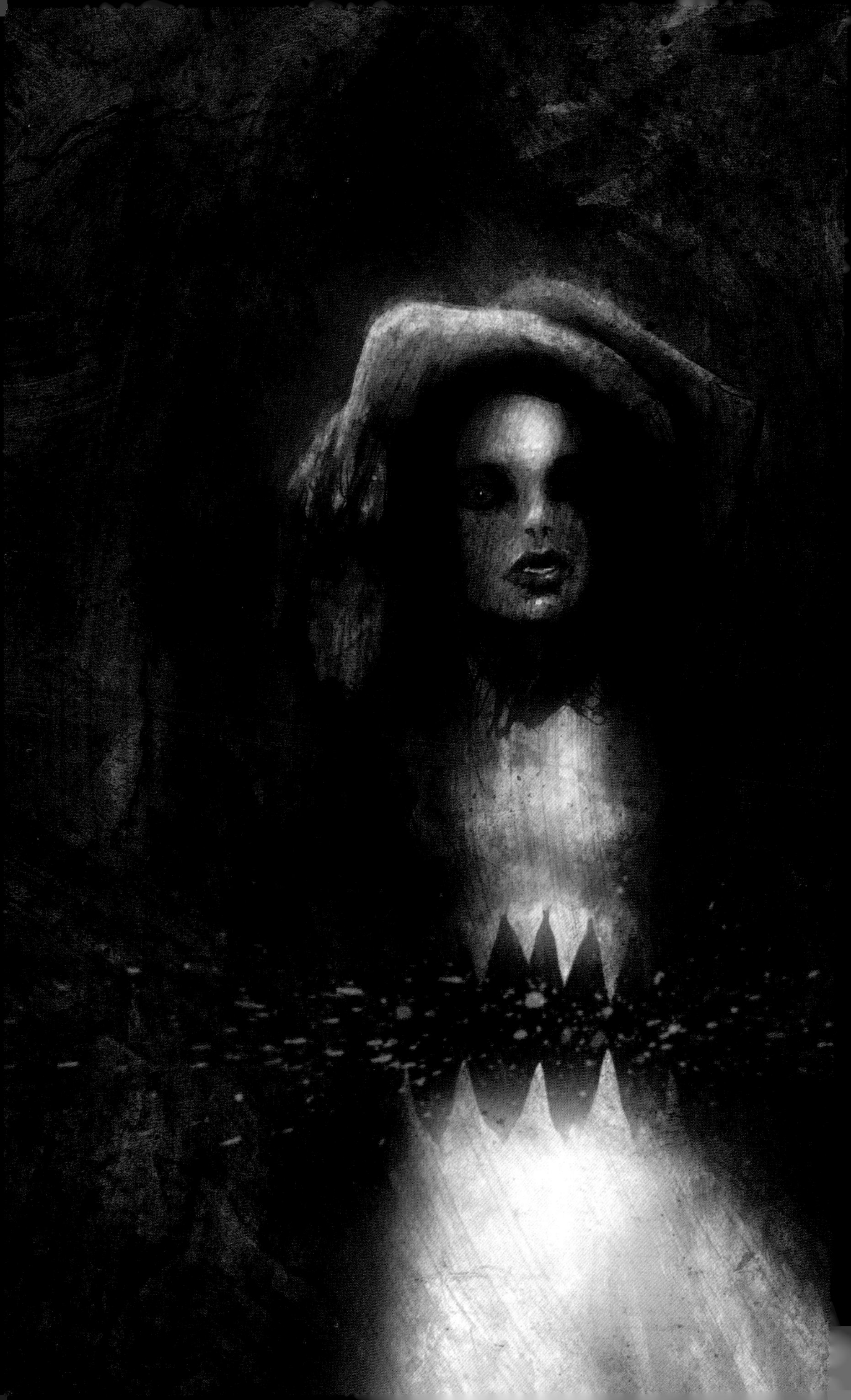

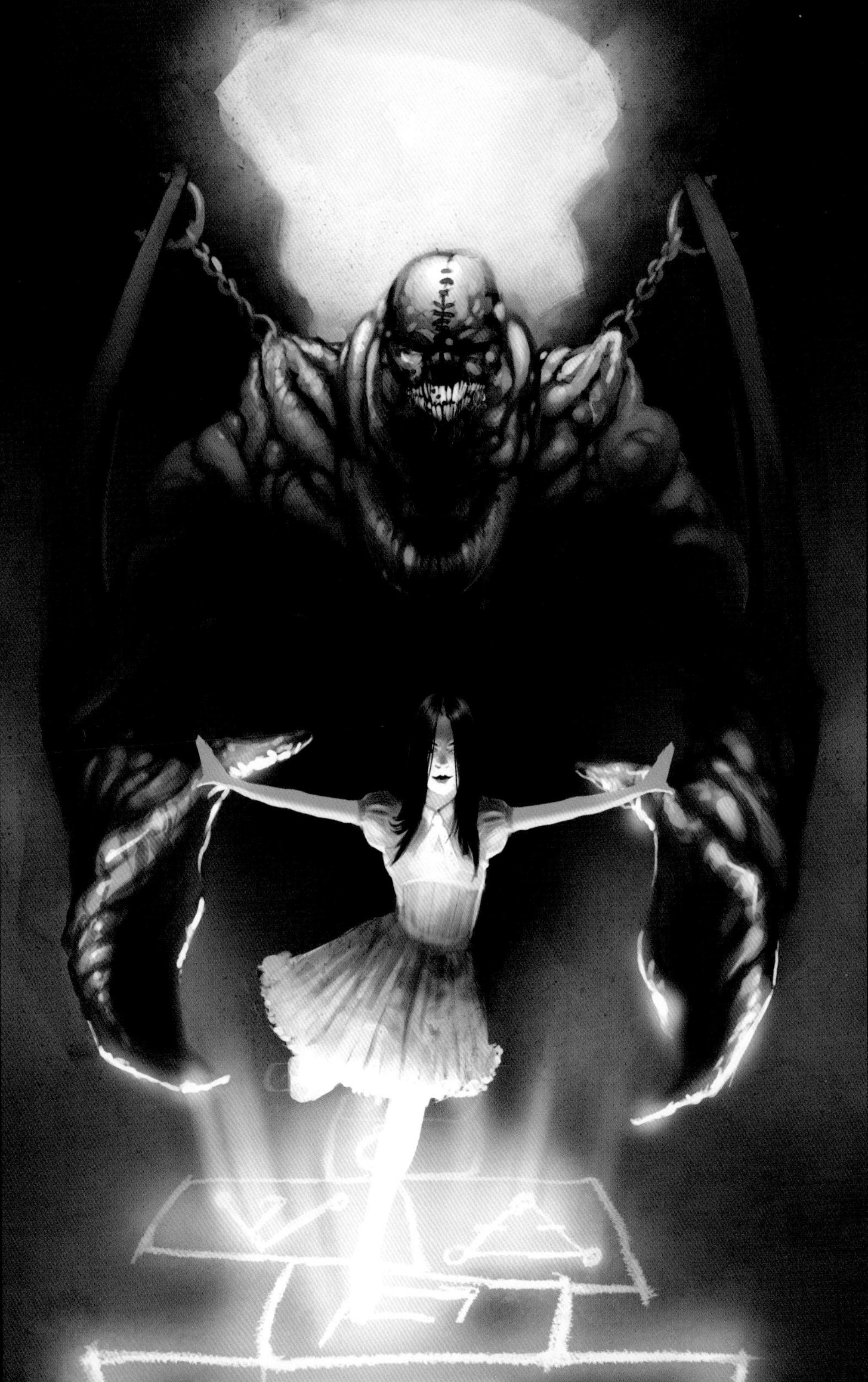

Opposite Page: Issue no. 1 Variant, Art by Steven Perkins
This Page: Issue no. 1 Variant, Art by Scott Keating

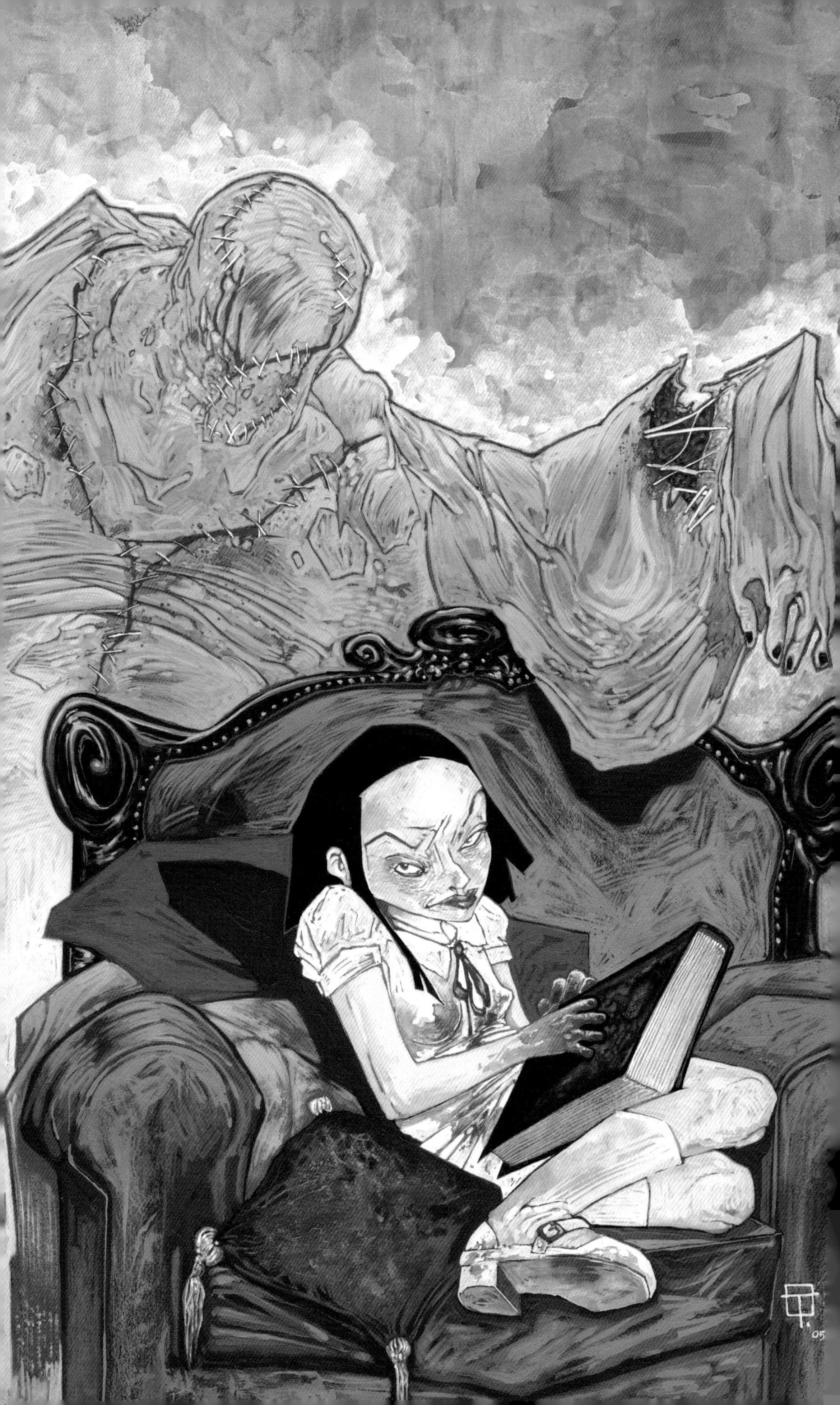

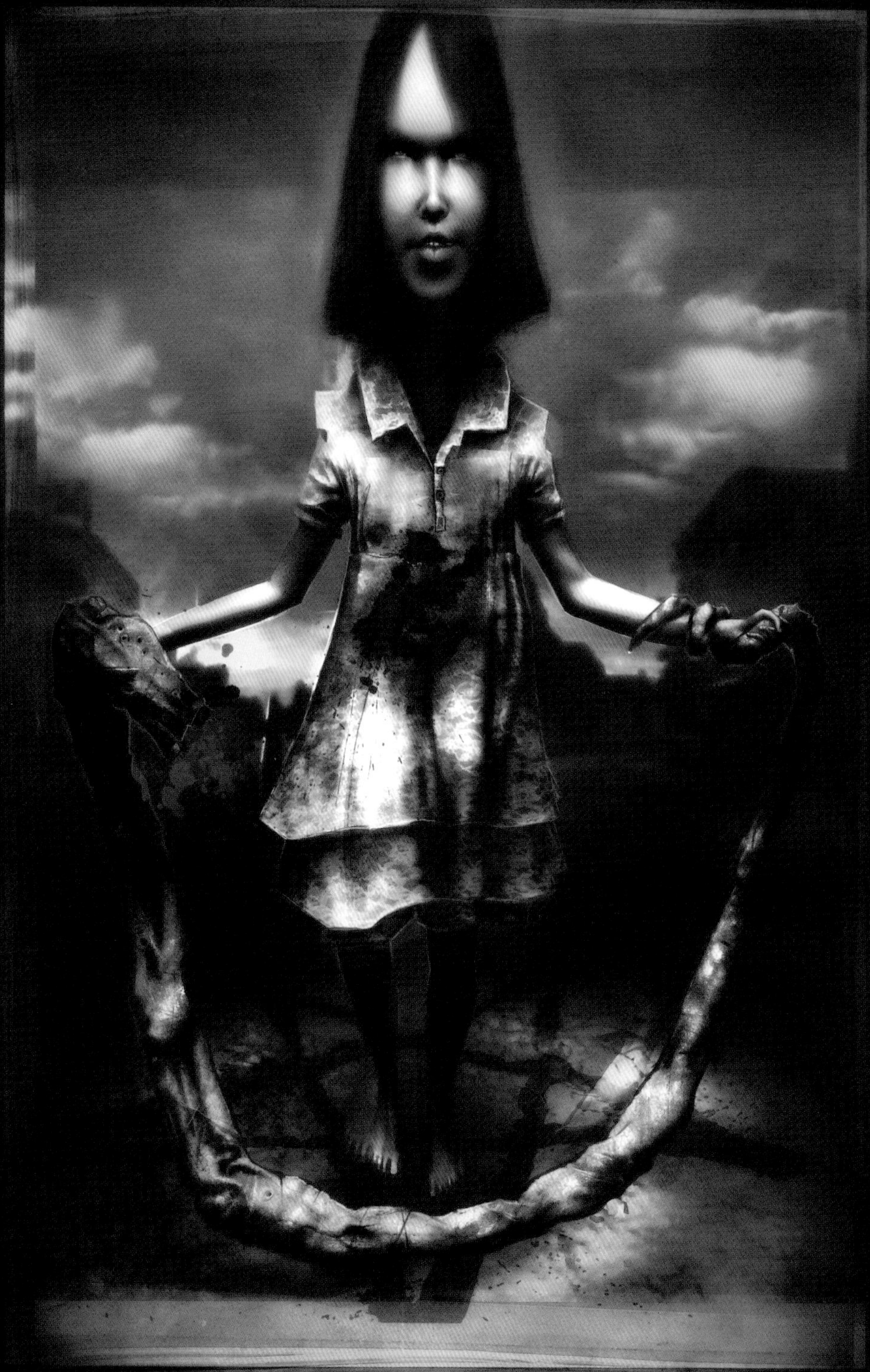

Opposite Page: Issue no. 1 Variant, Art by Ted McKeever
This Page: Issue no. 1 Retailer Incentive, Art by Loïc Zimmerman

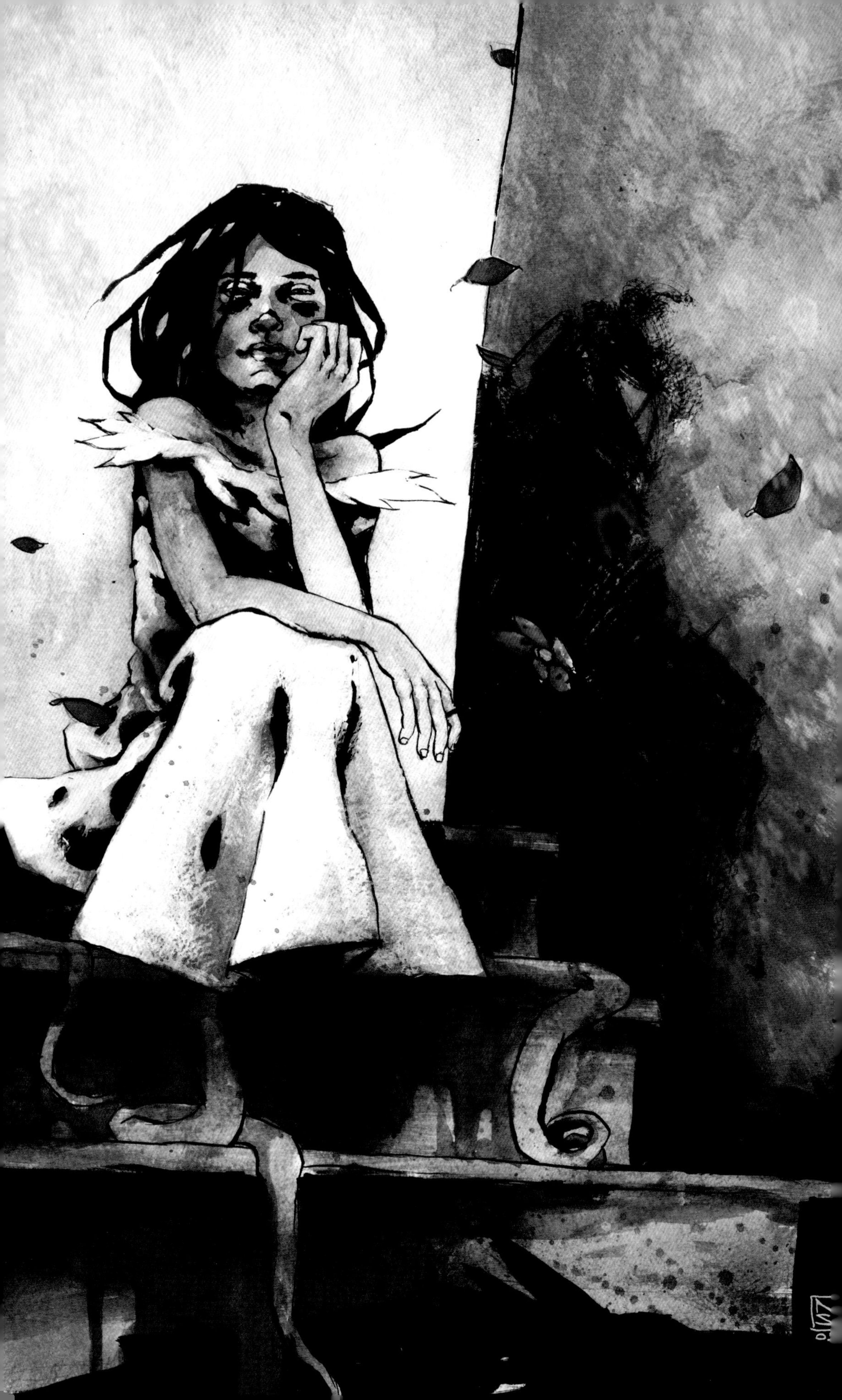

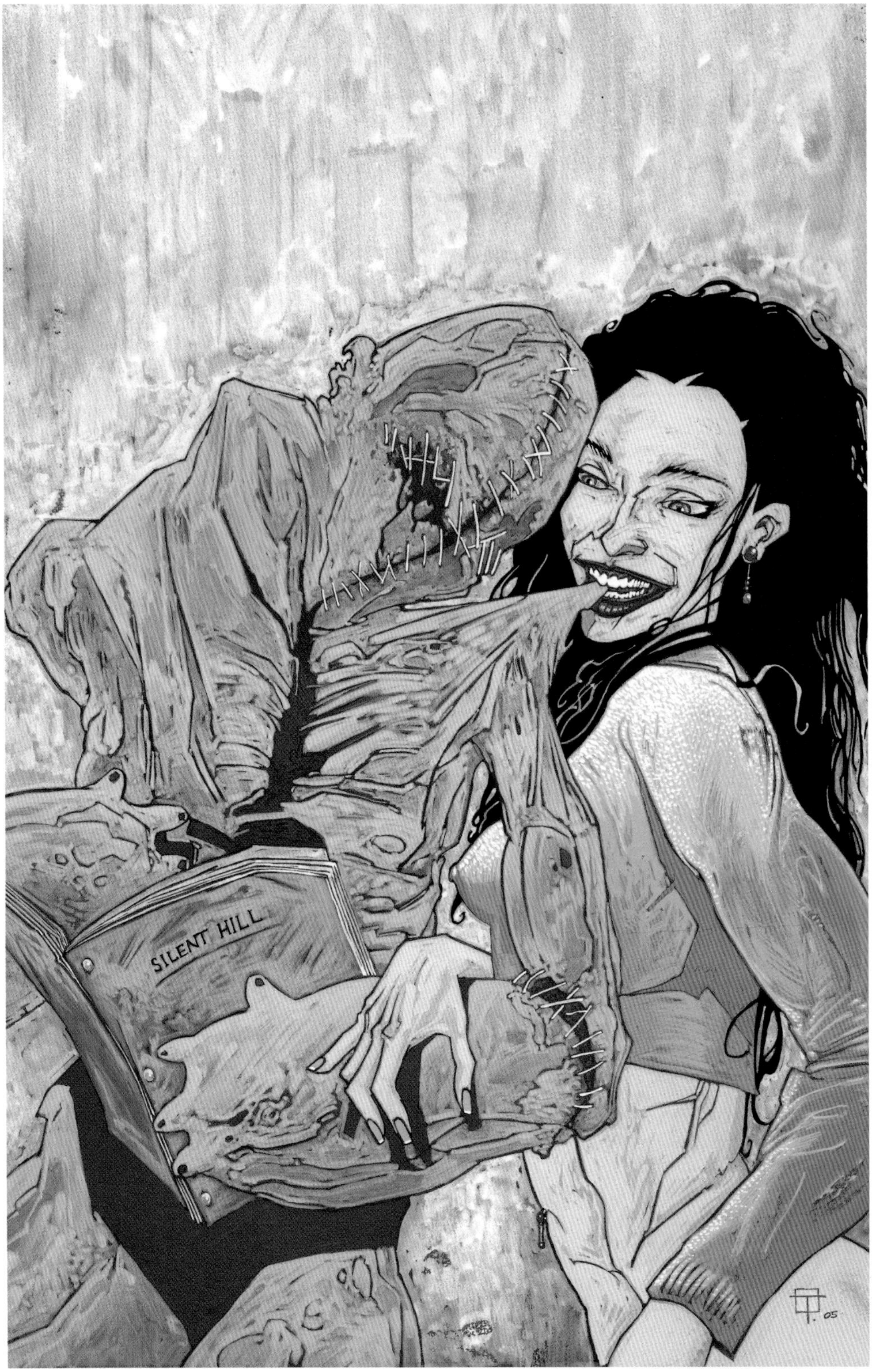
SILENT HILL

Opposite Page: Issue no. 2, Art by Nick Stakal
This Page: Issue no. 2 Variant, Art by Ted McKeever
Next Page: Issue no. 3, Art by Chris Bolton

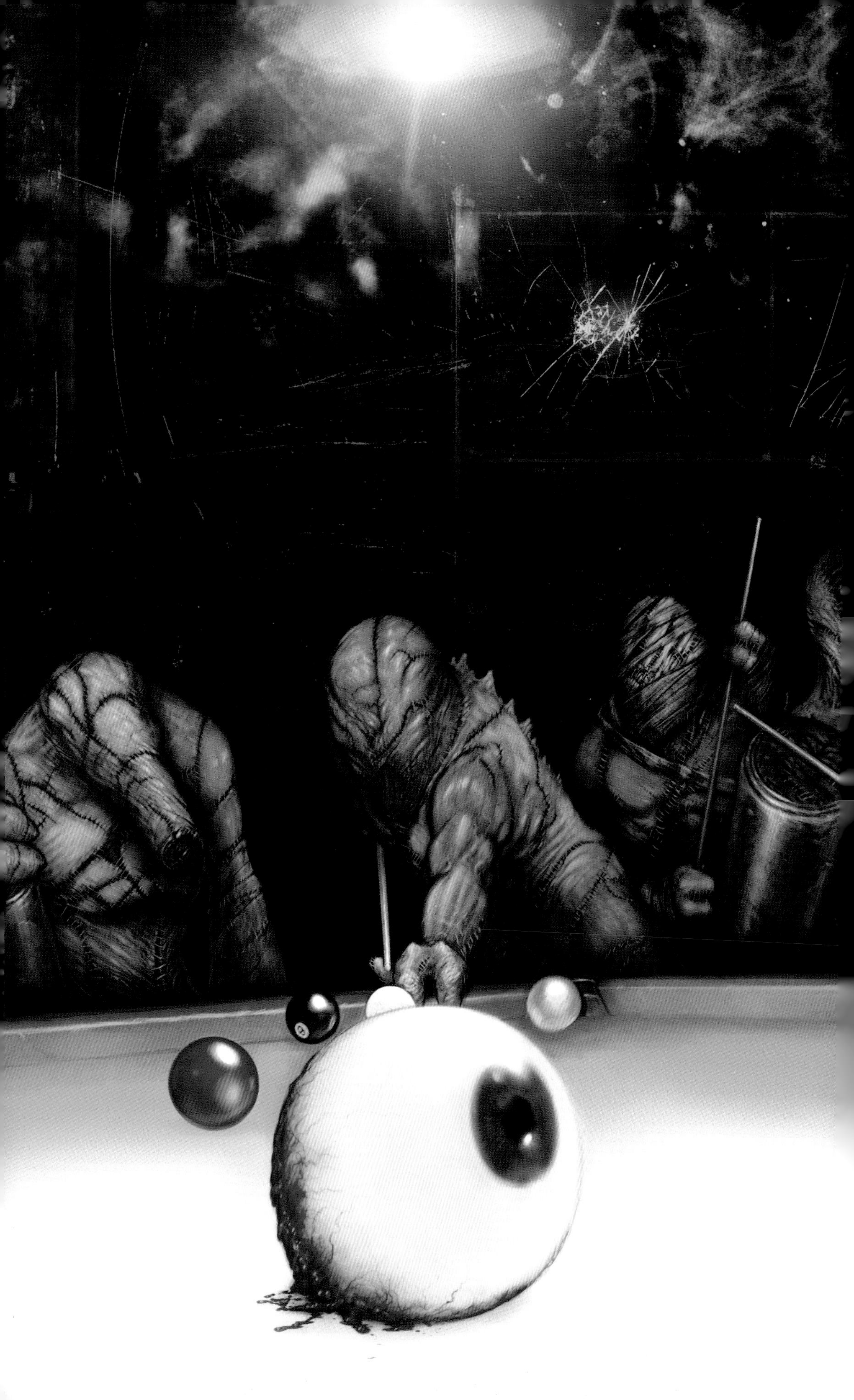

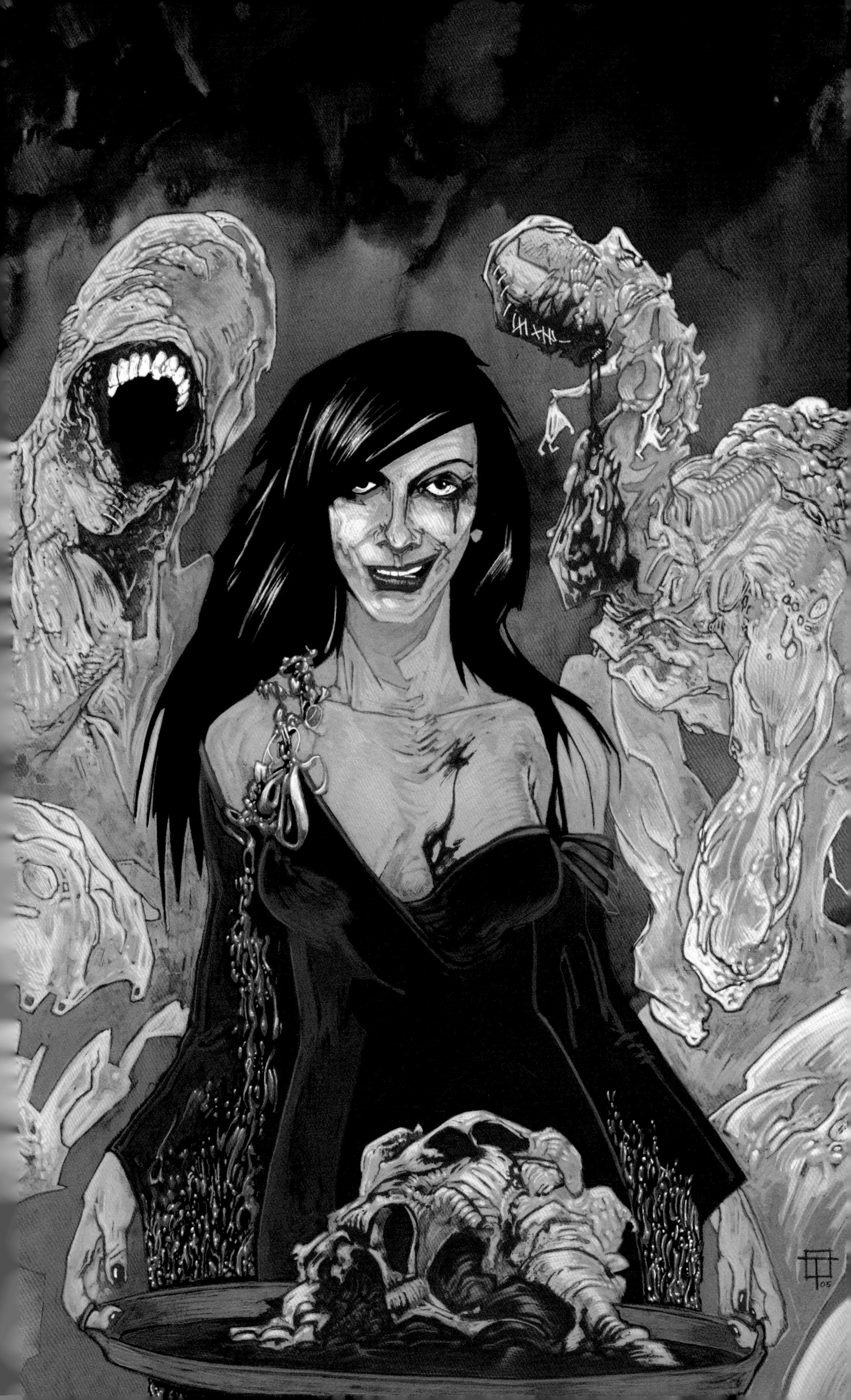

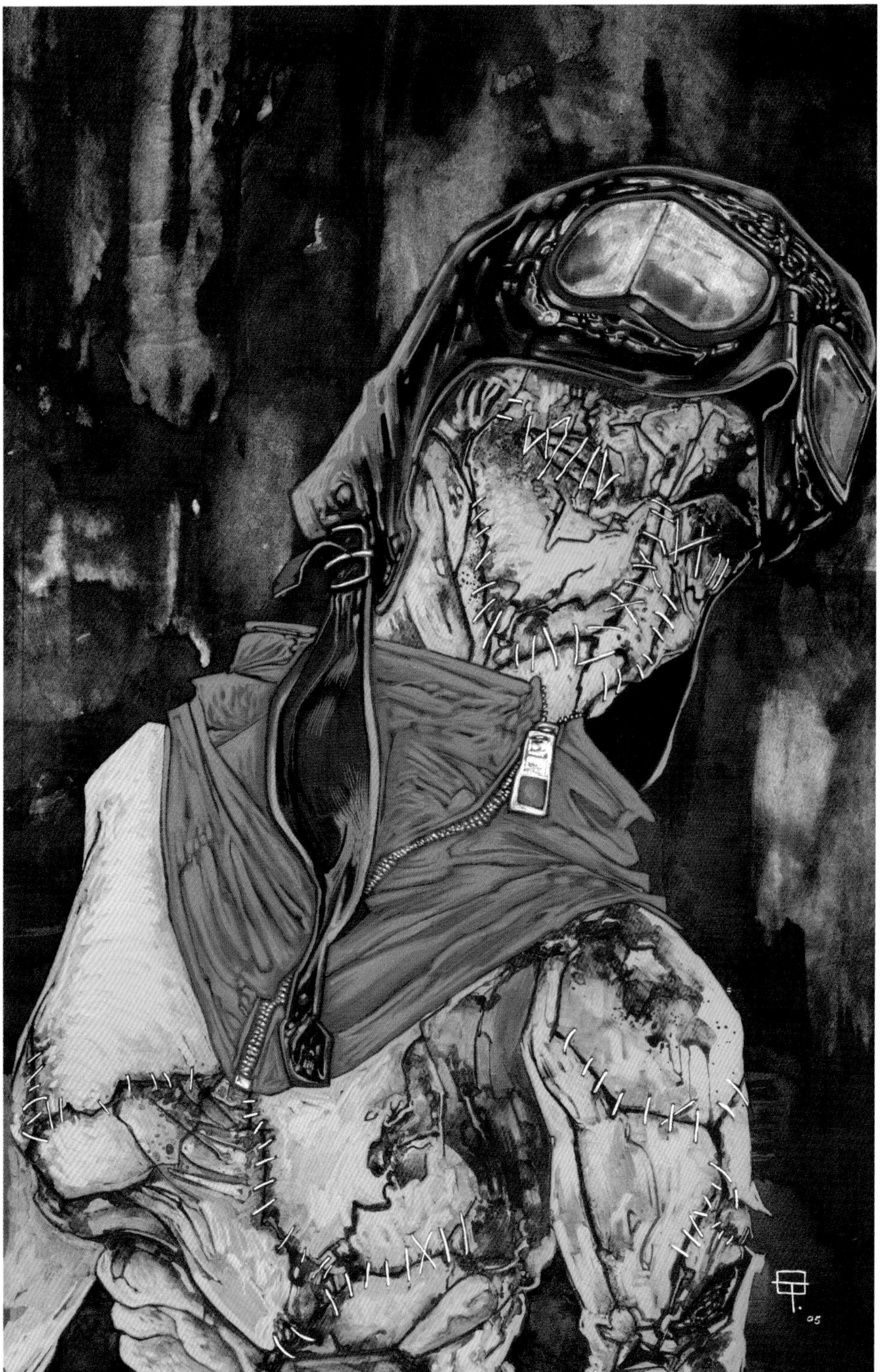

Previous Page: Issue no. 3 Variant, Art by Ted McKeever
This Page: Issue no. 4 Variant, Art by Ted McKeever
Opposite Page: Issue no. 4, Art by Nick Stakal

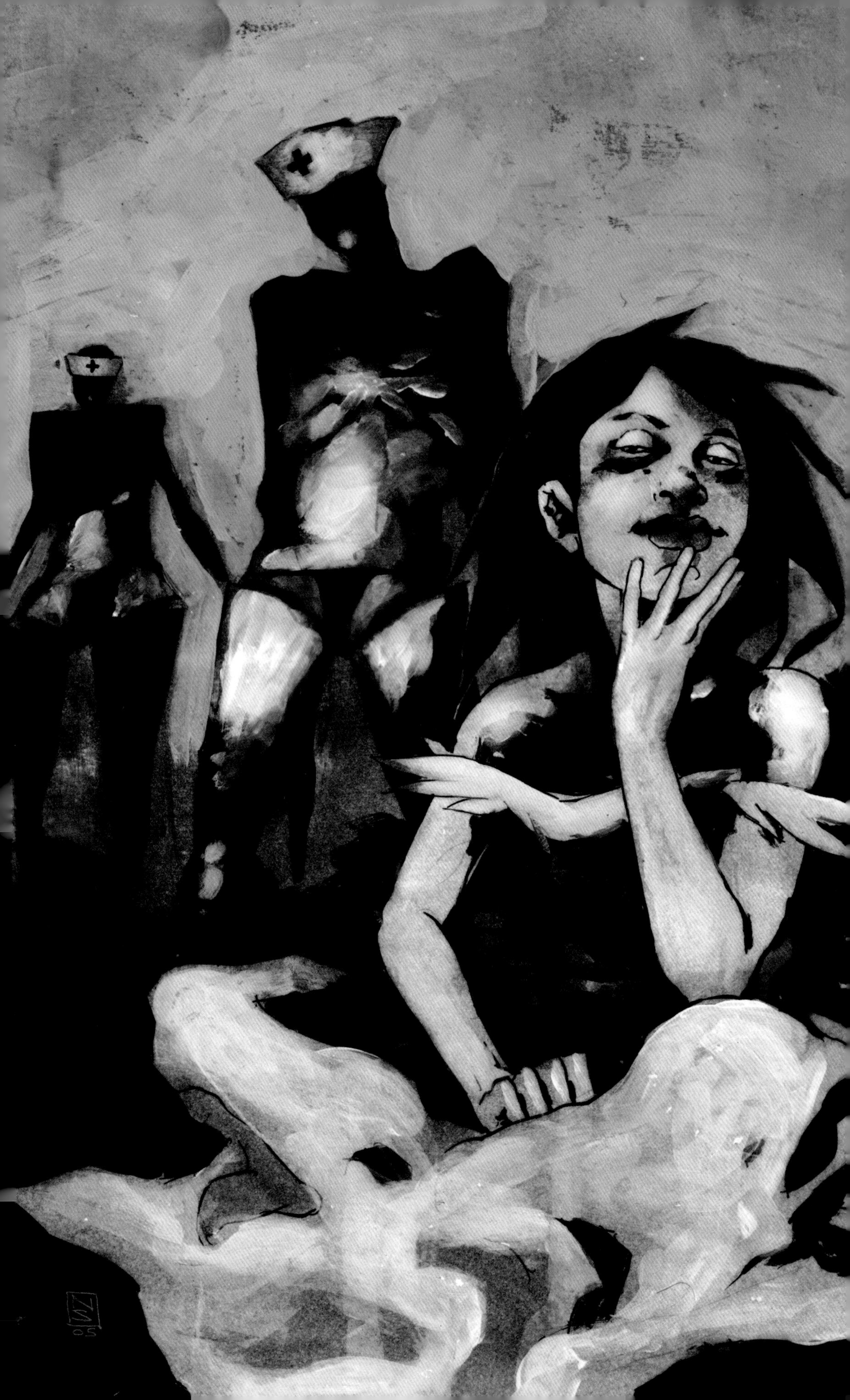

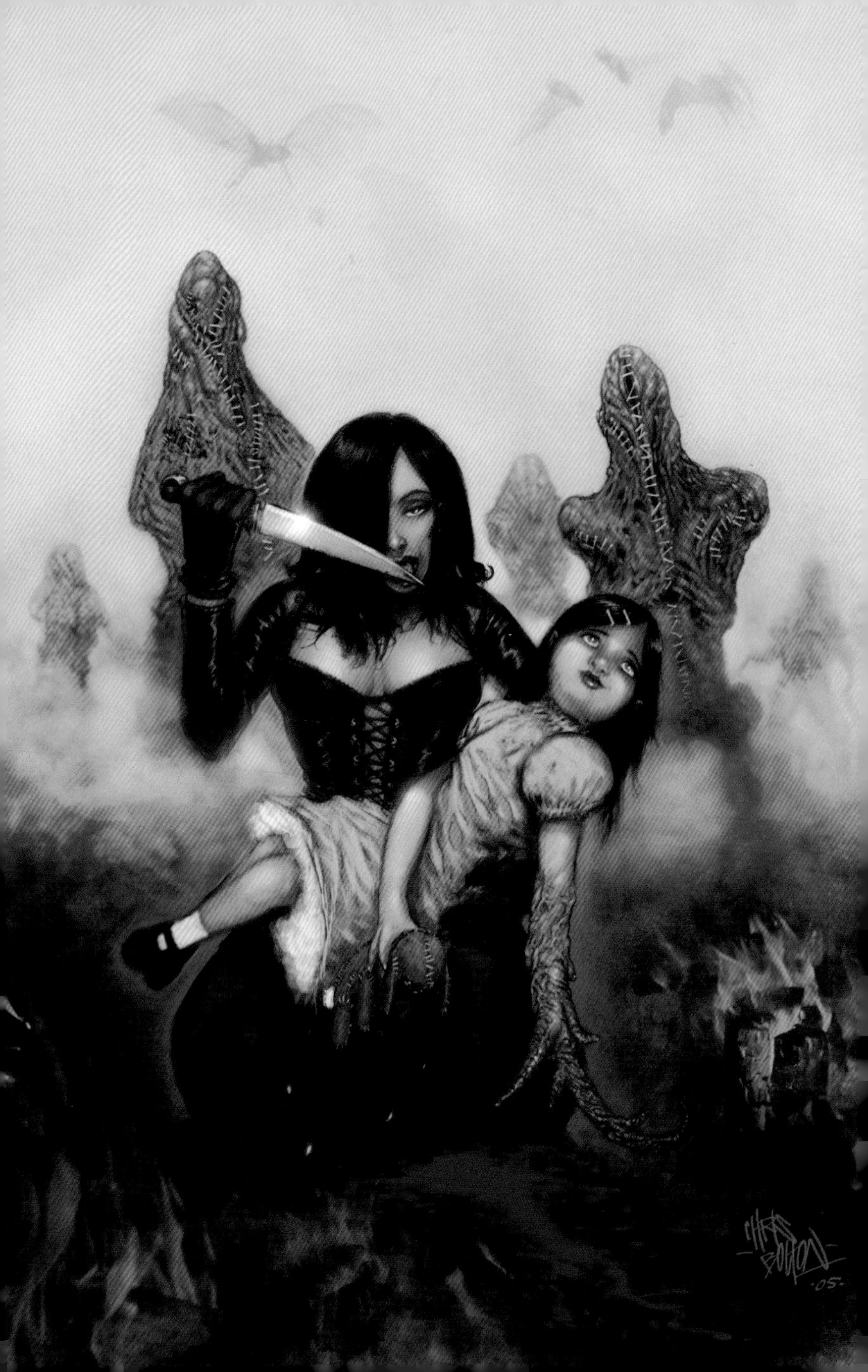
CHRIS BOLTON
·05·

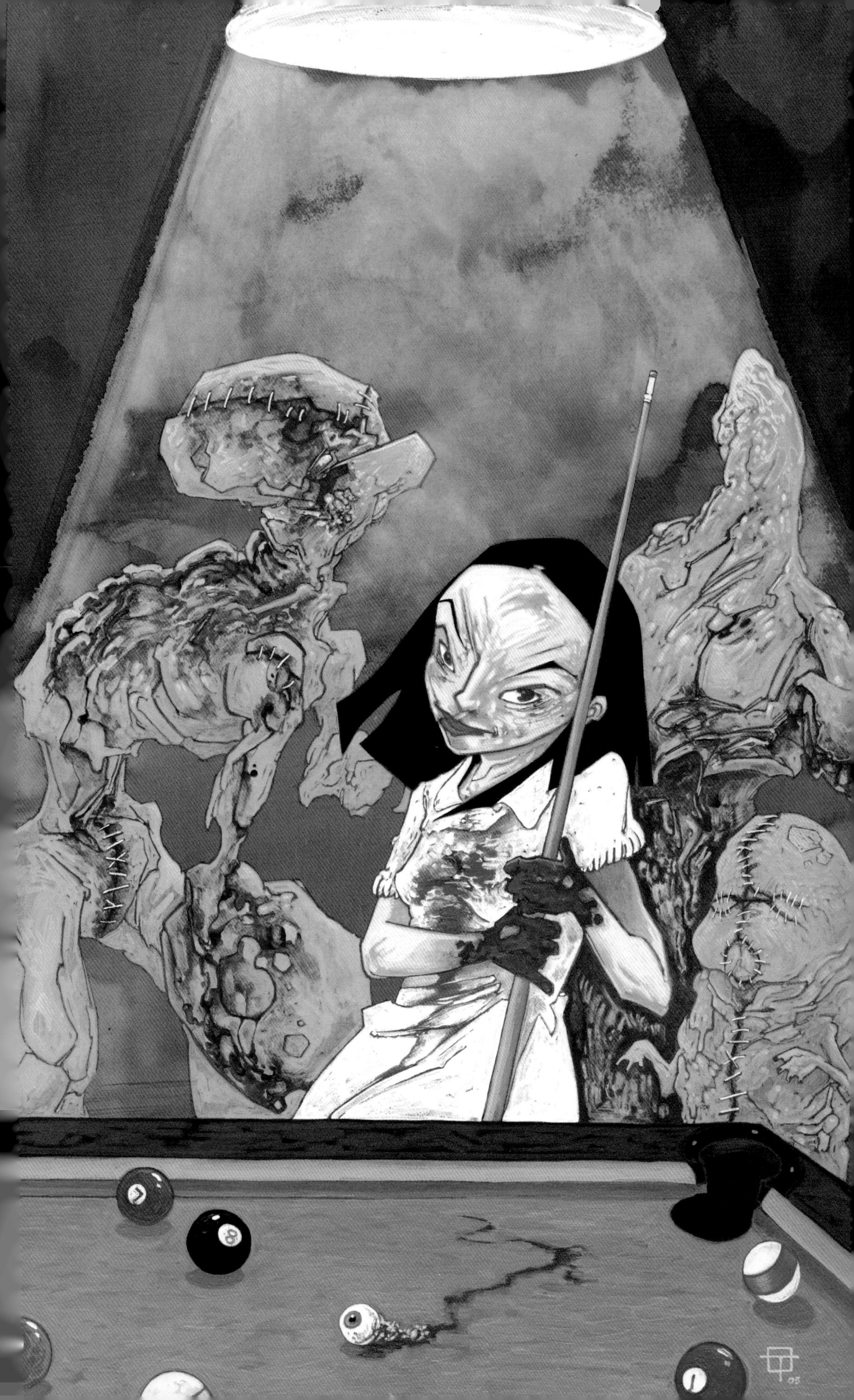

More Silent Hill Books from IDW Publishing:

Silent Hill: Dying Inside

Story by Scott Ciencin • Art by Ben Templesmith, Aadi Salman

Troy Abernathy doesn't believe in ghosts or demons—except those of the mind. The glory-seeking doctor's world is shattered when he brings patient Lynn DeAngelis to Silent Hill. There they confront the source of her seeming delusions... and find themselves trapped in a realm of unspeakable terrors!

ISBN: 1-932382-24-0 • $19.99 • Full Color • 136 Pages

SILENT HILL
THREE BLOODY TALES
SCOTT CIENCIN
SHAUN THOMAS
NICK STAKAL

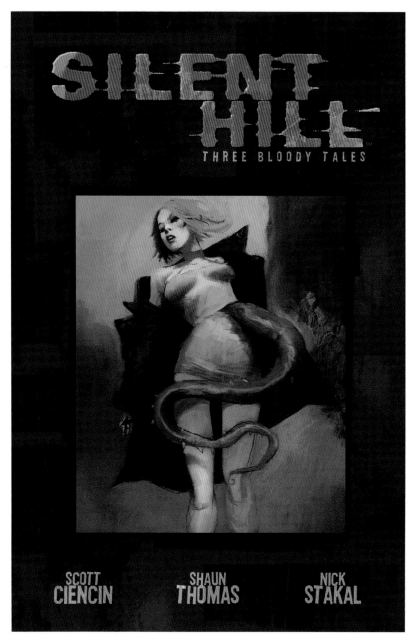

Silent Hill: 3 Bloody Tales

Story by Scott Ciencin • Art by Nick Stakal, Shaun Thomas

This blood-soaked volume collects IDW Publishing's three chilling one-shots based on Silent Hill, the smash-hit Konami videogame series. In "Among the Damned," a young, guilt-ridden soldier meets a doomed soul that will either change his life or end it. In "Paint It Black," a painter finds his dark muse in Silent Hill, until a group of cheerleaders arrive and the attacks begin. "The Grinning Man" tells the tale of the terrifying title character, who faces off against a State Trooper one day away from retirement.

ISBN: 1-933239-16-6 • $19.99 • Full Color • 152 Pages

IDW®

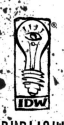

WWW.IDWPUBLISHING.COM